Respecting Life

Theology and Bioethics

Neil Messer

scm press

© Neil Messer 2011

Published in 2011 by SCM Press
Editorial office
13–17 Long Lane,
London EC1A 9PN, UK

SCM Press is an imprint of Hymns Ancient and Modern Ltd
(a registered charity)
13A Hellesdon Park Road, Norwich,
Norfolk NR6 5DR, UK

www.scm-canterburypress.co.uk

British Library Cataloguing in Publication data

A catalogue record for this book is available
from the British Library

978 0 334 04333 1

Typeset by *Church Times*
Printed and bound by
CPI Antony Rowe, Chippenham,
Wiltshire

Contents

To my friends and colleagues at the University
of Wales, Lampeter, 2001–09.

Acknowledgements

This book is the fruit of work done in various contexts over a number of years, and many people have helped in various ways to make it possible. Material in several chapters was presented at conferences, seminars and colloquia, including: the College of Health Care Chaplains Study Conference, Durham, July 2004; the Society for the Study of Christian Ethics Annual Conference, Oxford, September 2004; colloquia held at St Deiniol's Library, Hawarden, by the Centre for Religion and the Biosciences, University of Chester, November 2005 and November 2007; the National Conference on End of Life Issues, Aintree University Hospitals Trust, November 2007; the Association of Teachers of Moral Theology, Leeds, November 2007; the Faraday Institute, Cambridge, April 2008; the Societas Ethica Annual Conference, Lammi, Finland, August 2008; a conference on Eastern Orthodox and Western Christian Approaches to Bioethics, Durham, April 2009; and various departmental seminars at the University of Wales, Lampeter. I am grateful for the opportunities to give these presentations, and for the valuable comment and discussion that followed.

I thank friends and colleagues who have read and commented on parts of the book or on papers that have been incorporated into it, especially Mark Bratton, David Clough, Celia Deane-Drummond, Corinna Delkeskamp-Hayes, Simon Oliver and Angus Paddison. I have learned a good deal from them and many others over the years, but of course they are in no way responsible for what I have failed to learn. Thanks also to Natalie Watson at SCM Press for her enthusiastic support for this project and her forbearance in agreeing to extend the deadline for its completion, and to her and her colleagues for all their help in the production of the book.

Some chapters incorporate material from previous publications, and permission is gratefully acknowledged from copyright holders and publishers to use the following: from Oxford University Press for 'Christian Engagement with Public Bioethics in Britain: The Case of Human Admixed Embryos', *Christian Bioethics* 15.1 (2009), pp. 31–53 (in Chs 1 and 2); from the Editor of *Crucible* for 'Morality, the State and Christian Theology', *Crucible* (April–June 2009), pp. 16–23 (in Chs 2 and 10); from Continuum International Publishing Group for material from '"Ethics", "Religious Ethics" and "Christian Ethics": What Are Scholars For?', in *Theology and Religious Studies: An Exploration of Disciplinary Boundaries*, ed. Maya Warrier and Simon Oliver, London: T & T Clark, 2008, pp. 149–65 (in Ch. 2) and 'Medicine, Science and Virtue', in *Future Perfect? God, Medicine and Human Identity*, ed. Celia Deane-Drummond and Peter Scott, London: T & T Clark, 2006, pp. 113–25 (in Ch. 5); from Darton, Longman and Todd for material from Ch. 10 of *Theological Issues in Bioethics: An Introduction with Readings*, London: Darton, Longman and Todd, 2002 (in Ch. 2); from Grove Books Ltd, for material from *The Ethics of Human Cloning*, Cambridge: Grove Books, 2001 (in Ch. 3); from Sage Publications for 'Healthcare Resource Allocation and the "Recovery of Virtue"', *Studies in Christian Ethics* 18 (2005), pp. 89–108 (Ch. 7). Chapter 6 is a revised version of 'Humans, Animals, Evolution and Ends', in Celia Deane-Drummond and David Clough (eds), *Creaturely Theology: On God, Humans, and Other Animals*, London: SCM Press, 2009, pp. 211–27.

The dedication acknowledges a debt of a very particular kind. I learned my trade as an academic theologian in the department of Theology and Religious Studies at the University of Wales, Lampeter (recently incorporated into the University of Wales: Trinity St David). I had the privilege to be a member of that Department during an extraordinarily rich and stimulating time in its history and owe a very great deal to those who led it and who shared in its work during that time. I remain profoundly grateful for the friendship and collegiality I experienced there and for all I learned during those eight years. Since moving to the University of Winchester in 2009 I have found a thoroughly congenial home in its Department of Theology and Religious Studies and the wider university community, and I thank my colleagues here for their support and friendship.

A dominant theme of this book is that Christian theology and ethics must be located not only in the academy but also – indeed, first and foremost – in the Church. It is therefore only right to thank also the Christian communities in which my family and I have been located during the past few years: St Thomas' Methodist Church, Lampeter; Llandeilo United Reformed Church; the United Church, Winchester; and the University Chaplaincies in Lampeter and Winchester.

I am deeply thankful for another, closer circle of human community, that of my family. Within the past year this family has suffered the loss of my mother, Eunice Adela Connon, who died suddenly, shortly after her eighty-second birthday. I am increasingly conscious how much her human and Christian character is reflected in various ways in the perspectives, commitments and interests that I bring to the work presented here. And finally most heartfelt thanks, as ever, to and for Janet, Fiona and Rebecca, whose presence and love have sustained me through both hard and good times while this book has been in the making.

Winchester
September 2010

Introduction

Bioethical issues are rarely out of view in Western societies. Novel developments in biology, biotechnology and health care continue to raise new ethical problems: within the past few years, for example, legal provision for research on human-animal hybrid (or 'human admixed') embryos has been made in the UK amid much controversy,[1] while in the USA, political and legal disputes about the Federal funding of human embryonic stem cell research continue.[2] At the same time, more familiar issues such as abortion, animal experimentation, assisted dying and health care resource allocation frequently reappear on the public agendas of Western countries.[3]

These are issues of concern for Christian churches, because they raise fundamental questions about the nature and value of human life, what it means for humans to flourish, how suffering should be understood and faced, how death should be approached, how a human community should share its resources justly and how humans should relate to the non-human world, all of which are close to the heart of Christian faith and practice. It is no surprise,

---

1 Human Fertilisation and Embryology Act 2008.

2 For details, see below, p. 109, n. 11.

3 There is no clear consensus in the literature as to the exact definition and scope of the term 'bioethics'. Sometimes, for instance, a distinction is made between 'medical ethics' and 'bioethics' – the latter having a particular focus on new developments in biotechnology and high-tech medicine – but this usage is by no means universal, and others understand 'bioethics' more broadly. I follow the latter course, understanding the term to include reflection on a wide range of ethical issues raised by the biosciences, biotechnology and medicine.

therefore, that as bioethics emerged as a discipline in the latter part of the twentieth century, Christians played a large part in shaping it and Christian churches took a serious interest in bio-ethical issues and debates.[4] Within theological ethics, there continues to be a rich vein of reflection on bioethical issues from a variety of theological traditions.[5] This book is intended as a contribution to that ongoing conversation and reflection, from the perspective of the theological tradition outlined in the following paragraphs. As my examples illustrate, however, these are also matters of concern for a wider public, giving rise to some of the most vigorous arguments about policy and legislation in many Western countries. Much of the discussion in this book also has this wider public (or publics) in view, responding to issues raised in debates about law and policy, and trying to enable Christians and churches to contribute constructively and faithfully to such debates – even though, as I shall observe later, that can be a problematic exercise for a variety of reasons.

My own ecclesial, social and political context has shaped my approach to these questions in complex ways. I belong to the United Reformed Church, a small 'nonconformist' denomination in the UK – that is, one with historical roots in a seventeenth-century separation from the established Church of England.[6] Its name signals that the United Reformed Church is the product of recent unions between various nonconformist groups in the UK,

---

4 Albert R. Jonsen, *The Birth of Bioethics*, Oxford: Oxford University Press, 2003, pp. 34–64.

5 The range can be seen from the following illustrative examples from Orthodox, Catholic, Anglican, Lutheran and Reformed theologians: John Breck, *The Sacred Gift of Life: Orthodox Christianity and Bioethics*, Crestwood, NY: St Vladimir's Seminary Press, 1999; Lisa Sowle Cahill, *Theological Bioethics: Participation, Justice and Change*, Washington, DC: Georgetown University Press, 2005; Robin Gill, *Health Care and Christian Ethics*, Cambridge: Cambridge University Press, 2006; Gilbert Meilaender, *Body, Soul and Bioethics*, 2nd edn, Notre Dame, IN: University of Notre Dame Press, 1998; Agneta Sutton, *Christian Bioethics: A Guide for the Perplexed*, London: T & T Clark, 2008; Allen Verhey, *Reading the Bible in the Strange World of Medicine*, Grand Rapids, MI: Eerdmans, 2003.

6 For an excellent historical account of the United Reformed Church and its precursors in the UK, see David Cornick, *Under God's Good Hand: A History of the Traditions Which Have Come Together in the United Reformed Church in the United Kingdom*, London: United Reformed Church, 1998.

which shared a Reformation heritage but had developed it in contrasting ways. It thus brings together – sometimes uneasily – a range of diverse strands within the Reformed tradition, showing the influence (for example) of both Calvinist and Radical Reformation traditions, as well as later developments such as the eighteenth-century Evangelical Revival. The unions that brought the denomination into being have also left it with a strong sense of ecumenical commitment.[7] At the same time, its recent history, in common with many Western European churches, has been one of decline in numerical strength and social influence.

Christian churches in the UK cannot avoid the reality that they are minority participants in public bioethical debates – as they are in many, though not all, other Western contexts – and their contributions to these debates are by no means universally welcomed.[8] Not surprisingly, this means that public debates in this context tend to be framed rather differently from the way that a Christian theological tradition would habitually approach them, in ways that (as I argue in Chapter 1) display various unsatisfactory features and characteristic forms of distortion. In this situation, one question facing a Christian community concerned about bioethical issues is how those issues might be addressed in ways that cohere with its deepest commitments of faith and practice; a second is whether and how it ought to engage with public debates that are unlikely to be framed according to anything like the same commitments or moral vision. This book is an attempt to address both these questions by reflecting on the terms of theological and public engagement with bioethical issues, and offering a series of theological engagements with particular substantive issues. The latter can be understood in a variety of ways: as part of the academic

7 It is also possible, however, that the URC's recent history, including these unions, has involved a loss of ecclesiological and moral coherence; for a sharp critique to that effect, see Romilly Micklem, 'The Failure of Moral Discourse: The Epistemological Crisis in the United Reformed Church', unpublished PhD dissertation, University of London, 2010.

8 See for example Mark Henderson, 'Benefits Are Years Off, but it's a Victory for Scientific Freedom', *The Times*, 20 May 2008, p. 4.

theologian's service to the Christian community, attempting to express and focus that community's reflection on bioethical questions; as contributions to academic discourse on bioethics; as contributions to the Church's public witness on these issues; and as 'worked examples' showing how my proposals for theological and public engagement in the first two chapters might work out in practice.

The ecclesial, social and political context described above gives rise to various influences on the theological and ethical approach of this book, three of which stand out as particularly important. First, and most obviously, my approach is located within a Reformed theological tradition. Thus, a major conversation partner through much of the book is the most influential twentieth-century theologian of that tradition, Karl Barth, together with those from a variety of churches influenced by him. Much of the constructive argument in this book is implicitly or explicitly an attempt, in Barth's words, 'to understand the Word of God as the command of God' in relation to a range of substantive bioethical questions.[9] Second, partly under the influence of the Radical Reformation heritage in my own ecclesial tradition, I have learned from Stanley Hauerwas – and through him from John Howard Yoder, the most prominent recent English-speaking theologian of that tradition – that the Church, with its distinctive narratives and practices, should be the primary place where Christians can learn what a moral vision shaped by the gospel looks like, and how, by God's grace, to live by that vision.[10] Third, again under the influence of Hauerwas, as well as the philosopher Alasdair MacIntyre and others, I have learned to think about a life lived by that Christian vision in terms of the virtues and character that it calls

9 Karl Barth, *Church Dogmatics*, ET ed. Geoffrey W. Bromiley and Thomas F. Torrance, 13 vols, Edinburgh: T & T Clark, 1956–75, vol. III.4, p. 4.

10 See for example Stanley M. Hauerwas, *The Peaceable Kingdom: A Primer in Christian Ethics*, rev. edn, London: SCM Press, 2003; Stanley Hauerwas and Samuel Wells (eds), *The Blackwell Companion to Christian Ethics*, Oxford: Blackwell, 2004; Mark Thiessen Nation, *John Howard Yoder: Mennonite Patience, Evangelical Witness, Catholic Convictions*, Grand Rapids, MI: Eerdmans, 2006.

for.[11] Therefore Thomas Aquinas, as well as Karl Barth, is a frequent conversation partner, and my own arguments are worked out in dialogue with other, particularly Catholic, Christian traditions as well as my own.

Different chapters reflect these influences to varying extents. This is a function partly of the fact that some of these chapters originated as essays written over a period of several years, during which my thinking changed and developed, and partly of the different contexts in which those essays were written. However, I believe that underlying the varying emphases is a basic coherence. In brief: if the divine command is understood as God's gracious call, inviting and summoning us to become all we are meant to be as God's creatures, reconciled sinners and heirs of God's promised good future, this raises questions not only about acts and decisions, but also about the character of human life, community and society, and about the particular qualities, habits and moral skills that God's transforming grace brings about in people and communities. [12]

11 Stanley Hauerwas and Charles H. Pinches, *Christians Among the Virtues: Theological Conversations with Ancient and Modern Ethics*, Notre Dame, IN: University of Notre Dame Press, 1997; Alasdair MacIntyre, *After Virtue: A Study in Moral Theory*, 2nd edn, London: Duckworth, 1985; Jean Porter, *The Recovery of Virtue: The Relevance of Aquinas for Christian Ethics*, London: SPCK, 1994. For an extensive and valuable recent treatment of MacIntyre's thought, see Thomas D. D'Andrea, *Tradition, Rationality and Virtue: The Thought of Alasdair MacIntyre*, Aldershot: Ashgate, 2006. My intellectual debt to MacIntyre also extends to his central claim in *After Virtue* about the 'traditioned' nature of human reason, including moral reason (see below Chapter 1), but not – as will be clear from the first two kinds of influence that I have cited above – to his way of setting up the relationship between philosophical inquiry and Christian revelation: see D'Andrea, *Tradition, Rationality, and Virtue*, pp. 388–93, and MacIntyre, 'What Has Christianity to Say to the Moral Philosopher?', in Alan J. Torrance and Michael Banner (eds), *The Doctrine of God and Theological Ethics*, London: T & T Clark, 2006, pp. 17–32.

12 A number of commentators in recent years have found more common ground in the theological projects of Barth and Aquinas, the main representatives of two of these strands, than has often been thought: for example Eugene F. Rogers, *Thomas Aquinas and Karl Barth: Sacred Doctrine and the Natural Knowledge of God*, Notre Dame, IN: University of Notre Dame Press, 1995; Stanley Hauerwas, *With the Grain of the Universe: The Church's Witness and Natural Theology*, Grand Rapids, MI: Brazos, 2001, pp. 163–7, 205–15. Furthermore, as Nigel Biggar has argued, Barth's account of the command of God need not be understood as solely preoccupied with acts and decisions, but can also include questions of virtue and character, understood in the way I have in view here: Nigel Biggar, *The Hastening that Waits: Karl Barth's Ethics*, Oxford: Clarendon Press, 1993, pp. 132–9.

The book is in two parts. The first, 'Terms of Engagement', consists of two chapters in which I develop a proposal for addressing bioethical questions theologically, and consider how such an approach might engage with public debates. The first, 'Reframing the Questions', begins by mapping some characteristics of contemporary public discourse about bioethics, with particular reference to arguments about human admixed embryos in the context of recent UK legislation on human fertilization and embryology. I argue that such debates display various unsatisfactory features: first, a set of attitudes and aspirations reflecting what Gerald McKenny has called the 'Baconian project',[13] to subject the material world (including the human body) to human control with the aims of minimizing suffering and maximizing individual autonomous choice; second, the assumption of a sharp dichotomy between 'public reason' and a private realm of non-rational preference and belief; third, what MacIntyre has described as an 'interminable' character, because the rival protagonists base their arguments on different and incompatible premises. This critical analysis of such debates suggests that Christians and churches wishing to engage with them would be unwise simply to accept the terms in which they are customarily framed; rather, a reframing of the questions will be required.

Taking my cue from MacIntyre, Hauerwas and others, I argue that this reframing requires the recovery of a 'traditioned' mode of moral reasoning, located in a community with a distinctive character and narrative. In particular, this chapter begins to articulate how the questions might be reframed within the kind of Christian tradition outlined above, whose narrative describes humans and the world as God's good creatures, broken by sin and evil, yet reconciled to God in Christ and promised ultimate fulfilment in God's good future. Christian thinking and action in relation to bioethics must be located within the frame of reference

---

13 Gerald P. McKenny, *To Relieve the Human Condition: Bioethics, Technology and the Body*, Albany, NY: State University of New York Press, 1997, pp. 17–21.

supplied by this narrative, but in the face of the new problems raised by biology, biotechnology and health care, the narrative cannot simply be repeated: it must be retold, its significance rethought and renegotiated, in relation to the new situations and challenges that the Christian community faces. This requires of the community a kind of 'practical wisdom' formed by the biblical witness to Christ. The discussions of particular practical issues in bioethics in Part 2 can all be understood as attempts to articulate and foster that practical wisdom. The development of such a biblically formed practical wisdom cannot be reduced to a standard procedure, which could too easily become a presumptuous attempt to contain the word and command of God. Faithful response to the biblical witness to Christ must have a certain flexibility and contextual character about it, and the discussions of practical issues in Part 2 accordingly do not follow a uniform scheme. However, Chapter 1 concludes with an elaboration of one approach originally proposed in a previous book,[14] and used at various points in this one: a set of five 'diagnostic questions' that can be asked about a wide range of practices and projects in the bioethical field, to aid the community's discernment of what constitutes faithful response to the Christian narrative in relation to those practices and projects.

Having articulated this theological approach to bioethical questions, I turn in the next chapter, 'Public Engagement', to the question of how such theological thinking should be brought into contact with public bioethical debates. First, I ask what might be meant by 'public' engagement or debate, and follow David Tracy, Duncan Forrester and others in recognizing the variety of 'publics' to which theological ethics might be addressed. Next, I argue with reference to Karl Barth and Dietrich Bonhoeffer that the Church's divine mandate to care for the 'penultimate' realm of this world, in which the gospel is to be proclaimed and heard, gives it the best

---

14 Neil Messer, *Selfish Genes and Christian Ethics: Theological and Ethical Reflections on Evolutionary Biology*, London: SCM Press, 2007, pp. 229–35.

of reasons to attempt this engagement.[15] I survey a range of modes in which a Christian bioethic might engage with the 'public' of a pluralist society, and argue – in dialogue with Stanley Hauerwas, Michael Banner, Duncan Forrester and others[16] – for a form of engagement that gives full weight to the distinctive moral vision of the Christian tradition and the distinctive context of Christian practice that renders the moral vision both intelligible and persuasive. The chapter concludes with some brief comments about the kind of contribution that a distinctively Christian bioethic might make to public debates in late modern Western societies.

Part 2, 'Theological Engagements', offers theological treatments of a broad range of current bioethical issues. Chapter 3, 'Human Reproductive Cloning', begins with a brief account of the nuclear transfer cloning technique that achieved sudden public prominence with the cloning of Dolly the sheep in 1997. The cloning of Dolly, and subsequently mammals of other species, quickly provoked a public debate about the prospect of using the technique to try and clone humans. In these discussions, a distinction is customarily made between 'reproductive cloning', using cloning by nuclear transfer to produce a new human being, and 'therapeutic cloning', using the same technique not to produce a new human being, but to generate cell lines that could be used in medical research or the treatment of disease. Chapter 3 focuses on reproductive cloning, while 'therapeutic cloning' is discussed in the following chapter.

Having outlined the cloning technique, I turn to the ethical analysis of reproductive cloning, arguing first that the consequen-

---

15 Karl Barth, *Church and State*, ET, London: SCM Press, 1939; Barth, 'The Christian Community and the Civil Community', in *Against the Stream: Shorter Post-War Writings 1946–52*, ed. Ronald Gregor Smith, London: SCM Press, 1954; Dietrich Bonhoeffer, *Ethics* (*Dietrich Bonhoeffer Works*, vol. 6), ET ed. Clifford J. Green, Minneapolis: Fortress Press, 2005.

16 For example Michael Banner, *Christian Ethics and Contemporary Moral Problems*, Cambridge: Cambridge University Press, 1999; Duncan Forrester, *Christian Justice and Public Policy*, Cambridge: Cambridge University Press, 1997; Hauerwas, *The Peaceable Kingdom*.

tialist forms of analysis prominent in public debates fail to get to the heart of the matter. I develop a theological-ethical analysis through the lens of the five diagnostic questions set out in Chapter 1. My analysis suggests that cloning, as an exercise of near-total control over the genetic identity of the clone, represents what the political philosopher Michael Sandel describes as 'the one-sided triumph of willfulness over giftedness, of dominion over reverence, of molding over beholding'.[17] The moral meaning implicit in this practice can therefore be understood as a striving after god-like power and mastery over the world and ourselves, which has the tragic and ironic effect of alienating us from God. Furthermore, such an exercise of control over the genetic identities of cloned children is antithetical to the attitude of 'welcoming the stranger' that should characterize our attitude to our children: as Hauerwas has argued, children are gifts precisely because they refuse to be exactly what we would like them to be, thus teaching us to love them as others who are not under our control.[18] Finally, the dark history of eugenics shows that a drive towards the genetic control of humans all too easily goes hand in hand with an intolerance of those whose genetic inheritance is considered undesirable, including ethnic minorities and people with genetic impairments. Drawing on the work of Alistair McFadyen,[19] I suggest that the Christian doctrine of sin can illuminate the dynamics at work in such processes, and should serve as a warning about the dangers for some marginalized and vulnerable sections of society if technologies of genetic control were to become widely and routinely available.

Chapter 4, 'Embryonic Stem Cells and Human Admixed Embryos', also begins with a brief account of the two fields of

---

17 Michael J. Sandel, *The Case against Perfection: Ethics in the Age of Genetic Engineering*, Cambridge, MA: Harvard University Press, 2007, pp. 85–6.

18 Stanley Hauerwas, *Truthfulness and Tragedy: Further Investigations into Christian Ethics*, Notre Dame, IN: University of Notre Dame Press, 1977, p. 153.

19 Alistair McFadyen, *Bound to Sin: Abuse, Holocaust and the Christian Doctrine of Sin*, Cambridge: Cambridge University Press, 2000.

biomedical research named in the title, before moving on to a theological and ethical analysis of each. The central issue with embryonic stem cell research is that although many of its therapeutic goals are good and important in themselves, the production of embryonic stem cells involves the destruction of embryonic human life. While a consequentialist ethical analysis would most likely conclude that the benefits of the therapeutic goals would far outweigh the harm of destroying the embryos used in the research, this will not do for a theological analysis. It must be asked whether the destruction of embryonic human life can ever be justified even for a good and important goal. I argue that standard ways of framing this question by distinguishing between human beings and persons, and asking whether embryos meet the criteria of personhood, are theologically unsatisfactory because they involve an unwarranted attempt to set limits on our moral concern. However, I am also doubtful about Christian attempts to establish the intrinsic dignity of all human life, embryos included, on the grounds that all humans bear the image of God (Gen. 1.26–28). There are good exegetical and hermeneutical reasons for thinking that the ethical implications of the *imago dei* are not best expressed in terms of intrinsic human dignity. In theological perspective, the basic reason why we should value other humans is that they are neighbours whom God has given us to love. This suggests a different kind of ethical analysis from standard accounts, because 'neighbour', theologically understood, is not a bounded category whose limits we are entitled to define: we have to reckon with the possibility that the embryos who might be destroyed in stem cell research, as well as the patients whose lives might be saved, are neighbours whom we are called to love. In the light of this, I argue with reference to Karl Barth's treatment of the protection of life that it is very doubtful whether the killing of embryos to benefit others could ever be permitted or commanded by God.

While research on human admixed embryos has attracted similar critiques, on the assumption that it entails destroying entities that are or might be human, a good deal of the ethical concern in recent debates has been excited by the fact that admixed embryos are *not* unambiguously either human or non-human. Some critics of this research have argued that by blurring the species boundary between humans and non-humans, it undermines human dignity. From a theological standpoint, however, I question the notion that human dignity depends on our difference from other species. Nor am I fully persuaded by the theological argument that making admixed embryos goes against God's creative purposes by mixing the 'kinds' in which living creatures are made. In preference to these lines of argument, I examine the character of the practice of making human admixed embryos through the lens of the diagnostic questions set out in Chapter 1. I conclude that there is as yet no good reason to think that this practice could be mandated by the theological ethic set out in this book.

While the previous chapter addresses the ethical issues raised by some very new and high-profile areas of biomedical research, Chapter 5, 'Medicine, Science and Virtue', explores an ethical issue experienced in more routine medical research: the legitimacy or otherwise of involving human participants in clinical research that is intended to benefit future patients, but not (directly) the participants themselves. The starting point is Franklin G. Miller and Howard Brody's critique of 'clinical equipoise' – uncertainty within the medical profession as to whether an experimental therapy is more effective than proven treatments – as a condition of the ethical acceptability of clinical trials of new therapies.[20] Miller and Brody argue that the concept of clinical equipoise rests on a confusion between clinical medicine and clinical research, which are in fact fundamentally different activities for which different ethical frameworks are appropriate. This claim is investigated by considering both clinical medicine and scientific research as 'practices' in Alasdair MacIntyre's sense of that term,[21]

---

20 Franklin G. Miller and Howard Brody, 'A Critique of Clinical Equipoise', *Hastings Center Report* 33.3 (2003), pp. 19–28.
21 MacIntyre, *After Virtue*, p. 187.

and asking what virtues are necessary to sustain each. I argue that medicine and research can indeed be considered as distinct practices, each with its own characteristic 'map' of virtues, albeit with considerable overlap between the virtues characteristic of each. There are, furthermore, theological reasons for thinking that each is worth doing. However, it would be a mistake to separate the two too sharply. Not only are they connected by virtues, such as justice, which are probably needed to sustain any imaginable practice; they are also bound together by the reliance of modern medicine upon the results of scientific research. The standard way of connecting medicine and science in modernity is by means of the 'Baconian project' outlined in Chapter 1: the use of science and technology to gain mastery over the material world for the relief of suffering and the expansion of individual choice. This way of connecting medicine with science is evident in Miller and Brody's treatment, but from a Christian theological perspective, it is a distorted way of making the connections. I propose an alternative, theologically informed, account of the relationship between medicine and science and sketch out a few of its implications.

Modern biomedical research, of course, depends not only on the use of human participants, but much more heavily on the use of non-human animals in laboratory experimentation. This raises questions about whether, and with what limits, humans are entitled to use animals in this way, and more generally how we might give an account of the proper human treatment of non-human animals. In Chapter 6, 'Humans, Animals, Evolution and Ends', I argue that a theologically satisfactory answer to these questions must be teleological in character: our treatment of non-human animals ought to be oriented towards our, and their, proper ends. If that is so, how might we learn what those ends are? It might seem that modern biology can supply at least a partial answer, performing a role analogous to that of Aristotelian biology in the natural law theory of Thomas Aquinas. For example, natural selection tends to favour the evolution of traits conducive to survival and reproduction, which might seem to suggest that survival and reproduction are among the chief ends of any living species. One major difficulty with this, however, is that unlike Aristotelian biology, modern biology by and large proceeds by a methodological exclusion of teleology. That is one reason why, since Darwin's time, attempts to construct an evolutionary ethic have foundered on the problem of the relationship between 'is' and 'ought'. I maintain that if we are to think theologically about the proper human treatment of non-human animals, our talk of teleology must be located within an understanding of God's purposes in creating, redeeming and reconciling the world, as those purposes are made known in Christ. Within such a theological frame of reference, insights from evolutionary biology can be critically appropriated to contribute to our moral understanding of the relationship between humans and non-human animals. The chapter concludes by exploring the implications of one key biblical text – Isaiah's vision of the peaceable kingdom (Isa. 11.6–9) – for our understanding of God's purposes in respect of humans and animals, and the significance of that understanding for our treatment of non-human animals here and now.

In Chapter 7, 'Healthcare Resource Allocation and the "Recovery of Virtue"', I begin by mapping different levels of the problem of health care resource allocation: micro, macro and international. I argue that two standard approaches to the issue of distributive justice in health care, the quality-adjusted life year (QALY) approach[22] and the social-contract approach developed by Norman Daniels,[23] are unsatisfactory for reasons identified by MacIntyre, as outlined in Chapter 1. Although the virtue theory articulated by MacIntyre and others has been influential in many areas of health care ethics, there seems to have been relatively little discussion of the difference it might make to the problems of resource allocation. The potential of such an approach is explored

---

22 For example Alan Williams, 'Economics of Coronary Artery Bypass Grafting', *British Medical Journal* 291 (1985), pp. 326–9.

23 Norman Daniels, *Just Health Care*, Oxford: Oxford University Press, 1985.

in the later sections of the chapter. Two apparently promising ways of bringing virtue ethics into the discussion are examined and found wanting to greater or lesser extents. First, I argue that Beauchamp and Childress' account of the virtues, in a book mostly dedicated to expounding their 'Four Principles' framework, makes little substantive contribution to this issue.[24] Second, the 'liberal communitarian' system of resource allocation proposed by Ezekiel Emanuel,[25] while a considerable improvement on the account of Beauchamp and Childress, remains problematic in some respects. An alternative Christian account is developed by identifying significant influences that might shape the 'political prudence' which would enable Christian communities to form sound judgements about distributive justice in health care. The chapter concludes with some remarks about the relationship between this tradition-constituted account and the wider public sphere of policy-making and practice.

The point of departure for the final chapter, 'Beyond Autonomy and Compassion: Reframing the Assisted Dying Debate', is the public debate provoked by recent proposed legislation to permit assisted dying in the UK. I observe that in that debate, arguments both for and against the proposed legislation were commonly framed in terms of respect for autonomy and compassion for suffering patients. I critically examine this way of framing the debates and find it wanting from the perspective of a Christian theological ethic. Arguments from *autonomy* are open to various criticisms: in particular, they rely on assumptions about our ownership of our own lives which are unsustainable if we understand ourselves as God's creatures, accountable to God for the life that has been entrusted to us. The idea of *compassion* in play in these debates, and deployed in much public rhetoric in favour of assisted dying, is sometimes presented as an expression of Chris-

---

24 Tom L. Beauchamp and James F. Childress, *Principles of Biomedical Ethics*, 6th edn, New York: Oxford University Press, 2009, pp. 30–63.

25 Ezekiel J. Emanuel, *The Ends of Human Life: Medical Ethics in a Liberal Polity*, Cambridge, MA: Harvard University Press, 1995.

tian love of neighbour. It is, however, a partial and distorted notion of what love of neighbour entails. A more complete account of Christian love for the suffering, and of our proper responsibility for our own and one another's lives, must be set in the context of the Christian narrative and the ultimate hope that it promises. I argue that in this perspective, assisted dying cannot be understood as a properly faithful response to the biblical witness to Christ. However, this witness to Christ calls Christian churches to live – more faithfully than they have sometimes done – as communities in which proper responsibility for our own and each others' lives can be exercised, in which Christian love for all, particularly those who suffer, is a lived reality and in which people are enabled to hope even in the face of suffering. Unless these forms of faithful Christian practice are evident, spoken Christian opposition to assisted dying is unlikely to carry much weight.

Taken together, the six chapters in Part 2 illustrate how the theological ethic articulated in Part 1 can be fruitfully brought to bear on a range of bioethical issues from the beginning to the end of life, both those raised at the cutting edge of biomedical research and those concerned with the routine practice of health care, and can offer resources for addressing both the Christian community and a range of wider publics.

Part 1

Terms of Engagement

1

Reframing the Questions

In 2007, the UK Government published draft legislation to update the existing law on fertility treatment, embryo research and related areas,[1] and an amended version of this draft bill became law in 2008.[2] One of the new provisions in this legislation allowed for the creation of human-animal hybrid (or 'human admixed') embryos for research purposes under licence.[3] Not surprisingly, this proved highly controversial and provoked vigorous debate. As a result, the work of the Parliamentary Select Committee on the draft legislation and the evidence it received provide an instructive sample of the arguments deployed in public bioethical debates in one contemporary Western context.[4] In this chapter, I shall use this example to diagnose what I hold to be problematic features of such contemporary ethical debates, which require reframing from a theological standpoint. The substantive ethical issue of human admixed embryo research is addressed in Chapter 4.

---

1 Human Tissue and Embryos (Draft) HC Bill, 2006–07 (Cm 7087), online at http://www.official-documents.gov.uk/document/cm70/7087/7087.pdf (accessed 8 September 2010).

2 Human Fertilisation and Embryology Act 2008, online at http://www.opsi.gov.uk/acts/acts2008/pdf/ukpga_20080022_en.pdf (accessed 12 August 2010).

3 For more detail on the types of admixed embryo provided for in the Act, see below, pp. 109–11.

4 Joint Committee on the Draft Human Tissue and Embryos Bill, Report on the Human Tissue and Embryos (Draft) Bill, 2006–07, HL Paper 169-I, II. Online at http://www.parliament.uk/business/committees/committees-archive/humantissue/ (accessed 8 September 2010). Hereafter: Report on the HTE (Draft) Bill.

The debate on human admixed embryo research

Arguments in support of human admixed embryos

As might be expected, much of the most enthusiastic support for legislation permitting the making of human admixed embryos came from the biotechnology industry, the biomedical research community and patient organizations. Not surprisingly, by far the most common arguments for permitting this research appealed to the *benefits* to be gained from it, particularly the prospect of understanding and perhaps developing treatments for various debilitating and fatal diseases and the potential benefit to the British economy.[5] It was acknowledged that no one could be certain whether new treatments would eventually emerge from this research, and that some of what was being discussed (such as the creation of 'true hybrids' by combining human and animal gametes) did not currently have important medical or scientific applications. However, supporters argued that since it could not be predicted in advance which lines of research would prove fruitful, the legislation must be permissive enough to allow scientists to respond quickly to new developments.[6] Restrictive legislation would risk losing the benefits promised by this research, to the detriment of seriously ill patients, their families and the economy. Advocates of the research claimed that the potential benefits of permissive legislation were not offset by disproportionate risks or harms: research using admixed embryos would pose no particular safety risks over and above those that were common and easily dealt with in embryological work.[7]

In short, the arguments in favour of permitting research on human admixed embryos were largely couched in terms of the

---

5 Academy of Medical Sciences, *Inter-Species Embryos*, London: Academy of Medical Sciences, 2007; Report on the HTE (Draft) Bill, vol. II, pp. 1–18, 237–48, 264–5, 402–5, 410–13.

6 Report on the HTE (Draft) Bill, vol. II, pp. 1–18, 415–18, 429–32.

7 Academy of Medical Sciences, *Inter-Species Embryos*, pp. 26-7.

positive consequences of such a move. This is not to say, of course, that all of those advocating permissive legislation were thorough-going consequentialists. Some probably were; others acknowledged the existence of non-consequentialist moral principles, such as those derived from a human rights framework, which set limits to what ought to be done in biomedical research, but did not believe that these would prohibit research on human admixed embryos.[8] As one contribution to the debate put it, there were 'no substantive ethical or moral reasons not to proceed' with such research within a framework similar to the legislation already governing human embryo research in the UK.[9]

Arguments against human admixed embryo research

The other side of the debate had a rather different character. Some of the opposition to permissive legislation was, indeed, couched in terms of consequences. Some opponents questioned the claims about the benefits promised by human admixed embryo research, and were less sanguine than its advocates about the risks that it entailed.[10] Much more characteristically, though, the case against permissive legislation relied on deontological arguments that were held to prohibit the creation and use of human admixed embryos. For example, many opponents argued that creating a part-human, part-animal entity would blur the boundary between humans and non-human species, thereby undermining the distinctive dignity and moral regard to which humans are entitled.[11] Others made claims about the moral status of human embryos, holding that as genetically distinct human individuals, embryos should be

---

8 For example: Report on the HTE (Draft) Bill, vol. II, pp. 1–18.

9 Academy of Medical Sciences, *Inter-Species Embryos*, p 38.

10 For example: Report on the HTE (Draft) Bill, vol. II, pp. 328–9, 375–83, 401–2; Bio-Centre: the Centre for Bioethics and Public Policy, *The New Inter-Species Future? An Ethical Discussion of Embryonic, Fetal and Post-Natal Human-Nonhuman Combinations*, London: BioCentre, 2007, p. 57.

11 BioCentre, *The New Inter-Species Future?*, pp. 24, 26; Report on the HTE (Draft) Bill, vol. II, pp. 328–9, 383–7, 387–95, 466–76.

accorded the same moral regard as other human individuals. If we recognize absolute moral principles that prohibit us from doing certain things to children or adults – for example, subjecting them to lethal experiments for the benefit of others – then we should not do those things to human embryos either.[12] Some, acknowledging the well-known debate and controversy about the moral status of the human embryo, argued for a 'precautionary principle' whereby, if there is doubt as to its moral status, it should be treated *as if* it had the same status as a human child or adult.[13]

To a large extent, therefore, the moral issue between the two sides in this debate was whether there are absolute and exceptionless moral principles that prohibit the creation of human admixed embryos. Some of those who held that there are such principles based their arguments on explicitly Christian theological premises. Some appealed to the doctrine of the *imago dei* to support claims about human dignity and the status of the embryo.[14] Others argued that to create human admixed embryos would transgress the limits of legitimate human action in the world by 'making something which God has not made.'[15] But, of course, such explicitly theological premises appeared easy for advocates of permissive legislation to dismiss. It is often stated in such debates that arguments like these are the religious convictions of a minority, which must be respected as far as possible, but should not be allowed to determine public policy or impede scientific and medical progress. For example, the journalist Mark Henderson wrote on the day after one of the parliamentary votes on the legislation: 'As cybrids are supported by all the country's leading scientific institutions, a ban would have suggested that this considered consensus matters less to Parliament than the vocal concerns of a religious minority.'[16]

---

12 Report on the HTE (Draft) Bill, vol. II, pp. 211–22, 375–83.

13 BioCentre, *The New Inter-Species Future?*; Report on the HTE (Draft) Bill, vol. II, pp. 445–52.

14 Report on the HTE (Draft) Bill, vol. II, pp. 281–2, 316, 328–9, 395–7.

15 Report on the HTE (Draft) Bill, vol. II, p. 251.

16 Mark Henderson, 'Benefits Are Years Off, but it's a Victory for Scientific Freedom', *The Times*, 20 May 2008, p. 4.

Other opponents argued on the basis of moral premises that were not (explicitly) theological, either to avoid being written off in this way or because they were not arguing from the perspective of a particular faith tradition.[17] Several appealed, for instance, to the existence of universal human rights and their expression in international treaties and conventions.[18] Others claimed that there is a widely felt repugnance about such research, which reflects a moral wisdom deeper than scientific knowledge, and should be taken as a warning not to proceed.[19] In this debate, however, many of these arguments did not make much more headway than the explicitly theological ones. Appeals to the 'wisdom of repugnance' were written off by supporters of admixed embryo research as 'a rationalization of a prior decision that something is wrong – a decision whose basis is not always transparent'.[20] And arguments based on universal human rights became entangled in the difficult question of whether human embryos are among the *bearers* of such rights. Even when an answer in the affirmative is supported by philosophical arguments that do not depend on explicitly theological premises, it is vulnerable to being written off as a faith stance held by a religious minority – though it is worth noting in passing that it is not only this side of the debate which relies on contested claims about the moral status of human individuals.[21]

In short, the debate on human admixed embryo research seemed

---

17 Report on the HTE (Draft) Bill, vol. II, pp. 295–6, 368–74, 383–7, 401–2.

18 Report on the HTE (Draft) Bill, vol. II, pp. 295–6, 401–2, 445–52.

19 Report on the HTE (Draft) Bill, vol. II, p. 299, citing Leon R. Kass, 'The Wisdom of Repugnance', *New Republic* 216.22 (2 June 1997), pp. 17–26.

20 Academy of Medical Sciences, *Inter-Species Embryos*, p. 30.

21 The Academy of Medical Sciences responded to the argument that blurring the species boundary would undermine human dignity by remarking that '[i]f the concept of "human dignity" has content, it is because there are factors of form, function or behaviour that confer such dignity or command respect. Either hybrid creatures would also possess these factors or they would not. If they do possess these factors, they would also have a specific type of dignity analogous or identical to human dignity that other creatures lack; if not, they would not' (*Inter-Species Embryos*, p. 29). The claim that humans possess distinctive dignity or command respect by virtue of possessing 'factors of form, function or behaviour' is, of course, a widely held philosophical position, but hardly an uncontroversial one.

to have approached stalemate: a stand-off between those who held that there were moral principles which should absolutely prohibit such research and those who denied that there were such principles, either because they did not acknowledge the existence of any absolute principles whatsoever or because they believed that any absolute principles which do apply to biomedical research would not rule out this work. One reason this stand-off seemed so difficult to resolve was that the various positions in the debate relied, implicitly or explicitly, on fundamental, but vigorously contested, claims about such things as the nature and grounds of human dignity and the moral significance to be attached to membership of the human species. The various parties in the debate took divergent and sometimes incommensurable views on these matters, and it was not clear whether, and how, these basic differences could be settled. That being the case, it was dauntingly difficult for all the protagonists to find enough common ground to settle their differences about the practical ethical questions. It was hardly surprising that the Joint Committee – having taken extensive evidence about the ethics of human admixed embryo research, and looked at the issue with great care – reported that they were 'unable to reach a consensus on this point', and could only recommend that it be put to a free vote in Parliament.[22]

It is not quite stalemate, however, as is evident from remarks made by the Government's Chief Medical Officer in his evidence to the Committee. Speaking generally about the regulation of human embryology research, he affirmed that 'there is a spectrum of opinion in society which feels very deeply about such matters, and their views have to be respected'.[23] However, when pressed to

22 Report on the HTE (Draft) Bill, vol. I, p. 50.
23 Report on the HTE (Draft) Bill, vol. II, p. 100. In this connection, it is worth noting that the Joint Committee apparently took with some seriousness the thought that such moral convictions, including those stemming from faith traditions, 'have to be respected'; certainly, their decision to organize an evening forum for 'those organisations representing faith groups or others with particular ethical perspectives' (Report on the HTE (Draft) Bill, vol. I, pp. 92–104) suggests a level of commitment to listening to those voices in the debate.

defend what was then the Government's position that the creation of 'true hybrids' should be prohibited, he said, 'I think there are two strands. One is the ethical and the other is the scientific, and then it is a question of whether the scientific arguments are so compelling as to overcome the ethical concerns that some people would have ...'[24] This appears to mean that the moral principles which would prohibit such things as the creation of true hybrid embryos are to be regarded as matters of personal conviction, which ought as far as possible to be respected by public policy-makers, but which can and should be set aside if the stakes are high enough. In the case of true hybrids, it was simply that the stakes were not judged to be high enough to justify disregarding 'the ethical concerns that some people would have'. Now since the forms of suffering that biomedical research is supposed to address are widely regarded with horror and dread, the stakes will often seem high enough to justify disregarding the moral objections of some members of society. Therefore, even though it might be acknowledged in theory that there are moral principles which set clear limits on what ought to be done, public ethical debates about biomedical research in this kind of climate tend to be susceptible to a drift towards consequentialist forms of rationality. The subsequent shift in the Government's position on true hybrids would seem to be a case in point.

In this section I have attempted to sketch some of the characteristics of public debates about bioethical questions in a contemporary UK context. It will be obvious that if my sketch is at all accurate, it represents a state of affairs that is hardly satisfactory from a Christian perspective. Later in the chapter, I shall suggest how a Christian tradition might respond to this state of affairs. Before doing so, however, it will be helpful to try and understand a little more fully some of the influences that have contributed to the character of contemporary public ethical debates.

---

24 Report on the HTE (Draft) Bill, vol. II, p. 101.

Some features of contemporary bioethical debates

I suggest that three related intellectual and cultural features of modernity, though often unnoticed and unacknowledged, have considerable influence over the terms and character of public debates such as the one described in the last section.

The 'Baconian project'

The first is the set of assumptions and aspirations that Gerald McKenny has called the 'Baconian project', after the early modern philosopher and politician Francis Bacon.[25] It should be emphasized that these assumptions and aspirations are not to be found fully formed in Bacon's own works; rather, what is meant is that his influence set in train a series of intellectual and cultural developments that have given rise to the project as we find it. One of Bacon's motivations, according to McKenny, was the practical concern, found in Puritan Christianity, to serve God in everyday life by loving one's neighbour. He argued that the natural sciences had a crucial role to play in making this practical service of God possible, because they made it possible to achieve control over nature for human benefit. Now in Bacon's time, his Protestant Christian context supplied a rich notion of what was *meant* by 'human benefit', and placed limits on what was permissible, even in pursuit of that benefit. But subsequently, Bacon's vision was progressively secularized and narrowed down. In particular, under the influence of eighteenth-century utilitarianism, human benefit became increasingly identified with pleasure and the absence of pain. Then, in the nineteenth century, the Romantics' emphasis

---

25 Gerald P. McKenny, *To Relieve the Human Condition: Bioethics, Technology and the Body*, Albany: State University of New York Press, 1997, pp. 17–24; Robert Song, 'The Human Genome Project as Soteriological Project', in Celia Deane-Drummond (ed.), *Brave New World? Theology, Ethics and the Human Genome Project*, London: T & T Clark, 2003, pp. 164–84 (pp. 173–6); Allen Verhey, *Reading the Bible in the Strange World of Medicine*, Grand Rapids, MI: Eerdmans, 2003, pp. 151–3.

on 'inwardness' and the importance of individual self-expression meant that increasing importance came to be attached to individual choice. According to McKenny, the outcome of this process, in our time, is that Western cultures place enormous value on the use of science and technology to achieve control over nature – and 'nature', of course, includes our own bodies – with two over-riding aims: to relieve suffering and to maximize individual choice.

None of the critics of this project wishes to deny the genuine goods that come from science, technology and medicine. But if our use of science and technology is informed and directed by a 'Baconian' vision, certain important problems result. One arises from the utilitarian reduction of human benefit to pleasure and the absence of pain. With that frame of reference, it comes to seem obvious that the relief of suffering is an *over-riding* good, and it becomes increasingly difficult to acknowledge that there could be other human goods, which might be in conflict with the relief of suffering and might sometimes be more important. In many public bioethical debates, there is an unspoken assumption that the relief of suffering trumps almost any other consideration. This helps to explain the pressure, noted in the last section, to judge that the scientific and medical stakes are high enough to over-ride moral objections to practices such as human embryo research. It also helps to explain the over-heated rhetoric, sometimes heard in these debates, about the massive benefits of such research and the callous inhumanity of those who would place restraints on it.

A Christian theological ethic is committed to a richer understanding of the human good than the utilitarian calculus of pleasure and the absence of pain. Furthermore, Christian ethics must, I think, take issue with another assumption of the Baconian mindset, namely the tendency to regard the material world as indifferent or inimical to human interests, and lacking any inherent moral significance of its own. On that view the material world – including, as I have said, our own bodies – can properly be subdued by scientific and technological means in the service of human benefit. By contrast, the Christian tradition understands

27

the material world as God's good creation, brought into being for God's good purposes. As such, the material creation (including human bodily life) has its own value and its own proper ends and goals, which our human choices and actions ought to respect. For these two reasons, while it goes without saying that the relief of suffering is a hugely important part of the Christian calling to love one's neighbour, a Christian ethic must resist the assumption that it is the only or over-riding good that we should pursue.

The public/private dichotomy

The second characteristic that can be discerned in the debate about inter-species embryos is a sharp dichotomy between the public and the private, and, mapped onto that division, an equally sharp one between reason and faith. As Simon Oliver has argued, a set of complex historical and cultural influences has given rise to a widespread assumption in modern societies that faith commitments (and 'faith' can be understood very broadly) are matters of purely private, non-rational choice.[26] Members of society are free to hold such beliefs and practise them in the privacy of their homes and their faith communities, but in the public realm of policy and legislation, society cannot allow its decisions to be made on the basis of such private, supposedly non-rational beliefs. Rather, it must strive to make its decisions on the basis of publicly accessible reason.[27]

If such a division is made between the private realm of non-

---

26 Simon Oliver, 'What can Theology Offer to Religious Studies?', in Maya Warrier and Simon Oliver (eds), *Theology and Religious Studies: An Exploration of Disciplinary Boundaries*, London: T & T Clark, 2008, pp. 15–29.

27 John Rawls is commonly taken to be one of the leading philosophical exponents of this dichotomy (see esp. his *Political Liberalism*, expanded edn, New York: Columbia University Press, 2005), though his view is on any account far more nuanced than the simple public/private opposition evident in public debates such as the one in view in this chapter: see, for example, Peter Sedgwick, 'The Public Presence of Religion in England: Anglican Religious Leaders and Public Culture', in Nigel Biggar and Linda Hogan (eds), *Religious Voices in Public Places*, Oxford: Oxford University Press, 2009, pp. 235–59. For an argument that the later writings of Rawls allow a significant place for religious arguments in public

rational preference and belief and the realm of public rationality, to which realm does moral deliberation belong? It appears to straddle both, rather uncomfortably. As the debate about human admixed embryos illustrates, public policy has to be made – and defended – about what are obviously moral questions. But the answers that citizens give to those questions often seem to be deeply rooted in the kinds of conviction and belief that are assumed to be private and non-rational. It is tempting for a political community to try and resolve this tension in one of two ways. One is to make policy that prescinds as far as possible from any decision about substantive moral issues, aiming instead for procedural settlements that leave everyone free to act according to their own 'private' convictions. The other is to decide the moral issues using arguments that conform as closely as possible to what is considered admissible in the realm of public rationality. Now – at any rate in the present, bioethical, context – the form of reasoning that is thought to qualify most unequivocally as rational is natural-scientific reasoning. So when moral issues are debated in this kind of context, the arguments that most easily gain admission to the public forum are those that look most like natural-scientific arguments. And that often means consequentialist arguments, since they promise to settle moral questions by means of calculations about testable empirical claims. This could well be one reason why the default position for public bioethical arguments, at any rate in contemporary Britain, is some form of consequentialism.

One problem with such a default to consequentialism is that it risks ignoring the greater part of the relevant data. It is not self-evident that the only relevant 'data' for moral deliberation are the likely consequences of our actions and the value we attach to those consequences. So unless it can be shown that these *are* the only factors that need be considered, this move risks solving the

---

reason, see Nigel Biggar, 'Not Translation but Conversation: Theology in Public Debate about Euthanasia', in Biggar and Hogan, *Religious Voices in Public Places*, pp. 151–93 (esp. pp. 174–84). As these and other commentators make clear, a good deal hangs on what exactly is meant by publicly accessible reason.

problem of moral deliberation by misrepresenting it. A related, and deeper, problem is that this default to consequentialism rests on a dubious assumption about what it means to be 'rational'. The default to consequentialism is an attempt to make public moral debate as 'rational' as possible by making it as 'scientific' as possible (in a fairly narrow sense of 'scientific'). But we should at least consider the possibility that this is inappropriate: that moral rationality operates by different procedures and criteria from natural-scientific rationality – at least as rational, at least as rigorous, but *different*. And that brings me to the third characteristic of current bioethical debates to which I wish to draw attention.

The interminability of moral debate and the failure of the Enlightenment project

In the early 1980s Alasdair MacIntyre drew attention to the *interminability* of many modern moral debates: they cannot be brought to a conclusion, because those on the different sides of the argument do not have enough common ground to enable them to agree how to settle their differences.[28] As is well known, he attributed this feature to the failure of the 'Enlightenment project' in ethics. The project of justifying moral language, concepts and claims philosophically without reference to received traditions or appeal to authorities, he argued, is an incoherent project, because it is an attempt to isolate our moral language from the tradition of thought and practice that has given rise to that language and within which it makes sense. If the account I gave earlier was accurate, recent British debates about human admixed embryos are a case in point: only moral arguments that are not supported by appeals to particular traditions are considered admissible in the public forum, and the differences between the rival positions

---

28 Alasdair MacIntyre, *After Virtue: A Study in Moral Theory*, 2nd edn, London: Duckworth, 1985, pp. 6–11.

turn out to be unresolvable because their arguments are based on incommensurable premises.

It is worth noting in passing here that one of the key insights of *After Virtue* concerns the 'traditioned' character of all human reason. According to MacIntyre, it just is the case that 'all reasoning takes place within the context of some traditional mode of thought, transcending through criticism and invention the limitations of what had hitherto been reasoned in that tradition; this is as true of modern physics as of medieval logic'.[29] As I have already suggested, one of the problems with the default to consequentialism in public bioethical debate is that it tends to force moral discourse into modes of thought and argument alien to the tradition of reasoning within which that discourse belongs. Perhaps this happens because many of the participants, particularly if their education and training have been predominantly scientific and technological, are not as self-aware as they might be about the traditioned character of their own habitual modes of reasoning.

Faced with the failure of the Enlightenment project and its preferred modes of moral reasoning, the only alternative to a Nietzschean counsel of despair, according to MacIntyre, is to recover and reappropriate the kind of tradition-based moral reasoning that was displaced by the Enlightenment project.[30] In *After Virtue*, he identifies this as an Aristotelian tradition of the virtues, in which moral reasoning and the formation of character take place in a moral community with a shared narrative and tradition. In later works, he has developed a more explicitly Thomist account of the moral tradition that needs to be recovered, and has been willing to make more confident claims about the place of such a revived Thomism in contemporary public moral debate.[31] But for the present, my interest in MacIntyre's analysis in

---

29 MacIntyre, *After Virtue*, p. 222
30 MacIntyre, *After Virtue*, ch. 9.
31 MacIntyre, *Whose Justice? Which Rationality?*, London: Duckworth 1988; *Three Rival Versions of Moral Enquiry: Encyclopaedia, Genealogy and Tradition*, London: Duckworth,

After Virtue is that it has proved attractive to many Christian theologians – most famously (and prolifically) Stanley Hauerwas – who regard the Christian Church as a moral community in something like a MacIntyrean sense.[32] If the Christian community is regarded in this way as the locus of moral formation and tradition-constituted moral reasoning, it makes a considerable difference to the way in which Christians should think and act in relation to bioethical issues. In the next section I shall explore more fully what that difference might look like.

Christian bioethical reasoning: a proposal

The Christian Church has a shared narrative, told in its Scriptures and repeatedly retold and re-enacted in its worship and preaching, which represents humankind and the cosmos we inhabit as created, reconciled and redeemed by the God who is made known to us in Jesus Christ. As Colin Gunton has observed, its doctrine of creation has enabled the Christian tradition to say some distinctive and important things about God, humanity and the world.[33] Christians affirm that God created all that exists out of nothing and pronounced the whole creation 'very good' (Gen. 1.31). The goodness of creation is not merely instrumental – as if God needed the creation in order to make up some deficit in the divine being – but in and for itself. If the created order is good in and for itself, then it is worthy of attention and care for its own

---

1990. See, further, Thomas D. D'Andrea, *Tradition, Rationality and Virtue: The Thought of Alasdair MacIntyre*, Aldershot: Ashgate, 2006, part II, who emphasizes the basic continuity and coherence of MacIntyre's project through these works.

32 See, for example, Stanley Hauerwas, *A Community of Character: Towards a Constructive Christian Social Ethic*, Notre Dame, IN: University of Notre Dame Press, 1981; Stanley Hauerwas and Charles H. Pinches, *Christians among the Virtues: Theological Conversations with Ancient and Modern Ethics*, Notre Dame, IN: University of Notre Dame Press, 1997; Stanley Hauerwas and Samuel Wells (eds), *The Blackwell Companion to Christian Ethics*, Oxford: Blackwell, 2004.

33 Colin E. Gunton, *The Triune Creator: A Historical and Systematic Study*, Grand Rapids, MI: Eerdmans, 1998, pp. 8–13.

sake, which is one reason why Christians should never fall prey to a Gnostic hatred or suspicion of the material world.

Furthermore, the cosmos is created for a purpose: it has an ultimate destiny in God's good purposes which is related to its origins, but 'is something more than a return to its beginnings'.[34] The Christian tradition has also understood humankind to have a distinctive place within the creation, expressed by the affirmation that humans are created in the image and likeness of God (Gen. 1.26–28). Much ink has been spilled over the doctrine of the *imago dei*; I take it to denote a distinctive calling in the world, which springs from a distinctive relationship to God.[35] One aspect of this distinctive calling, as Gunton argues, is a role in enabling the non-human creation to glorify and praise its Creator.[36]

The Christian tradition, however, also has to reckon with the presence of various kinds of evil in the world, including human sin.[37] In his impressive study of the latter, Alistair McFadyen has argued that if it is properly understood as a theological category rather than merely a synonym for moral transgression, the Christian doctrine of sin has real and indispensable explanatory power in relation to the pathological in human affairs.[38] Sin can be

---

34 Colin E. Gunton, 'The Doctrine of Creation,' in Colin E. Gunton (ed.), *The Cambridge Companion to Christian Doctrine,* Cambridge: Cambridge University Press, 1997, pp. 141–57 (p. 143).

35 This reading is articulated more fully below in Chapter 4 (pp. 118–21) and is influenced particularly by Nathan MacDonald, 'The *Imago Dei* as Election: Reading Genesis 1:26–28 and Old Testament Scholarship with Karl Barth', *International Journal of Systematic Theology* 10.3 (2008), pp. 303–27. For a contrasting view (though with some common ground), see J. Richard Middleton, *The Liberating Image: The* Imago Dei *in Genesis 1*, Grand Rapids, MI: Brazos, 2005.

36 Gunton, *Triune Creator*, pp. 12–13 and ch. 9.

37 Although in this summary statement I mention sin and evil before God's work of reconciliation, I follow Karl Barth (for example *Church Dogmatics* vol. IV.1, pp. 388–9) and others in giving theological and epistemological priority to the latter: see, further, Neil Messer, *Selfish Genes and Christian Ethics: Theological and Ethical Reflections on Evolutionary Biology*, London: SCM Press, 2007, Chapters 7 and 8.

38 Alistair I. McFadyen, *Bound to Sin: Abuse, Holocaust and the Christian Doctrine of Sin*, Cambridge: Cambridge University Press, 2000.

schematized in many ways,[39] but McFadyen argues that at root it should be understood as idolatry: a fundamental refusal of the right relationship of love, joy and praise to which we are called by God. From this basic distortion in our 'vertical' relationship with God spring pervasive distortions in the 'horizontal' dimensions of our life together in the world, alienating us from ourselves, one another and the non-human creation. This basic refusal of right relations with God, neighbours and world, however, is not a matter of free and unconstrained individual choice.[40] One of the insights articulated in the Western Christian doctrine of original sin is that we are all born into this alienated condition, to which we also make our own contribution by our choices and actions.

We also have to reckon with forms of distortion and brokenness that are found beyond the bounds of human creatures and so-cieties, a claim articulated by biblical texts such as Romans 8.18–25, where the whole creation is said to be 'subjected to futility' and 'in bondage to decay'. It is hard to understand in any detail what this might mean for parts of the creation remote in place or time from human influence,[41] but this Pauline language does at any rate signal both that sinful humanity has inflicted deep damage on the non-human world within its reach, and that the created order as a whole, not only fallen humankind, stands in need of the transformation and ultimate fulfilment promised by its Creator.

The existence of sin and evil in the world means, in Colin Gunton's words, 'that creation's purpose can only be achieved by its redirection from within by the creator himself'.[42] According to

39 For example Barth's account of sin as pride, sloth and falsehood: *Church Dogmatics*, vol. IV.1–3.

40 See, further, Messer, *Selfish Genes*, pp. 156–8, 184–95.

41 For attempts to do so, see Messer, *Selfish Genes*, pp. 196–202, and 'Natural Evil and Theodicy after Darwin', in Michael Northcott and R. J. Berry (eds), *Theology after Darwin*, Carlisle: Paternoster Press, 2009, pp. 139–54. For a critical response to these attempts, see Christopher Southgate, *The Groaning of Creation: God, Evolution and the Problem of Evil*, Louisville, KY: Westminster John Knox Press, 2008, pp. 28–35, and Christopher Southgate, 'Natural Theology and Ecology', in Fraser Watts and Russell Re Manning (eds), *The Oxford Companion to Natural Theology*, Oxford: Oxford University Press, forthcoming.

42 Gunton, 'The Doctrine of Creation', p. 143.

the Christian narrative, this 'redirection' is achieved in and through the divine-human person of Jesus Christ. The reconciliation accomplished by God in and through Christ's incarnation, life, death and resurrection promises the transformation of our distorted relations with God, one another and the world, making possible relationships with God characterized by love, joy and praise, renewed forms of human community and society characterized by love of our neighbours, 'good news to the poor' (Luke 4.18) and just and peaceable relations with our non-human fellow creatures. This good news is in Dietrich Bonhoeffer's words God's 'ultimate' or last word to us,[43] which summons us to respond to Christ's reconciling work on our behalf, and directs us to the fulfilment of God's good purposes for us and all creation in God's promised good future.

Karl Barth summarizes the task of Christian ethics as 'understand[ing] the Word of God as the command of God'.[44] This calls for the Christian community's moral vision to be formed at the most fundamental level by the narrative of the gospel, but that moral vision continually faces new questions and challenges. As Oliver O'Donovan has observed, developments in medicine and biotechnology can give rise to genuinely new situations,[45] which means that Christian moral discernment can never simply be a matter of repeating the narrative and what has been said in the

---

43 Dietrich Bonhoeffer, *Ethics* (*Dietrich Bonhoeffer Works*, vol. 6), ET ed. Clifford J. Green, trans Reinhard Krauss, Charles C. West and Douglas W. Stott, Minneapolis: Fortress Press, 2005, pp. 146–70.

44 Barth, *Church Dogmatics*, vol. III.4, p. 4. The language of divine command has unhappy connotations, appearing to many critics to suggest an ethic that is (among other faults) arbitrary, unpredictable and opaque to reason. However, if the 'word of God' is the whole gospel of God's creating, reconciling and redeeming work made known in Christ, then the command of God is far from the capricious inscrutable divine *fiat* that critics sometimes imagine. It is better understood as God's gracious call, setting us free to become all for which we were created and inviting us towards the ultimate fulfilment promised to us and the world in Christ; see further Nigel Biggar, *The Hastening that Waits: Karl Barth's Ethics*, Oxford: Clarendon Press, 1993, pp. 19–25.

45 Oliver O'Donovan, *Resurrection and Moral Order: An Outline for Evangelical Ethics*, 2nd edn, Leicester: Apollos, 1994, pp. 92–3.

past about its implications. The story of God's creating, reconciling and redeeming work revealed in Christ must be continually retold and reappropriated, its significance rethought and renegotiated, by Christian communities facing these new situations and challenges. (There is nothing unique about bioethics in this regard, of course: throughout Christian history, every new context in which the Church has found itself has necessitated this rethinking and renegotiation of the meaning and significance of its tradition. The newness of some bioethical issues in our time is no more than a particularly clear and sharply focused example of what is generally the case.) Faithful response to the narrative of God's creating, redeeming and reconciling work requires the Christian community to learn the skills and habits of discernment that will enable it to recognize, in an ever-changing world, those forms of life which constitute a faithful response to that narrative; or to put it another way, to cultivate the virtue of 'practical wisdom' that is itself God's gracious gift, the fruit of the 'Spirit of wisdom and understanding' (cf. Isa. 11.2) at work among God's people. The development of such a biblically formed practical wisdom cannot be reduced to a fixed procedure or scheme, which would risk becoming a presumptuous attempt to control the word and command of God. It must retain a certain provisionality, openness and humility, characteristics that I seek to maintain in the following proposal.

In short, faced with a new possibility like human admixed embryo research, the Christian community must ask itself: *Can this practice be part of a life lived in faithful response to the narrative that forms this community and its tradition – the story that centres on Jesus of Nazareth, whom Christians confess as Messiah and Son of God?* Three possible answers to that question can be distinguished. First, it could be the kind of practice that is blatantly *opposed* to the Christian story – the kind of practice that instead serves the ends of chaos and destruction. Second, it could be *in line* with the Christian story – the kind of practice that *can* be part of a life directed towards God's good future. Or, third, it could be the kind of practice that is an attempted *substitute* for God's good and loving work in the world, to solve the problems caused by the sin and evil of the world without reference to the help that God offers. In Christian perspective, this kind of attempt, however well intentioned, is a basic and tragic mistake, one dimension of the sin of *pride*.[46]

However, distinguishing between the second and third of these possibilities – the kind of practice that could be in line with God's work in the world, and the ultimately self-defeating attempt to set up a substitute for God's work – will often be far from straightforward. In the light of the Christian narrative which, I have said, must shape and guide the community's moral vision, some 'diagnostic questions' may be proposed that may help Christian communities with this kind of difficult moral discernment.[47]

1 *Is the project a way of acting that conforms to the* imago dei, *or an attempt to be 'like God' (*sicut deus*) in the sense promised by the serpent in the story of the Garden of Eden (Gen. 3.5)?* This question is influenced by Dietrich Bonhoeffer's theological exposition of the Fall narrative of Genesis 3.[48] Human action in conformity to the *imago dei* would embody a level-headed acknowledgement of human finitude – a recognition that we are creatures, not gods – but also a willingness to live up to the divine mandate to live and act in the created world in which God has set us, to care for it and to take responsibility for its well-being before God. The attempt to be 'like God', by contrast, springs from a forgetfulness or denial of our creaturely limits, an assumption that we can and may do anything that we choose. The problem with projects done in this spirit is not so much the prospect of failure (some might fail, but

---

46 Karl Barth, *Church Dogmatics*, vol. IV.1, pp. 458–78.

47 The 'diagnostic questions' proposed here are an adaptation and expansion of the approach first outlined in Messer, *Selfish Genes and Christian Ethics*, ch. 9.

48 Dietrich Bonhoeffer, *Creation and Fall: A Theological Exposition of Genesis 1–3* (Dietrich Bonhoeffer, *Works*, vol. 3), ET ed. John W. de Gruchy, trans. Douglas Stephen Bax, Minneapolis: Fortress Press 2004, pp. 111–14.

not necessarily all) as the price of success. As Bonhoeffer observes, the serpent in the Fall narrative is not lying when he promises the humans the 'knowledge of good and evil', but in gaining that knowledge, they become alienated from God, one another, themselves and the created world.[49]

2   *What attitude does the project manifest towards the material world (including our own bodies)?* This question too draws on Bonhoeffer, this time the fragment 'Ultimate and Penultimate Things' in his *Ethics*.[50] The 'ultimate' is God's last word to us, the word of justification in Christ. This last word is 'at the same time the judgment on the penultimate ways' by which we might attempt to reach God (p. 150). Yet in the light of the ultimate, the penultimate, 'all that precedes the ultimate – the justification of the sinner by grace alone – and that is addressed as penultimate after finding the ultimate' (p. 159), becomes important, not in its own right, but precisely because it is pen*ultimate*. Bonheoffer identifies two 'extreme' or erroneous ways of relating the ultimate to the penultimate. The first he calls 'radicalism', which 'sees only the ultimate, and in it sees only a complete break with the penultimate' (p. 153). In the light of the ultimate, 'radicalism' would do away with the penultimate altogether. But though this seems to give utmost weight to God's grace, it in fact ends up denying it: 'The ultimate word of God, which is a word of grace, becomes here the icy hardness of the law that crushes and despises all resistance' (p. 153). The other 'extreme' solution Bonhoeffer calls 'compromise', which places the ultimate 'completely beyond daily life [so that] in the end [it] serves only as the eternal justification of all that exists' (p. 154); it is 'to have no say in the formation of life in the world' (p. 156). Both of these solutions, says Bonhoeffer, are extreme in the same sense:

---

49 Bonhoeffer, *Creation and Fall*, pp. 113–36.

50 Bonhoeffer, *Ethics*, pp. 146–70. Page references in brackets in this and the following paragraphs refer to this work.

they make the penultimate and the ultimate mutually exclusive ... Both wrongly absolutize ideas that are necessary and right in themselves ... One absolutizes the end, the other absolutizes what exists. Thus creation and redemption, time and eternity, fall into an insoluble conflict. (p. 154)

Each is exposed as un-Christian in the light of Jesus Christ, who unites what the extremes of 'radicalism' and 'compromise' divide. 'In Jesus Christ, we believe in the God who became human, was crucified, and is risen' (p. 157). The incarnation displays God's love for the created world, the crucifixion is the judgement of God on fallen humanity, and the resurrection makes known the promise of God's good future. To absolutize one of these elements of the Christian confession over against the others would invite one of the extremes: absolutizing the incarnation would lead to compromise; absolutizing the cross or the resurrection would lead to radicalism. A theological ethic that is not to fall into one or other error must be built on a faith in Christ that gives proper weight to his incarnation, his death and his resurrection, and holds them together rather than setting them against one another.

In the bioethical sphere, the extreme solution that Bonhoeffer calls 'radical' finds its counterpart in some kind of *hatred* of the material. This hatred could take various forms. One would be a kind of pseudo-asceticism that sought to escape the physical as far as possible.[51] Another would be to regard physical nature as indifferent or even potentially hostile to our own interests, in which case it must be subjected, violently if necessary, to our wills. Earlier I identified this attitude with the 'Baconian project'. 'Compromise', in Bonhoeffer's sense, finds a bioethical counterpart in the tendency to *reduce* everything to the material, either denying that

---

51 *Pseudo*-asceticism, because I take it that the ascetic traditions of Christianity, rightly understood, do *not* spring from the fear or hatred of the material creation, but from the aim of valuing it properly and proportionately in the light of God's promised good future.

there is more to human life than physical existence in this material world or bracketing out anything beyond the material so that it has no significance for human life here and now. This form of 'compromise' gives rise to the assumption that to solve any human problem whatever, we have nowhere else to look but our own skill and cleverness – particularly our scientific and technological cleverness. A more theologically adequate attitude to the physical will hold together what these extremes tend to separate. It will recognize the material world as good and worth taking trouble over, yet flawed and in need of transformation, and will not make the mistake of thinking that physical life in the present material world exhausts what humanity has to hope for.

3   *What attitude does the project embody towards our neighbours?*
The love of God and neighbour are at the heart of the transformed 'vertical' and 'horizontal' relationships promised by the gospel, as has been recognized since New Testament times (Mark 12.28–34 par.; Rom. 13.8–10). Indeed, there is a long history of Christian reflection that has regarded love of neighbour as the summation of all moral obligation. This overstates the case: as Richard Hays has argued, the moral witness of the New Testament is too complex and diverse to be reduced to a single category, even one as rich as love,[52] and a Christian ethic developed in response to the New Testament's witness to Jesus Christ must reflect that diversity. Nonetheless, love of neighbour is clearly a central theme in Christian ethics.

Talk of neighbour-love in the context of ethical debates about health care and biotechnology, however, raises the complex question of the relationship between love and justice, perhaps most famously addressed by Reinhold Niebuhr's argument that to attempt to instantiate love in the political life of a fallen world is both naïve and dangerous; justice is the best approximation that

---

52 Richard B. Hays, *The Moral Vision of the New Testament*, Edinburgh: T & T Clark, 1997, pp. 200–3.

can be achieved in 'immoral society'.[53] Critics have responded that the 'realism' expressed in Niebuhr's dichotomy of love and justice too easily becomes a rationalization of the interests of the powerful.[54] In any event, it is not necessary to settle the issue of the relationship between love and justice in political ethics for a question about our attitudes to our neighbours to be serviceable as one of our diagnostic questions. The point of these questions is to aid the Christian community's discernment of whether proposed projects and practices in health care and biotechnology can be part of a faithful response to the narrative of the Christian gospel, and it is not hard to imagine some technological projects that would embody attitudes and actions towards our neighbours that were clearly against the grain of that narrative.

Christian reflection on loving one's neighbour has often given particular emphasis to the love of those neighbours who are vulnerable, suffering and in need, and this brings us to the next diagnostic question.

4   *Is the project good news to the poor, the powerless, those who are oppressed or marginalized in any way?* Who stands to gain from it and at whose expense? What effect will it have on those who are on the margins of our societies and communities: will it tend to marginalize them further, or to draw them in to the heart of things? The question is simpler to ask than to answer, because an adequate answer to it will require close attention to the social, economic and political context in which the project takes place, and must include an account of its intended and unintended effects. Here there is a proper place for attention to the consequences of scientific and technological projects – but, of course, set in the context of a much richer and wider-ranging theological

---

53 For example Reinhold Niebuhr, *Moral Man and Immoral Society*, New York: Scribners, 1932, pp. 257–77.

54 For example Duncan B. Forrester, *Christian Justice and Public Policy*, Cambridge: Cambridge University Press, 1997, p. 219.

and ethical analysis than is allowed for by the consequentialist forms of public rationality that I criticized earlier.

5   *What attitude does the project manifest towards past failures?* Many of the human problems to which our technological projects are addressed are caused, at least in part and maybe in quite complex ways, by human error, weakness or wickedness – in other words, by aspects of human *sin*. If we try to solve our problems without recognizing our collective responsibility for having caused them, we risk not solving them, but compounding them. Karl Barth's analysis of the sin of pride is illuminating in this regard. One dimension of pride, as it is revealed to us in the light of Christ's reconciling work, is the pride of self-help: not wanting to be helpless, we cling to the illusion that we 'can and must be [our] own helper[s]',[55] and thereby turn away from the true help that God offers us. Human action intended to address the consequences of sin, if it is to avoid this danger, must be done in what could be called a *repentant* spirit. Technological projects that are addressed to human problems and needs must be accompanied by an honesty about past failures, a recognition that things will have to be different in the future, and an openness to the help that will be needed in *making* things different – from whatever source that help might come. If technological projects are approached in such a spirit, of course, Christian traditions will have something important and distinctive to offer by way of the moral and spiritual resources that can sustain such an attitude to technological action in the world.

In the last part of this chapter I have argued that a Christian moral response to contemporary bioethical questions and challenges requires the cultivation of a biblically formed practical wisdom that will enable Christian communities to discern what constitutes a faithful response to the narrative of God's creating, reconciling

---

55 Barth, *Church Dogmatics*, vol. IV.1, p. 459.

and redeeming work made known in Christ. That narrative supplies the overarching frame of reference for all the engagements with substantive bioethical issues offered in Part 2 of this book. The 'diagnostic questions' set out here are one tool that can help Christians and churches to discern what constitutes a faithful response to the Christian narrative in the face of particular bioethical problems, and are deployed to that end in some of the chapters in Part 2. However, I have already emphasized that faithful response to the biblical witness to Christ cannot be a matter of devising some universal method or procedure which, if properly applied, is guaranteed to give the right answer in every case. So the basic question of what constitutes a faithful response to the Christian narrative is in the background, explicitly or implicitly, throughout Part 2 of the book, but a variety of approaches, of which these diagnostic questions are just one, is adopted in different chapters to bring that Christian narrative to bear on the various practical issues addressed.

2

Public Engagement

In Chapter 1 I described the new – or apparently new – ethical problems raised by the scientific and technical advances that make it possible to create human admixed embryos. I argued that a theological vision of humanity and the cosmos, centred on the Christian narrative of God's work in the life, death and resurrection of Christ, gives a distinctive moral perspective on problems such as these. As subsequent chapters will show, the same is true of more familiar bioethical problems such as assisted dying. Yet in many modern societies, including Britain, these are also public questions, debated in various forums, in many ways and through a variety of media. Within the past few years, both assisted dying and admixed embryo research have been the subject of legislative proposals in the UK Parliament, the latter successful, the former as yet unsuccessful. Discussions about proposed legislation have in both cases been foci for vigorous debates in the news and current affairs media, including skilful media campaigns by interested parties and pressure groups.[1] The issues have also been raised and debated through literary and dramatic media,[2] as well as being the objects of academic discourse in a variety of fields. In liberal, pluralist and supposedly secular societies like modern Britain,[3] the

---

1 For a sample of the media campaign, see the website of the pressure group Dignity in Dying, http://www.dignityindying.org.uk/ (accessed 9 September 2010).

2 For example Frank McGuinness, *A Short Stay in Switzerland* (2009), dir. Simon Curtis, BBC1, 25 January.

3 'Supposedly' secular, because I take what David Ford holds of our world in general to be true of modern Britain in particular, that it 'cannot truthfully be described simply as

conceptual and moral horizon of these debates is unlikely to be in any simple way the horizon supplied by the Christian vision sketched in Chapter 1. Indeed, I have already argued in Chapter 1 that from a Christian standpoint, the terms of public debate on these questions manifest various deeply rooted and serious kinds of distortion. If this is the case, should Christian communities whose moral response to these issues is formed by their distinctive theological vision attempt to engage with wider public debate in all its various forms, and how should they go about it?

Which 'public'?

Talk of 'public engagement', though, oversimplifies the matter, because it has become a commonplace among public theologians that theology potentially has a number of different 'publics' to en-gage. This thought is perhaps most famously expressed in David Tracy's frequently cited taxonomy of society, the academy and the Church as the three publics of theology.[4] Tracy correlates these three publics with a threefold classification of the discipline of theology into fundamental, systematic and practical theology, primarily addressed to academy, Church and society respectively.[5]

Almost three decades after its publication, Tracy's formulation is still in use as a map of public theology's field of operations. For example, in a tribute to the Scottish public theologian and ethicist Duncan Forrester (of whom more later), Andrew Morton shows how Tracy's taxonomy informs Forrester's conception of the task of public theology.[6] As Morton points out, however, Forrester does

---

"religious" or simply as "secular"; it is simultaneously and complexly both'. David F. Ford, 'The Responsibilities of Universities in a Religious and Secular World', *Studies in Christian Ethics* 17.1 (2004), pp. 22–37 (p. 24).

4 David Tracy, *The Analogical Imagination: Christian Theology and the Culture of Pluralism*, London: SCM Press, 1981, Ch 1.

5 Tracy, *Analogical Imagination*, Ch 2.

6 Andrew Morton, 'Duncan Forrester: A Public Theologian', in William F. Storrar and Andrew R. Morton (eds), *Public Theology for the 21st Century: Essays in Honour of Duncan B. Forrester*, London: T & T Clark, 2004, pp. 25–36.

not acknowledge such a tidy mapping of disciplines or modes of theology (fundamental, systematic and practical, or – alluding to Rowan Williams – 'celebratory, communicative and critical') onto the three publics.[7] Theology done among any of the three publics, or any combination of them, will operate to some degree in all three modes.

Tracy's taxonomy of 'publics' is helpful as an initial reminder that talk of 'public engagement' conceals a multiplicity of audiences or conversation partners, and potentially also a range of modes of engagement. Two caveats, though, must be entered. The first and more trivial is that this threefold division is clearly oversimplified. This is most obvious in the case of 'society', which – it hardly need be said – is a highly complex and heterogeneous entity. Not only are there great disparities between the relatively rich and powerful and the relatively poor and powerless in most societies, so that Morton can write of Forrester's Scottish context that 'the most and the least powerful people … constitute in effect two publics'.[8] 'Society' can also be broken down in any number of ways into subgroups. Tracy himself subdivides it into the realms of 'technoeconomic structure', 'polity' and 'culture'.[9] Going further, in relation to the issues in view in this book, 'public theology' might be addressed to a society as a whole in so far as it is engaged in debates about policy and legislation, to those with particular roles and responsibilities in the legislative and policy process, to particular professional groups such as doctors, nurses and other health care professions, to particular institutions such as those delivering health care, to particular interest and lobby groups such as the pharmaceutical industry or patient support groups, and so on.

The more fundamental caveat concerns the assumptions underlying Tracy's exposition of his taxonomy in *The Analogical Imagina-*

---

7 Morton, 'Duncan Forrester', pp. 31–2; Rowan Williams, *On Christian Theology*, Oxford: Blackwell, 2000, pp. xii–xvi.

8 Morton, 'Duncan Forrester', p. 33.

9 Tracy, *Analogical Imagination*, pp. 6–7.

tion, and in particular the criteria by which each type of theology is recognized as a genuinely public activity – that is to say, the criteria by which its claims to truth and meaning are assessed. In Tracy's perspective, fundamental theology, done primarily with reference to the academy, is the most straightforwardly public, because it is concerned with 'the articulation of fundamental questions and answers which any attentive, intelligent, reasonable and responsible person can understand and judge in keeping with fully public criteria for argument'.[10] The others are more problematic: systematic theology, for example, is typically 'confessional' in character, done primarily with reference to the Church, and systematic theological claims are typically judged in terms of their congruence with the Christian faith tradition. For Tracy, this raises the question whether systematic theology can truly be described as 'public':

> What, from the seemingly disparate stance of fundamental theology, can one argue on obviously public grounds for the public status of all good systematic theology? If one's answer must finally be that no plausible argument can be made for the public status of systematics, then the latter should be disowned as not really a 'confessional' but an entirely private option.[11]

In fact, he goes on to argue that systematic theology *does* have such a public character, because it is a hermeneutical activity concerned with the interpretation of religious 'classics';[12] but the point for the present discussion is that the validity and adequacy of any theological activity are to be judged by universal criteria (those of 'any attentive, intelligent, reasonable and responsible person') external to the tradition itself. In Chapter 1, with reference to

---

10 Tracy, *Analogical Imagination*, p. 63.
11 Tracy, *Analogical Imagination*, p. 82.
12 Tracy, *Analogical Imagination*, chs 3–5.

MacIntyre's account of the 'traditioned' nature of human reason, I questioned whether such universal criteria, external to traditions, exist. As will become clear in the present chapter, the theological tradition articulated in this book is profoundly suspicious of the use of external, non-theological criteria to judge the adequacy of theological reasoning: in a theological approach influenced by Karl Barth, one of my principal conversation partners, the adequacy of theological reasoning can only properly be judged against the divine revelation to which it is theology's business to respond.

As Kristen Heyer points out, in his more recent thinking, Tracy has responded to the challenge of anti-foundationalism and the critiques of postliberal theologians such as George Lindbeck by moving away from the search for universal criteria of justification, and adopting a conversational model of theological reasoning, while still wishing to retain a notion of public rationality.[13] While issues remain about what might be meant by public rationality and how it might be recognized, this shift does at any rate indicate that one can take Tracy's taxonomy as a helpful reminder of the range of different conversation-partners to which a theological bioethic might be addressed, without thereby being committed to the account of the justification of theological claims which originally accompanied that taxonomy.

The discussion of public engagement in this chapter, then, potentially has a range of audiences and conversation partners in view. The 'public' of the Church is not in question in the present chapter, or indeed elsewhere in this book: it is taken as read that the Church is the primary public of theology, and that when theological claims are advanced in other 'public' domains, they are advanced in some sense on behalf of the Church. So when individual Christians, including theological ethicists, engage with (for example) policy debates *on the strength of their Christian commitment*, they are in some sense representing the Church. This

---

13 Kristen E. Heyer, 'How Does Theology Go Public? Rethinking the Debate Between David Tracy and George Lindbeck', *Political Theology* 5.3 (2004), pp. 307–27.

is not the same thing as saying that they are formal representatives of institutional churches or hierarchies, mandated to represent those institutions' officially determined positions: a good deal of Christian public engagement neither need nor should be officially mandated in this way. Nor is it to exclude the possibility that Christians might play other roles in public debates – for example, as spokespersons of professional bodies or health care institutions. It is simply to say that to speak and argue as a Christian, on the basis of one's Christian faith, just is to speak and argue as a member of a Christian community that is the bearer of a tradition of faith. As Oliver O'Donovan puts it:

> A theologian, for example, who is invited to participate in an exercise of secular deliberation about matters of social concern, has no independent standing to give advice. Such a one either speaks for and out of the church (not for its hierarchy or synods, of course, but for its faith and tradition) or is a false prophet.[14]

One major preoccupation of this chapter is Christian engagement with what Tracy calls 'the realm of polity':[15] public debates about policy and legislation, as those debates are played out in the news and current affairs media, in parliamentary debates and committees, and so forth. Another aspect of public engagement important for the issues in view in this book is with professional communities, particularly of doctors, nurses and other health care professionals. Related to the sphere of professional communities is the realm of the institutions in which those professionals practise health care: hospitals and other health care organizations, the

---

14 Oliver O'Donovan, *The Desire of the Nations: Rediscovering the Roots of Political Theology*, Cambridge: Cambridge University Press, 1996, p. 188. For an interesting and illuminating discussion of this statement and its implications for public engagement with bioethics, see Gilbert Meilaender, 'Against Consensus: Christians and Public Bioethics', *Studies in Christian Ethics* 18.1 (2005), pp. 75–88.

15 Tracy, *Analogical Imagination*, p. 6, and ch. 1 *passim*.

health care system as a whole and those administering it, and so forth. Other specific 'publics' with which Christians might engage in bioethical debates can of course be envisaged,[16] but those mentioned will suffice to indicate both the range and the diversity of contexts in which Christian public engagement on bioethical matters might take place.

Should Christians and churches engage?

It might be asked, though, whether engagement with publics other than the Church *ought* to be encouraged at all. Perhaps the distortions of public moral discourse and practice diagnosed in Chapter 1 are so severe that Christians and Christian communities finding themselves in such contexts should engage with these distorted forms of ethics as little as possible. Stanley Hauerwas' radically ecclesial ethic, discussed later in this chapter, is sometimes taken by unsympathetic readers to recommend a withdrawal from the world into the counter-cultural moral community of the Church, a withdrawal encouraged by one reading of Alasdair MacIntyre's call in the closing pages of *After Virtue* for 'the construction of local forms of community within which civility and the intellectual and moral life can be sustained through the new dark ages which are already upon us'.[17] As we shall see later, however, Hauerwas' emphasis on the Church as radically distinctive moral community is better understood as commending a particular *mode* of engagement with the world than advocating a refusal of that engagement.

---

16 The pharmaceutical industry, for example, is a major player in the development of health care in Western countries, and a very powerful influence in public ethical and policy debates, as the example of the human admixed embryo debate discussed in Chapter 1 makes clear; yet there is little discussion among theological bioethicists about whether, and if so how, Christians might engage with this powerful body.

17 Alasdair MacIntyre, *After Virtue: A Study in Moral Theory*, 2nd edn, London: Duckworth, 1985, p. 263. For a perceptive discussion of this aspect of MacIntyre and Hauerwas in relation to these issues, see David Fergusson, *Community, Liberalism and Christian Ethics*, rev. edn, Cambridge: Cambridge University Press, 1998, chs 3 and 5.

In any event, the theological vision articulated in this book should lead us to answer the question 'Should Christians engage?' with an unequivocal 'Yes'. This can be clearly seen with reference to various essays of Karl Barth, written before and after the Second World War, in which in effect he addresses the question: In theological perspective, what is the state for?[18] His answer, in part, is that Church and state have a common centre – Barth uses the image of concentric circles, the 'inner circle' of the Church and the 'outer circle' of the state, both centred on Christ – and both will find their fulfilment in the coming kingdom of God. But this does not mean that either one is called to subsume the other. Church and state have their own distinct vocations in the divine economy, though their common centre and goal mean that there are analogies between them. One aspect of the state's vocation, theologically understood, is to create and maintain the conditions in which the Church can exercise *its* distinctive vocation of proclaiming the gospel. This is only one of the things to be said about the relationship between Church and state, but this one thing turns out to be illuminating for our present concerns.[19]

Before exploring the implications of this insight, it is important to correct a potential misunderstanding. To emphasize the state's vocation to maintain the space in which the Church can preach the gospel might give the impression that the Church's principal interest in the state is basically self-centred, that the Church needs

---

18 Karl Barth, *Church and State*, ET G. R. Howe, London: SCM Press, 1939; Karl Barth, 'The Christian Community and the Civil Community', in *Against the Stream: Shorter Post-war Writings 1946–52*, ed. Ronald Gregor Smith, London: SCM Press, 1954, pp. 13–50; William Werpehowski, 'Karl Barth and Politics', in John Webster (ed.), *The Cambridge Companion to Karl Barth*, Cambridge: Cambridge University Press, 2000, pp. 228–42.

19 As Werpehowski points out ('Karl Barth and Politics'), Barth argues not only that the state is called to protect its citizens from chaos and preserve a space in which the Church can preach the gospel, but also that it can itself be a parable of the coming kingdom of God, and is called to bear witness in its own way to that kingdom; see Barth, 'The Christian Community and the Civil Community'. The way in which Barth develops this line of thought would, I believe, tend to reinforce and enrich what I argue in outline here about Christian engagement with public bioethics.

the state's protection in order to pursue its own 'sectarian' goals. This could hardly be further from the truth. In this theological perspective, the gospel is God's promise of, and invitation to, the ultimate fulfilment of human existence that is made possible in Christ. So to say that the state is called to keep open a space in which the gospel may be proclaimed and received is to say that it has a vital role in creating the conditions in which true human fulfilment can be sought and found. This turns out to be a wide-ranging task, by no means restricted to facilitating narrowly 'religious' activities. Dietrich Bonhoeffer, following a similar line of thought in his discussion of the 'ultimate' and the 'penultimate', to which I referred in Chapter 1, puts it like this:

> The hungry person needs bread, the homeless person needs shelter, the one deprived of rights needs justice, the un-disciplined one needs order, and the slave needs freedom ... If the hungry do not come to faith, the guilt falls on those who denied them bread. To bring bread to the hungry is preparing the way for the coming of grace.[20]

So understood, the state's vocation to create the conditions in which the gospel can be proclaimed and received encompasses a wide-ranging concern for the conditions of human life. It includes something like the same range of concerns that the Catholic tradition of social ethics has in view when it uses the rather different language of the *common good*: 'the sum total of those conditions of social life which enable men to achieve a fuller measure of perfection with greater ease'.[21]

If the state has this vocation, then as Barth points out, there are

---

20 Dietrich Bonhoeffer, *Ethics* (Dietrich Bonhoeffer, *Works*, vol. 6), ET ed. Clifford J. Green, trans. Reinhard Krauss, Charles C. West and Douglas W. Stott, Minneapolis: Fortress Press, 2005, p. 163.

21 Second Vatican Council, *Declaration on Religious Liberty (Dignitatis Humanae)*, in Austin Flannery (ed.), *Vatican Council II: The Conciliar and Post-conciliar Documents*, rev. edn, Northport, NY: Costello, 1984, pp. 799–812, para. 6 (p. 803).

things that it can legitimately expect from the Church: to 'be subject' to those in authority (Rom. 13.1), and to pray for them and for all people (1 Tim. 2.1, 2).[22] But Barth, writing against the backdrop of National Socialism and the German 'Church Struggle', is emphatic that these forms of service do not call for political passivity or acquiescence in anything and everything that political leaders might choose to do. He argues that '"Be subject unto" does not mean directly and absolutely "to be subject to someone" but to respect him as his office demands'.[23] This means that if the state seriously betrays its vocation, then Christian respect and prayer for the governing authorities will take forms that those authorities will find highly unwelcome, including various forms of protest, opposition and resistance.

> Christians would, in point of fact, become enemies of any State if, when the State threatens their freedom, they did *not* resist ... If the State has perverted its God-given authority, it cannot be honoured better than by this *criticism* which is due to it in all circumstances.[24]

Barth even considers the possibility that prayer for the state, and the political responsibility which that implies, could require Christians to engage in revolution against tyrannical rulers.[25] For concrete examples of the unwelcome forms of service that Christians might be called to render to the state under the extreme conditions of a profoundly corrupted political order, one need look no further than the German Confessing Church's Barmen Declaration of 1934, largely drafted by Barth,[26] and Dietrich

---

22 Barth, *Church and State*, pp. 62–8.
23 Barth, *Church and State*, pp. 64–5.
24 Barth, *Church and State*, p. 69, emphasis original.
25 Barth, *Church and State*, pp. 79–80.
26 *Theological Declaration of Barmen* (1934), ET online at http://www.creeds.net/re formed/barmen.htm (accessed 30 August 2010).

Bonhoeffer's participation in the resistance movement in Nazi Germany, which led to his imprisonment and execution in 1945.[27]

This understanding of the Church's proper service to the state suggests why, under the very different conditions of contemporary Western democracies, it is so important that Christian communities participate in public policy debates about bioethical questions. The decisions that a society makes about bioethical questions have potentially far-reaching implications for the value that it places on human life and how that value is instantiated in the practice of health care and biomedical research. This is one sphere among many in which the decisions made by the political community have the potential to be either more or less adequate ways of fulfilling its penultimate vocation. Christians have every reason to try and help the political community fulfil its vocation more adequately in this sphere. That being the case, we must ask what forms of Christian engagement with public debates have the potential to help the political community fulfil its vocation more adequately.

How should Christians and churches engage?

If it is granted that Christians and Christian communities *should* engage, on the basis of their theological commitments, with the bioethical debates that take place in the various kinds of public context noted earlier, how should they go about it? A wide range of possible modes of engagement can be found in the literature on public theology and ethics and in the churches' practice of public engagement.[28]

---

27 Eberhard Bethge, *Dietrich Bonhoeffer: Theologian, Christian, Contemporary*, ET ed. Edwin Robertson, London: Collins, 1970, esp. Part 3.

28 For a fuller typology, see Neil Messer (ed.), *Theological Issues in Bioethics: An Introduction with Readings*, London: Darton, Longman and Todd, 2002, ch. 10, from which some of the material in this section is taken.

Seeking common ground: Beauchamp and Childress

At one end of the scale are those approaches to public ethics that avoid the use of explicitly theological language or presuppositions as far as possible, seeking instead to find moral ground common to all participants in the debate, or arguments that will be persuasive to as many parties as possible. This form of engagement might be motivated by theological convictions about the nature of ethics and the human capacity for moral understanding. For example, Courtney S. Campbell has argued that the Quaker theme of 'answering that of God in every person' leads James F. Childress to conclude that 'there may be *theological* reasons for not doing medical ethics theologically'.[29] This theological orientation is certainly consistent with Childress' role, in partnership with Tom L. Beauchamp, in developing one of the best-known and most influential 'common-ground' approaches to bioethics: the so-called 'four-principles' approach set out in successive editions of their best-selling and highly influential text, *Principles of Biomedical Ethics*.[30]

Beauchamp and Childress hold that there is a 'common morality', binding on all people everywhere, whose precepts are acknowledged by 'all persons committed to morality' in every place and culture.[31] The common morality is not the totality of morality: there are also 'particular moralities', such as the moral traditions of faith communities and the ethical codes of professional groups.[32] These more specific moralities may add to – but not, it seems, subtract from – the norms of the common morality.

According to Beauchamp and Childress, the common morality

29 Courtney S. Campbell, 'On James F. Childress: Answering That of God in Every Person', in Allen Verhey and Stephen E. Lammers (eds), *Theological Voices in Medical Ethics*, Grand Rapids, MI: Eerdmans, 1993, pp. 127–56 (p. 127, emphasis original).

30 Tom L. Beauchamp and James F. Childress, *Principles of Biomedical Ethics*, 6th edn, Oxford: Oxford University Press, 2009.

31 Beauchamp and Childress, *Principles*, p. 3.

32 Beauchamp and Childress, *Principles*, pp. 5, 6.

supplies four principles that serve as an adequate framework for deliberation and debate about biomedical ethics: *respect for the autonomy* of human persons, *non-maleficence* (a principle stating the obligation not to do harm), *beneficence* (a principle that states an obligation to do good) and *justice*.[33] The application of these principles to particular issues and cases in bioethics requires a process of *specification*, whereby more detailed rules are derived from the general norms stated by the four principles.[34] For example, the rule requiring patients' informed consent to clinical procedures is a specification of the principle of respect for autonomy, and the rule about informed consent can itself be further specified to deal with situations in which informed consent cannot be obtained (for example, where the patient is a young child or lacks the mental capacity to give consent). Furthermore, a number of different principles and rules might have a bearing on any particular situation, and some of these might be in tension or conflict with one another. For example, when a competent patient refuses treatment that is needed to save his or her life, the clinician faces a conflict between respect for autonomy, which requires that the patient's refusal be honoured, and beneficence, which requires that life-saving treatment be given. Beauchamp and Childress handle these conflicts by holding that the principles state not absolute, but *prima facie*, requirements, and they recommend a process of *balancing* to accord the appropriate weight to each relevant principle or rule and determine which should over-ride the other in cases of conflict.[35]

The origins of the four-principles framework were closely associated with the US Government's *Belmont Report* on the ethical

---

33 Beauchamp and Childress, *Principles*, pp. 12, 13. They acknowledge that there is much more to morality than principles, and also seek to give an account of rules, rights, virtues and moral ideals (pp. 13–14 and ch. 2). However, they 'treat principles as the most general and comprehensive norms' (p. 13), and the four principles accordingly provide the structure and much of the content of their account of biomedical ethics.
34 Beauchamp and Childress, *Principles*, pp. 16–19.
35 *Principles*, pp. 14, 15, 19–24.

principles governing clinical research, for which Beauchamp served as a consultant;[36] and it seems clear that one of Beauchamp and Childress' aims is to provide a simple and workable method of political deliberation and policy-making about bioethical issues in democratic societies. Their approach has also been widely used among some of the other 'publics' identified above, for example in ethical deliberation and decision-making in clinical settings and in the teaching of biomedical ethics to present or future health care professionals. Beauchamp and Childress's 'principlism' appears to lend itself to these forms of public deliberation and decision-making by supplying an agreed framework of principles, based on uncontroversial common ground, that can form the basis of deliberation and the resolution of disputes about controversial issues and hard cases.

The aim of securing a framework for moral debate and deliberation about difficult and complex matters in diverse pluralist societies is both laudable and important. However, from the theological perspective being articulated in this book, some critical questions may be asked about whether principlism can, in the end, achieve such an aim, and whether it is the most appropriate way to set up public bioethical debate. This critical questioning can be focused by noting that Beauchamp and Childress present their four principles as part of the common morality, 'applicable to all persons in all places ... we rightly judge all human conduct by its standards'.[37] On what is this claim to universal authority for the four principles grounded?

Beauchamp and Childress' favoured method of moral justification is the 'reflective equilibrium' approach advocated by John Rawls,[38] in which we begin with our 'considered judgments' (those in which we have most confidence and 'match, prune and adjust considered judgments and their specifications to render them

---

36 Albert R. Jonsen, *The Birth of Bioethics*, Oxford: Oxford University Press, 1998, pp. 102–4.
37 Beauchamp and Childress, *Principles*, p. 3.
38 John Rawls, *A Theory of Justice*, Cambridge, MA: Belknap Press, 1971, pp. 48–51.

coherent with the premises of our most general moral commitments'.[39] This method is intended to avoid an infinite regress in the attempt to justify the moral norms which we use in our deliberation and argument. Beauchamp and Childress posit their four principles as 'considered judgments' to be used in the search for reflective equilibrium. Consistently with the reflective equilibrium method, they do not attempt a normative defence of their choice of principles. However, 'considered judgments' are not purely arbitrary, so Beauchamp and Childress must have some reason for selecting these four principles as their starting point. Despite the fact that they distinguish between empirical and normative justifications, acknowledging that '[w]hatever is established empirically about universal norms, nothing follows about the normative justifiability of these norms',[40] it seems that their grounds for selecting these four principles as the considered judgements with which to begin bioethical reasoning are at least partly empirical. They claim that '[m]ost classical ethical theories include these principles in some form, and traditional medical codes presuppose at least some of them',[41] so that the four principles are good candidates for membership of the common morality which is said to be 'shared by all persons committed to morality'.[42]

However, there are reasons to doubt these empirical claims for the extensive reach of the four principles. In terms of 'classical ethical theories', for example, it is not obvious how respect for autonomy figures in, say, a Thomistic scheme of natural law and the virtues without a good deal of projection of modern categories back onto a mediaeval body of thought. And in contemporary discussion, some Christian contributions at any rate offer some critical questioning of the concept of autonomy,[43] a line of thought

---

39 Beauchamp and Childress, *Principles*, p. 382.
40 Beauchamp and Childress, *Principles*, pp. 392–6; quotation at p. 394.
41 Beauchamp and Childress, *Principles*, p. 12.
42 Beauchamp and Childress, *Principles*, p. 3.
43 See, for example, Allen Verhey, *Reading the Bible in the Strange World of Medicine*, Grand Rapids, MI: Eerdmans, 2003, pp. 210–13.

developed further below in Chapter 8, in which I argue with reference to assisted dying that 'respect for autonomy' is simply unhelpful language to use in thinking about the value and dignity of human beings. So it looks as though some historical and contemporary expressions of the Christian tradition supply *prima facie* counter-examples to the claim that 'all persons committed to morality' acknowledge the authority of all four principles. These counter-examples to the *empirical* claim about the reach of the four principles, of course, are also indications that there are significant traditions of thought and practice that on any reasonable view are 'committed to morality', but that would nonetheless call into question the *normative* claim that all people everywhere *ought* to recognize the authority of all four principles.

In principle, Beauchamp and Childress can acknowledge that the four principles are open to this kind of questioning, since in a Rawlsian search for reflective equilibrium, '[e]ven the considered judgments that we accept as landmark fixed points are … subject to revision'.[44] Furthermore, they do acknowledge the possibility that these principles might not, as a matter of fact, turn out to be acknowledged by 'all people committed to morality', and outline the kind of empirical investigation that could test this.[45] However, there seems to be a certain amount of internal tension concerning this point in their account, because for the most part they seem to work on the assumption that the search for reflective equilibrium will yield new specifications of the principles, but will not call the principles themselves into question. Thus, the reader is in effect invited to accept as given a set of principles that are asserted to be part of a universal common morality, an assertion that is not rigorously tested out in the ensuing discussion.

Such internal tensions in Beauchamp and Childress' account are perhaps an indication that principlism suffers from the difficulties attributed by MacIntyre and others to the modern project

---

44 Beauchamp and Childress, *Principles*, p. 382.
45 Beauchamp and Childress, *Principles*, pp. 392–4.

of moral justification in general.[46] MacIntyre's argument is that the attempt to develop a system of moral justification without acknowledging the traditioned character of human reason, and without locating one's moral discourse within a coherent tradition of enquiry, will inevitably give results that are to some extent incoherent. If the MacIntyrean critique of the modern project is correct, it suggests that the quality and coherence of public bioethical debate will not best be served by Christian engagement that relies on a 'common-ground' or 'common-morality' approach.

In any event, the Reformed perspective being articulated in this book could be expected to sit rather uncomfortably with common-ground approaches such as principlism, since this Christian tradition has often been suspicious of attempts to gain some kind of autonomous human knowledge of the good in order to guide decision-making and living. This suspicion is expressed with particular sharpness by Karl Barth: commenting on the serpent's promise in Genesis 3.5 ('You will be like God, knowing good and evil'), he notoriously remarks, 'What the serpent has in mind is the establishment of ethics.'[47] For Barth, such attempts to gain autonomous moral knowledge are an aspect of the sin of pride, which, in alienating us from God, cuts us off from the true knowledge and the true help that we need. As we shall see later in this chapter, this emphatically does not mean that there is no true knowledge or insight about the good to be found outside the walls of the Church or the writings of theologians, nor (of course) that everything said within the Church or by theologians is true, wise and right. It is quite possible that many of the insights into the human good that Beauchamp and Childress schematize as aspects of the 'common morality' are genuine and true insights. The point, however, is that humans cannot pretend to know this independently of what is made known by God in and through Christ, and any putative insight into the good must be assessed in the light of

---

46 MacIntyre, *After Virtue*. See further above, Chapter 1.
47 Barth, *Church Dogmatics*, vol. IV.1, p. 448.

that divine revelation. So the kind of theological critique suggested by Barth and others does at any rate place a serious question mark against the project of developing a universal, tradition-neutral system of ethical principles by which to adjudicate public disputes about bioethical issues.

Some Christians might acknowledge this but still hold that common-ground modes of public engagement are necessary for strategic or tactical reasons. For example, they might conclude that public discourse is so shaped by the kinds of assumptions about public reason which underpin Beauchamp and Childress' account that Christians will only get a hearing in the public forum if they play the game according to those rules. Something like the tactical adoption of a 'common-ground' approach is advocated by the German Reformed theologian Ralph Charbonnier, who observes that Christian contributions to public debates must be both 'authentically "Christian" and at the same time contextualised'.[48] Contextualization, he argues, often requires Christians to 'leave [the] theological aspects [of their ethical reasoning] unmentioned' in order to 'render the ethical insights which were derived from the hermeneutic processes plausible' in a pluralist context.[49] This, though, assumes that those ethical insights *can* be detached from the context in which they were developed, and still retain their intelligibility and plausibility. If I was right to claim in Chapter 1 that moral reasoning, like other forms of reasoning, is inescapably 'traditioned', then the attempt to separate the conclusions of that reasoning from the narrative and tradition that have given rise to them risks rendering those conclusions less intelligible, or at any rate less interesting.[50] Furthermore, as Nigel Biggar has argued,

---

48 Ralph Charbonnier, 'The Contribution of the Protestant Church in Germany to the Pluralist Discourse in Bioethics: The Case of Stem Cell Research', *Christian Bioethics* 14.1 (2008), pp. 95–107 (p. 100).

49 Charbonnier, 'The Contribution of the Protestant Church', p. 99.

50 For a cautionary tale about these risks, see Neil Messer, '"Ethics", "Religious Ethics" and "Christian Ethics": What Are Scholars For?', in Maya Warrier and Simon Oliver (eds), *Theology and Religious Studies: An Exploration of Disciplinary Boundaries*, London: T & T Clark, 2008, pp. 149–65 (p. 157). The point at issue here has a long history, of course: an

Christians have good reason to challenge the claim that God-talk is by definition non-rational or irrational and therefore inadmissible in the forum of public argument and deliberation.[51]

Christian distinctiveness: Banner and Hauerwas

I have argued that rather than seeking some tradition-neutral common ground on which to conduct their public bioethical engagement, Christians should allow both their moral reasoning and their public engagement to be determined by the distinctive perspectives and claims of their tradition. One model for such engagement is the approach described by Michael Banner as a 'dogmatic Christian ethics', by which he means an ethic firmly rooted in the revelation of God in Jesus Christ.[52] Taking his cue from Karl Barth, Banner is highly critical of what he calls 'apologetic Christian ethics': that is, any account of Christian ethics which seeks to justify itself and its conclusions in terms of any other system, such as what I have described as the 'common moral ground' approach. For Banner, the only accountability that Christian ethics should acknowledge is to 'the kingdom of Jesus Christ'.[53] This does not mean, however, that Christian ethics is incapable of engaging with other systems and positions in the public arena. It can do so in a variety of ways: for example, by '[asserting] what it knows to be good and right' (pp. 36–7), by denouncing

---

earlier instance of it, again in a bioethical context, can be found in an exchange between James Gustafson and Stanley Hauerwas quoted by Gerald McKenny and Jonathan Sande (eds), *Theological Analyses of the Clinical Encounter*, Dordrecht, Germany: Kluwer Academic Press, 1994, p. vii.

51 Nigel Biggar, '"God" in Public Reason', *Studies in Christian Ethics* 19.1 (2006), pp. 9–19; Nigel Biggar, 'Not Translation but Conversation: Theology in Public Debate about Euthanasia', in Nigel Biggar and Linda Hogan (eds), *Religious Voices in Public Places*, Oxford: Oxford University Press, 2009, pp. 151–93.

52 Michael Banner, *Christian Ethics and Contemporary Moral Problems*, Cambridge: Cambridge University Press, 1999, pp. 1–46. Page numbers in brackets in this and the next paragraph refer to this work.

53 Banner, *Christian Ethics*, p. 9, quoting Karl Barth, *Church Dogmatics*, vol. II.2, p. 527.

what it knows to be wrong, and by exposing the weaknesses and inconsistencies of other systems and approaches. But whenever dogmatic Christian ethics enters the public arena, 'it does so on the basis of its own distinctive premise … of faith in the life, death and resurrection of Jesus Christ' (p. 39).

Banner's own work illustrates some of these modes of engagement with public ethical issues, including one of the two with which this chapter began. His essay 'Christian Anthropology at the Beginning and End of Life' (pp. 47–85) frames a discussion of euthanasia within a classic Christian conception of martyrdom. Within that discussion, he gives a thoroughgoing critique of the case for voluntary euthanasia in terms of what he takes to be 'its own self-understanding', pointing out a number of serious flaws in that case as he has presented it (pp. 75–81; quotation from p. 81). But he also challenges the terms of that self-understanding, arguing that it 'expresses more regard for death than for life and … is determined by a doubtfulness about life's beginning and, above all, a fear of its end' (pp. 68–9). By contrast, the Christian anthropology presupposed in the practice of martyrdom 'properly expresses a respect for life and not death' (p. 68) and is shaped not by fear, but by the hope commanded in Jesus Christ's words in Revelation: 'Fear not, I am the first and the last, and the living one' (Rev. 1.17–18, quoted p. 48). This anthropology challenges us to '*breathe* in the atmosphere of redemption',[54] and implies practices like hospice care which can embody a hope not dependent on the prolongation of the patient's present life.

One criticism sometimes made of Banner is that while his theological writing, such as this essay on the beginning and end of life, is done clearly and consistently in the 'dogmatic' mode that he advocates, it is less clear how his public ethical engagement – such as his work on government committees and other public bodies

---

54 Banner, *Christian Ethics*, p. 71, quoting Karl Barth, *Ethics*, ET, Edinburgh: T & T Clark, 1981, p. 490, emphasis original.

– is informed by his dogmatic commitments. Robin Gill, for example, suggests that when Banner writes on moral issues about which he is not so involved in public policy debate, he typically takes an 'absolutist and particularist' position, whereas on issues in genetics and biotechnology, where he has had a good deal of involvement in the public forum,[55] he tends to adopt a 'realist' approach more similar to the one that Gill himself favours.[56] Celia Deane-Drummond develops a similar critique, from which she infers that a dogmatic Christian ethics informed by theologians such as Barth has limited potential for public engagement with contemporary bioethical problems.[57]

These critiques are not completely persuasive: as I have already noted, Banner argues that a dogmatic moral vision informed by faith in the gospel of Jesus Christ has the potential for a wide variety of engagement on the strength of its distinctive theological commitment. A dogmatic Christian ethicist could, for example, attempt to expose the weaknesses and inconsistencies of secular ethical stances (as Banner does in relation to arguments about euthanasia),[58] or could seek to identify, and make more explicit and coherent, principles already discernible in policy and legislation that are worthy of support (as he does in relation to animal biotechnology).[59] The point is that these and other forms of intervention will be motivated and directed by the Christian ethicist's dogmatic commitment. More consistency can be found in Banner's various engagements with ethical questions than critics such as Gill and Deane-Drummond allow. Nonetheless, it is probably true to say that there is more to be done to articulate *how* a basic

---

55 See, for example Animal Procedures Committee, *Animal Procedures Committee Report on Biotechnology*, June 2001, online at http://apc.homeoffice.gov.uk/reference/biorec.pdf (accessed 9 September 2010); Banner, *Christian Ethics*, pp. 204–24.

56 Robin Gill, *Health Care and Christian Ethics*, Cambridge: Cambridge University Press, 2006, pp. 50–5; quotation at p. 55.

57 Celia Deane-Drummond, *Genetics and Christian Ethics*, Cambridge: Cambridge University Press, 2005, pp. 32–7, 53–5.

58 Banner, *Christian Ethics*, pp. 68–82.

59 Banner, *Christian Ethics*, pp. 216–22.

theological commitment of the sort acknowledged by Banner shapes and informs the various engagements exemplified in his essays.

Another approach that places an equally strong emphasis on the distinctive character of Christian ethics is that of Stanley Hauerwas,[60] who has argued over many years that Christian ethics is concerned less with rules for making decisions and resolving moral quandaries than with character, virtue and moral vision. We do not develop virtue and character by abstract moral reasoning, but by belonging to a 'community of character' – a community that shares a narrative or story which gives it a distinctive moral identity.[61] The Church is called to be a 'community of character' whose identity is formed by the Christian story: 'Christian ethics is not first of all an ethics of principles, rules or values, but an ethic that demands we attend to the life of a particular individual – Jesus of Nazareth.'[62] This argues against approaches to public engagement that give priority to the search for common moral ground. The contribution Christians are called to make is of a very different kind: 'the first social ethical task of the church is to be the church.'[63] In other words, it is called to be an alternative *polis* or political community, displaying a different way of living together in faithfulness to its distinctive story. And this acted-out witness to the possibility of a different way of life is the most important and helpful thing that the Church can offer to the world.

The most important things that the Church is called to say about medicine are likely only to be fully intelligible in the context

---

60 For a selection of Hauerwas' *oeuvre* over many years, see Stanley Hauerwas, *The Hauerwas Reader*, ed. John Berkman and Michael G. Cartwright, Durham, NC: Duke University Press, 2001; for a recent summary account of his approach, see Stanley Hauerwas and Samuel Wells (eds), *The Blackwell Companion to Christian Ethics* Oxford: Blackwell, 2004, chs 1–4.

61 Stanley Hauerwas, *A Community of Character: Toward a Constructive Christian Social Ethic,* Notre Dame, IN: University of Notre Dame Press, 1981.

62 Stanley Hauerwas, *The Peaceable Kingdom: A Primer in Christian Ethics,* London: SCM Press, 1984, p. 76.

63 Hauerwas, *The Peaceable Kingdom,* p. 99.

of the corporate life that it is called to live in response to the story of Jesus Christ. For example, in an early essay co-authored with Richard Bondi, Hauerwas argues that euthanasia should indeed be morally prohibited, but not primarily for the pragmatic reasons that often feature prominently in policy debates. The most important reasons for a Christian refusal of euthanasia have to do with the Church's basic theological convictions, for example that life is God's gift and that our life together depends on trust to sustain it:

> Our unwillingness to kill ourselves even under pain is an affirmation that the trust that has sustained us in health is also the trust that sustains us in illness and distress; that our existence is a gift ultimately bounded by a hope that gives us a way to go on; that the full, present memory of our Christian story is a source of strength and consolation for ourselves and our community.[64]

But Christians cannot expect these convictions to make sense in public debate detached from the corporate life and worship of the Christian community which makes them intelligible. So, while the churches are indeed called to bear public witness to their basic theological convictions and the implications of those convictions, the most important way that they do this may not be by lobbying for or against changes in the law, but by being the kind of communities in which dying people can find the resources to endure pain, suffering and indignity.

Hauerwas' insistence that the Church is the fundamental locus of Christian ethics has given rise to the stock criticism that his approach is 'sectarian': that he recommends a withdrawal from the world into the Church, a preoccupation with the purity of the

---

64 Stanley Hauerwas and Richard Bondi, 'Memory, Community and the Reasons for Living: Reflections on Suicide and Euthanasia', in Stanley Hauerwas with Richard Bondi and David B Burrell, *Truthfulness and Tragedy: Further Investigations into Christian Ethics*, Notre Dame, IN: University of Notre Dame Press, 1977, pp. 101–15 (p. 111).

Church's corporate life and a disengagement from the moral problems and deliberations of the society outside its walls.[65] This charge is easily repudiated, as commentators such as Nigel Biggar and David Fergusson – neither an uncritical admirer of Hauerwas – have shown.[66] They both argue convincingly that Hauerwas' insistence on the centrality of the Church's distinctive practice and speech to Christian ethics is not an irresponsible *refusal* of engagement with the life of the secular *polis*, but an argument about the best and fullest way in which the Church can *exercise* its political responsibility in the world. As Biggar puts it:

> [Hauerwas] is convinced that the Christian Church has something to communicate to the world that is vital to its well-being, corporate and individual … This is why he is so relentlessly insistent that the Christian Church concentrate on thinking and living out its own story, instead of squandering itself in merely repeating in religious tones the moral platitudes that the world already takes for granted.[67]

However, while the charge of sectarianism does not stand up, there is a related danger that important emphases will be neglected in a radically ecclesial ethic of a Hauerwasian kind. There is a risk of focusing to such a large extent on the Church as alternative *polis* that we do not do enough to give a theological account of the secular *polis* as part of the 'penultimate' realm (to use Bonhoeffer's

---

65 See, for example, James Gustafson, 'The Sectarian Temptation', *Proceedings of the Catholic Theological Society of America* 40 (1985), pp. 83–94; Max L. Stackhouse, 'Liberalism Dispatched vs. Liberalism Engaged', *Christian Century* (18 October 1995), pp. 962–7. For Hauerwas' response to Gustafson, see Stanley Hauerwas, 'Why the "Sectarian Temptation" is a Misrepresentation: A Response to James Gustafson', in *The Hauerwas Reader*, pp. 90–110.

66 Nigel Biggar, 'Is Stanley Hauerwas Sectarian?', in Mark Thiessen Nation and Samuel Wells (eds), *Faithfulness and Fortitude: In Conversation with the Theological Ethics of Stanley Hauerwas*, Edinburgh: T & T Clark, 2000, pp. 141–60; Fergusson, *Community, Liberalism and Christian Ethics*, ch. 3.

67 Biggar, 'Is Stanley Hauerwas Sectarian?', p. 143.

language) in which, by God's grace, people may hear and respond to God's Word and God's liberating command. I wholeheartedly agree that, as Hauerwas puts it, 'the first social ethical task of the church is to be the church';[68] in saying this, though, one must not neglect the ways in which the Church's distinctive practice, speech and critical reflection can not only constitute a powerful witness to the secular *polis* but also challenge, inform and enrich the latter's moral discourse and practice. Furthermore, I shall argue later that the Church's distinctive understanding and practice should also equip it to discern words from God and signs of God's work in the world outside its own walls.

Hauerwas' recent book *Performing the Faith* perhaps illustrates the danger.[69] In two typically stimulating opening chapters, he claims Bonhoeffer as an earlier source of lessons he later learned from John Howard Yoder and Karl Barth about the political significance of the 'visibility' of the Church and the importance to politics of the Church's truthful witness. There is no reason to doubt Bonhoeffer's importance as a source of these insights, but in a discussion of Bonhoeffer and political ethics, it would be good also to have some reflection on important themes in Bonhoeffer's ethical writing such as the relationship of the ultimate to the penultimate and his treatment of 'natural life'.[70] What Hauerwas says, with reference to Bonhoeffer, about the political and ethical importance of the Church's distinctive witness in word and deed need not be denied: it is just that a theological account of 'the world', and of the Church's responsibility for the world in response to the creating, reconciling and redeeming work of God in Christ, is also needed.[71]

---

68 Above, n. 63.

69 Stanley Hauerwas, *Performing the Faith: Bonhoeffer and the Practice of Nonviolence*, London: SPCK, 2004.

70 Bonhoeffer, *Ethics*, pp. 146–218.

71 For a similar critique of Hauerwas, see also Fergusson, *Community, Liberalism and Christian Ethics*, pp. 72–9.

Aims and strategies for Christian public engagement

I have argued thus far that the Reformed theological approach to bioethics set out in this book calls for forms of public engagement that are distinctively and explicitly theological, and that are not limited to distinctively Christian speech, but are also embodied in distinctively Christian practice. But more needs to be said about the aims and strategies of such engagement: what forms of engagement might be in view in this approach? What should Christians hope to achieve by their engagement, and how should they go about it?

As I argued in my second section above with reference to Barth, part of the state's vocation is to keep open the space in which humans are able to respond to the word and command of God, which turns out to be a much more wide-ranging responsibility than might at first sight appear. The vocation of the Church and its members includes helping the state to fulfil *its* vocation. Understanding the Church's political vocation in this way could suggest a variety of appropriate strategies for public engagement; a few examples follow.

The first, in the light of MacIntyre's insight about the 'traditioned' character of moral reasoning, is to challenge the rules of public discourse, in so far as they depend on faulty assumptions about the nature of public reason. As I observed earlier, it is sometimes regarded as problematic if the convictions of 'religious minorities' have an influence on public policy. Underpinning this view seems to be the assumption that there is such a thing as an a-traditional public moral reason that is distinct from the 'sectarian' ethics of particular communities and faith traditions. If MacIntyre is correct, and *all* reasoning is inescapably done within the context of a tradition of enquiry, then moral arguments that purport to be tradition-free will in fact turn out to be in an obscure way the products of some moral tradition or other – or more likely, a confused mixture of traditions. And if *that* is true, then the clarity and coherence of public debate will be best served if the participants are as self-aware, clear and honest as they can be about the traditions that have shaped their reasoning.

It might be asked, though, whether this diminishes the possibility of public discourse and debate in a pluralist society. If the members of such a society acknowledge their debts to the traditions that form their moral reasoning, will this confine them to the bounds of their own traditions, so that they can only engage in reasoned argument with those who share their tradition; and will this have the effect of reducing public discourse and policy debate to a Babel of different traditions' incommensurable voices? There is no reason to draw such a despairing conclusion. As MacIntyre and others have argued, it is perfectly possible for different traditions to engage one another in argument and debate – only care is needed about the terms on which such engagements are set up.[72] What cannot be done, *ex hypothesi*, is to find some a-traditional standpoint from which to evaluate the rival claims of the different traditions. Rather, a genuine engagement of different traditions requires the adherents of those traditions to take the trouble to learn one another's intellectual and moral 'languages' – the thought-worlds and assumptions of the different traditions, the way in which their rationality functions, and so on.

My first proposal for public engagement, then, is to challenge the ground-rules of public discourse. But even if that challenge is not heeded, and public debate continues to be structured in the unsatisfactory ways diagnosed in Chapter 1, Christian communities do not lack possibilities for critical and constructive engagement. There are critical tasks to be performed, which, though they might seem rather negative, can nonetheless be helpful and important. For example, Christians should be at least as well placed as others to point out when arguments deployed in public debate are

---

72 See Alasdair MacIntyre, *Whose Justice? Which Rationality?*, London: Duckworth, 1988, pp. 370–88; Alasdair MacIntyre, *Three Rival Versions of Moral Enquiry: Encyclopaedia, Genealogy, Tradition*, London: Duckworth, 1990; Gavin D'Costa, *Theology in the Public Square: Church, Academy and Nation*, Oxford: Blackwell, 2005.

inconsistent, incoherent, have unacknowledged and troubling implications, and so on.[73] In Chapter 1, for example, I noted the un-argued assertion by the Academy of Medical Sciences, in the context of the debate about human admixed embryos, that if human individuals are possessed of dignity or entitled to respect, 'it is because there are factors of form, function or behaviour that confer such dignity or command respect'.[74] It is certainly open to Christians, as well as others, to point out that such a claim is far from self-evident, and requires some defence. Or again, in relation to the assisted dying debate, Christians might very well offer critical perspectives on some of the basic assumptions that often go unchallenged in public debates. As I suggest in Chapter 8, they might for example call into question the assumption that com-passion – undoubtedly an important virtue in health care, as in other walks of life – generates an *over-riding* obligation to relieve suffering by any means necessary. Those working within a Chris-tian tradition might well conclude that this is a distorted view with damaging implications, and there is every reason to call attention in public debate to this distortion.

In addition to such interventions in critical mode, it is open to Christians to offer a variety of more constructive contributions even to public debates structured in ways that they find highly un-satisfactory. One form that such constructive contributions might take is what Duncan Forrester has called 'theological fragments'.[75] By 'fragments' he means ideas, insights and practices which come from a 'quarry' of coherent Christian theology, which when intro-duced into the public arena can act as irritants, challenges and insights that move debate and practice in new directions. Forrester's

---

73 So Banner, *Christian Ethics*, pp. 36–9.

74 Academy of Medical Sciences, *Inter-Species Embryos*, London: Academy of Medical Sciences, 2007, p. 29.

75 Duncan Forrester, *Christian Justice and Public Policy*, Cambridge: Cambridge University Press, 1997; Duncan Forrester, *Truthful Action: Explorations in Practical Theology*, Edinburgh: T & T Clark, 2000, pp. 143–57. See also Storrar and Morton, *Public Theology for the 21st Century*.

examples are wide-ranging, including statements of faith like the Barmen Declaration (produced in 1934 by the German 'Confessing Church' in opposition to the ideology of the Nazi regime), insights such as the need for a concept of forgiveness in a criminal justice system and examples of practice like the South African Truth and Reconciliation Commission. Fragments in isolation from their quarry can be misunderstood or misused, so Christians have a twofold task of contributing fragments to the public arena, while at the same time continuing to do the basic theological work to maintain and develop the theological 'quarry'.[76]

For example, I have just suggested that Christians can and should challenge the conceptions of 'compassion' frequently in play in the assisted dying debate; the obverse of this critical task is to articulate a more adequate vision of love of neighbour, love which includes the kind of solidarity and care that will enable pain, suffering and indignity to be endured when they cannot be avoided. But this kind of 'theological fragment', of course, cannot just be a matter of argument or ideas. If it is, it is likely to be dismissed – with some justice – as empty words. It can and must also be a fragment of practice, of *enacted* love that gives dying people the resources which will sustain them. The hospice movement in at least some of its present forms owes a good deal to this Christian vision of love,[77] and the Christian contribution to the development of hospice care can well be understood as a hugely influential lived 'theological fragment'.

When Christians articulate aspects of their own tradition and its implications as clearly and truthfully as possible, even under conditions that do not seem particularly hospitable to Christian insights and perspectives, they might find that some of what they have to say resonates with other participants in the debate. At one

---

76 Forrester, *Truthful Action*, pp 155–6.

77 Shirley du Boulay, *Cicely Saunders: The Founder of the Modern Hospice Movement*, London: Hodder and Stoughton, 1984, though for an argument about tensions inherent in this Christian motivation, see David Clark, 'Originating a Movement: Cicely Saunders and the Development of St Christopher's Hospice, 1957–1967', *Mortality* 3.1 (1998), pp. 43–63.

level, this is hardly surprising, since a good part of the moral language and concepts available to participants in such debates in most Western contexts have their origins in Christian moral traditions, however distanced that language and those concepts have become from their origins. To articulate the tradition from which the language and concepts come could help to clarify them and render them more coherent.[78] At another level, too, Christians should not be surprised to find that some things they say resonate with others. A Christian community which confesses that 'Jesus Christ, as he is attested for us in holy scripture, is the one Word of God which we have to hear and which we have to trust and obey in life and in death'[79] is not entitled to think that the Word is only to be heard within 'the sphere of the Bible and the Church', as Barth puts it:

In the very light of this narrower and smaller sphere ... we cannot possibly think that He cannot speak, and His speech cannot be attested, outside this sphere ... We can and must be prepared to encounter 'parables of the kingdom' in the full biblical sense, not merely in the witness of the Bible and the various arrangements, works and words of the Christian Church, but also in the secular sphere, i.e. in the strange interruption of the secularism of life in the world.[80]

Discerning such 'true words' and 'parables of the kingdom' in public debates outside the sphere of the Bible and the Church may be a difficult and uncertain business, but if it is true that the 'penultimate' status of the secular *polis* makes it worth taking trouble over, then the Church must be prepared to undertake this discernment prayerfully and boldly, trusting in the guidance of the Spirit. Where it does discern 'true words' and 'parables of the king-

---

78 See further Chapter 8, pp. 224–7.
79 *Theological Declaration of Barmen*, art. 1.
80 Barth, *Church Dogmatics*, vol. IV.3.1, p. 117.

dom', there is every reason to continue conversations, forge ad hoc alliances in pursuit of the goals to which Christians' theological and moral commitments direct them, and so on.[81] One example of a 'true word' to be found in the secular bioethical arena is the sense of solidarity that, as Ruud ter Meulen observes in a recent essay, has played an important part in the ethos of the National Health Service in the UK since its inception, but that is seriously threatened by the more recent rise of market thinking within the NHS.[82] As ter Meulen argues, Christians have good reason to speak out, act and form alliances with others in order to strengthen and extend this threatened ethos of solidarity.[83]

Finally, it is worth reiterating the Hauerwasian theme that one of the most important things that Christian communities can do in relation to public debates is to live faithfully as Christian communities. This final proposal might appear to be in some tension with what has already been said. My previous proposals suggested various strategies for involvement in public arguments and debates, whereas this one might appear to be simply a call to 'come out from them and be separate from them' (2 Cor. 6.17). In fact, though, these proposals are not opposed to one another, but complementary. The context of Christian practice (centrally, the

---

81 There are some points of contact between this approach to public engagement and the account given by Celia Deane-Drummond, on the basis of a Thomistic virtue ethic, of the importance of the virtue of *wisdom* in contemporary bioethical thinking and public engagement: see, for example, her *Creation through Wisdom*, Edinburgh: T & T Clark, 2000, and *Genetics and Christian Ethics*, pp. 46–53. In Deane-Drummond's account, the human wisdom that is to be found in many places and contexts has its source and origin in the wisdom of God. Christians do not have a monopoly on wisdom; they should be ready to recognize it and acknowledge it in many different places and people, and to offer reminders and challenges when wisdom is ignored or forgotten in bioethical debate and practice. The account I am proposing, however, is perhaps more explicit that 'true words' and 'secular parables' are recognized as such by reference to God's revelation in Christ.

82 Ruud H. J. ter Meulen, 'The Lost Voice: How Libertarianism and Consumerism Obliterate the Need for a Relational Ethics in the National Health Care Service', *Christian Bioethics* 14.1 (2008), pp. 78–94.

83 See also below, Chapter 7 (pp. 210–11).

practice of worship),[84] as well as the community's reflection on that practice and its argument and deliberation about the implications of its tradition, is crucial in at least two ways. First, it is the context of moral and spiritual formation in which Christians can develop the practical wisdom that, among other things, will make them skilled in discerning 'true words' and 'parables of the kingdom' in public debates. Second, the Church's practice is crucial in making sense of what it has to say about ethical issues. A Christian community that has ethical claims to make about health care and biomedical research will be able to make those claims intelligibly, persuasively and with integrity *in so far as* its corporate life is lived in the way one would expect if the Christian story, and the things it says about health, wholeness and hope, were true. So a Christian contribution to public ethical debate and discourse will be at its most complete when it comprises *both* the articulation of the Church's distinctive moral traditions, as they impinge on the questions under discussion, *and* the context of distinctive Christian practice within which the things that are said make sense. Now if a Christian community finds itself in a cultural and historical situation that is profoundly at odds with the Christian tradition, then faithfulness to that tradition will require that community to speak and live in ways that appear radically countercultural. In such a situation, it could happen that the possibilities for critical and constructive engagement with public debates are radically circumscribed, because the cultural context sets ground rules for public discourse that are thoroughly inhospitable to the coherent articulation of a Christian tradition. In such circumstances, it could be that the only remaining possibility for faithful Christian engagement is to be 'a city built on a hill' (Matt. 5.14), offering a lived witness to a radically different way of practising human community. But this is not for the Church to determine,

---

84 See Hauerwas and Wells, *The Blackwell Companion to Christian Ethics*, chs 1–4; Samuel Wells, 'How Common Worship Forms Local Character', *Studies in Christian Ethics* 15.1 (2002), pp. 66–74.

and it should not *seek* such isolation. While other possibilities remain, it is the Church's business to make use of them, in order to help the *polis* to be part of the penultimate realm in which people can be prepared to receive God's Word.

Conclusion

In the last and the present chapters, I have argued (with particular reference to recent British examples) that public bioethical debates in the contemporary West display certain features that Christians – and others – should regard as unsatisfactory in important ways. I have suggested that these unsatisfactory features have deep roots in aspects of modern thought and culture, and often result in sufficiently distorted public discourse that Christians and churches wishing to engage with these debates would be unwise simply to accept the terms in which they are customarily conducted. Christian moral deliberation about such issues, taking its bearings from the narrative that gives the Christian community its distinctive identity, will look very different from the ways in which these questions are usually discussed in public. This state of affairs, though, does not condemn Christians to a choice between a sectarian withdrawal from the public forum and an enervating compromise with secular modes of thought. I have argued that Christians and churches have a wide range of options for faithful, critical and constructive engagement with public bioethics. Furthermore, there are good theological reasons for attempting such engagement, since the Church's very witness to God's justifying word in Christ gives it every reason to care for the 'penultimate' realm in which that word may be proclaimed and received. In the following chapters, I shall set out some detailed examples of theological engagements with specific bioethical issues and public debates, in order to illustrate the potential of the theological tradition articulated here for challenging, constructive and illuminating engagement with such debates, and to suggest more fully how such engagements might be conducted.

Part 2

Theological Engagements

3

Human Reproductive Cloning

The science of human cloning

While human cloning has been the subject of scientific and ethical speculation – and a staple science fiction scenario – for many years, it is only since the 1990s that it has seemed a serious possibility, calling for an ethical and policy response. The event that brought the prospect of cloning sharply into the public consciousness was the birth at the Roslin Institute in Scotland of Dolly the ewe, the first mammalian clone ever to be produced using genetic material from an adult. The cloning of Dolly made it seem plausible for the first time that virtually exact genetic copies of other mammals, including humans, could also be made.

The term 'clone', in this context, refers to an individual living organism that is genetically identical to another individual. Cloning is a widespread phenomenon in nature, used as a reproductive strategy by many plant and invertebrate animal species. However, it is not a natural means of reproduction for humans or other mammalian species, whose reproductive strategies are entirely sexual. The only limited form of cloning that occurs naturally in humans is the occasional and unpredictable occurrence of monozygotic (identical) twins, and more rarely triplets and quadruplets. Twinning occurs when the embryo splits into two or more at an early stage in its development. Since the cells of the early embryo are *totipotent* – that is, they have the potential to develop into any of the thousands of specialized cell types found in the foetus, child or adult, and into the cell types found in extra-embryonic tissues such as the placenta – if an early embryo splits, it is possible for each part to continue developing as a separate individual. Since all the cells in the embryo contain copies of the same genetic material, the resulting individuals will of course be genetically identical.

Artificial cloning has a longer history than is sometimes realized. The propagation of plants by cuttings, for example, is a form of cloning. In the 1950s and 1960s, some species of frog and toad were successfully cloned by nuclear transfer, essentially the same approach that was later used to clone Dolly.[1] Mammals, however, proved much more difficult to clone, and it was not until the 1990s that the Roslin group succeeded. Broadly speaking, there are two possible approaches to mammalian cloning. One is to divide an embryo *in vitro* into two or more parts and introduce the parts into the mother's womb, mimicking the natural process of twinning. This approach, though, is fairly limited in application. It would not, for example, allow the cloning of an already-existing individual. The more powerful technique, which has attracted such scientific and public interest since the birth of Dolly, is cloning by *somatic cell nuclear transfer* (SCNT). The nucleus, which contains almost all of the cell's genetic information, is removed from an egg cell *in vitro*. In its place, the nucleus of a cell from the individual to be cloned is inserted into the enucleated egg cell.[2] If the egg cell with its new complement of inserted genetic material is subjected to the right conditions, it can be 'tricked' into behaving as if it had just been fertilized by a sperm cell, and beginning the processes of cell division, growth, differentiation and so forth that normally occur in embryonic development. Since (with a few specialized exceptions) the nuclei of all cells in the body contain identical copies of the individual's genome (his or her genetic 'blueprint'), the embryo formed by this

---

1 Anon, 'A Timeline of the Evolution of Animal Breeding', online at http://www.clone safety.org/cloning/facts/timeline/ (accessed 21 July 2010).

2 The cell from the individual to be cloned can be taken from any tissue of that individual's body, hence 'somatic' cells, as opposed to the 'germ line' cells such as sperm and egg cells.

process is an almost exact genetic copy of the individual from which the nucleus was taken. The clone is not quite genetically identical to the original, because a very small amount of genetic material is found outside the nucleus, in the *mitochondria*: self-replicating structures within the cell, with a major role in the cell's energy metabolism, which have their own DNA. The mitochondria of the cloned embryo will come from the egg, so the mitochondrial genome of the clone will be different from that of the original. However, the nuclear DNA contains the overwhelming majority of the individual's genetic information, so the clone is to all intents and purposes an exact genetic copy of the 'donor' of the nucleus.

Since Dolly, a number of other mammalian species have been cloned, including sheep, goats, cows, pigs, rabbits, mice, cats and a gaur.[3] Cloning remains far from straightforward: Dolly was the only live birth in 277 attempts, and success rates remain low. Cloning has not been successful in all mammalian species on which it has been tried: some seem more resistant to nuclear transfer than others. Furthermore, birth defects, chronic illness and premature ageing and death have been reported in some cloned sheep and other animals.[4]

The work at the Roslin Institute was done in the context of research on animal genetic engineering. The cloning technique that produced Dolly was developed as a reliable way of reproducing animals that had been successfully genetically modified in some way – for example, to have genes for medically important human proteins inserted into their genomes in such a way that the proteins would be secreted into females' milk.[5] Many applica-

---

3 US Department of Energy, Office of Science, *Human Genome Project Information: Cloning Fact Sheet*, online at www.ornl.gov/sci/techresources/Human_Genome/elsi/cloning.shtml (accessed 10 September 2010).

4 US Department of Energy, Office of Science, *Cloning Fact Sheet*.

5 Ian Wilmut and Donald Bruce, 'Dolly Mixture: Cloning by Nuclear Transfer to Improve Genetic Engineering in Animals', in Donald Bruce and Ann Bruce (eds), *Engineering Genesis: The Ethics of Genetic Engineering in Non-Human Species*, London: Earthscan, 1998, pp. 71–6.

tions of animal cloning are still within the area of animal bio-technology and genetic engineering, though there are also other applications: for example, members of some endangered species have been cloned for conservation purposes, and in some countries cloning is available commercially to pet owners who wish to 'copy' pets that have died.[6] While animal cloning itself raises important ethical issues,[7] most of the ethical debate genera-ted by the development of the SCNT technique has focused on the prospect of human cloning.

The focus of scientific and medical interest in the application of the SCNT technique to humans has been on so-called 'therapeutic cloning': that is, the use of the technique to produce cloned embryos that would not be implanted in women's wombs, but used in the laboratory for a variety of research and treatment applications. These will be discussed more fully in the next chapter. By contrast, much of the media attention and public concern, particularly in the early days after the cloning of Dolly, has been on 'human reproductive cloning': using the cloning technique to make human babies. Many countries, including the UK, moved rapidly to legislate against human reproductive cloning and to negotiate international declarations and agreements against it.[8] To date, there have been no reliable reports of successful human reproductive cloning, though from time to time

---

6 Michael J. Sandel, *The Case against Perfection: Ethics in the Age of Genetic Engineering* Cambridge, MA: Harvard University Press, 2007, pp. 4–5.

7 Andrew Linzey, 'Ethical and Theological Objections to Animal Cloning', *Bulletin of Medical Ethics*, no. 131 (Sept. 1997), pp. 18–22.

8 For a brief overview of legislation and international agreements (from an observer highly unsympathetic to their general tone), see John Harris, *On Cloning*, London: Routledge, 2004, pp. 19–22. In the UK, the Human Reproductive Cloning Act (2001), which banned reproductive cloning, was repealed by the Human Fertilisation and Embryology Act (2008). The latter maintains the prohibition on human reproductive cloning, though concerns have been expressed that it includes a loophole that could allow reproductive cloning in an attempt to address certain forms of mitochondrial disease (see below, n. 10) without new primary legislation: Mark Henderson, 'Loophole in Embryology Bill Could Allow Cloning Without New Legislation', *The Times* (14 June 2008), online at http://www.timesonline. co.uk/tol/news/politics/article4133539.ece (accessed 12 September 2010).

there are unconfirmed reports of pregnancies and births resulting from cloning experiments. Specialists in the field typically take the view that the technical difficulties are so great, and the chances of success so low, that it is unlikely that anyone would yet be in a position to perform human reproductive cloning successfully.[9]

Why might anyone want to clone humans? The most obvious and likely motivation is to use cloning as an addition to the range of fertility treatments currently available. Some authors envisage cloning as a way of enabling heterosexual couples, who are unable to conceive naturally or by other fertility treatments, to have children genetically related to at least one partner. Indeed, if the egg were taken from the woman of the couple and the somatic cell nucleus from the man, the clone would be genetically related to both of them, since his nuclear DNA would come from the man and his mitochondrial DNA from the woman – though as I noted earlier, the mitochondrial genes only account for a tiny proportion of the total genetic material in the cell. Commentators also speculate that cloning could enable lesbian couples to have children genetically related to at least one partner, and single women to have genetically related children by cloning cells from their own bodies. Another use sometimes envisaged for reproductive cloning is to avoid the transmission of mitochondrial and metabolic disorders caused by mutations in the mitochondrial DNA.[10] Women can pass mitochondrial DNA mutations on to any children conceived using their eggs either naturally or by means of fertility treatments such as IVF, since progeny inherit their mitochondrial DNA from their (genetic) mother via the mitochondria in the mother's egg cells. Cloning, using donated egg cells from unaffected women, is envisaged as a way of circumventing this

---

9 See, for example, Andy Coghlan, 'Latest Human Cloning Claims Leave Sour Taste', *New Scientist* (22 April 2009), online at www.newscientist.com/article/dn17002-latest-human-cloning-claims-leave-sour-taste.html (accessed 10 September 2010).

10 See Robert Naviaux, 'Overview, the Spectrum of Mitochondrial Disease', selections online at www.umdf.org/site/c.otJVJ7MMIqE/b.5692879/k.3851/What_is_Mitochondrial_Disease.htm (accessed 10 September 2010).

problem: for example, a heterosexual couple could clone a child using an egg from a third-party donor and a somatic cell nucleus from the male partner, and the clone could be gestated and borne by the female partner.

For applications such as these, it is incidental that the cloned individual would be genetically identical to the person from whom the somatic cell nucleus was taken. The cloning technique would be used as a way for individuals or couples to have children when other means were impossible or carried the risk of serious inherited disease. (Genetically, of course, the children resulting from such cloning procedures would be the twin siblings of those from whom the genetic material was taken, not their offspring. They would be the genetic offspring of the nucleus donors' parents.)[11] However, other applications have been envisaged for which the genetic identity of progenitor and clone is essential. For example, it is conceivable that parents might wish to clone a sick child so that the clone could be a source of genetically matched cells or tissues, an extension of the controversial 'saviour sibling' cases made possible by currently available reproductive technologies.[12] There is also, of course, speculation about other cloning scenarios: that families would seek to replace deceased loved ones by cloning them, that high achievers would be cloned in the (almost certainly vain) hope that their clones would replicate their abilities and achievements, that people would seek a kind of immortality by cloning themselves, and so on.

The limits of consequentialist reasoning

As I noted in Chapter 1, public ethical and policy debates about developments in biomedical research are often dominated by arguments about the beneficial or harmful *consequences* that will

---

11 As Harris points out: *On Cloning*, p. 5.

12 See Human Fertilisation and Embryology Authority, 'Pre-implantation Tissue Typing ("Saviour Siblings")', online at www.hfea.gov.uk/preimplantation-tissue-typing.html (accessed 10 September 2010).

follow from various courses of action. This might be for various reasons: because those deploying these arguments adopt a consistently consequentialist approach to moral reasoning; or for tactical reasons, because it is assumed that consequentialist arguments will command wider agreement than other forms of argument that appeal to possibly contested moral principles or criteria; or because the existence of non-consequentialist principles or criteria is acknowledged, but they are thought not to impinge on the matter being discussed; or (as Mary Warnock suggests) because inviolable moral principles have a place in private morality but not public policy – 'it is the business of legislators to be consequentialist'.[13]

Arguments about the risk of harm have played a large part in the legislation and international agreements against human reproductive cloning. The current state of cloning technology is such that success rates are still only a few per cent at best, and cloning is thought to carry an increased risk of congenital abnormalities, chronic diseases and shortened lifespan. It is widely assumed that the risk of clones suffering severe harm far outweighs the benefits of reproductive cloning, given the current state of the art; even John Harris, one of the most enthusiastic advocates of human cloning, concurs that '[b]ecause of the present high failure rate and enhanced risk of malformations no sane person would lightly select reproductive cloning as a procreative pathway of choice'.[14] However, he does not agree with the majority view that these risks of harm justify legal prohibitions of cloning:

> We do not ban opportunities to procreate to those who, because of genetic or other risk factors have a higher than average chance of failure or malformations. In these cases we

---

13 Mary Warnock, 'The Politics of Religion,' *New Statesman* (10 April 2008), online at www.newstatesman.com/politics/2008/04/law-moral-religious-society (accessed 12 September 2010); see further Mary Warnock, 'Public Policy in Bioethics and Inviolable Principles', *Studies in Christian Ethics* 18.1 (2005), pp. 33–41.

14 Harris, *On Cloning*, pp. 144–5.

judge counselling and good information to be sufficient and I see no good argument for different principles or a different approach in the case of cloning.[15]

Harris believes that the eagerness for a legal ban owes more to widely held prejudices, fears and fantasies about cloning than to any good reasons.[16] Be that as it may, this argument about the risks of harm does not appear to justify a permanent prohibition in principle. If the cloning technique could be improved until the risks were no greater than those of natural conception, gestation and birth, would that mean that risk-based arguments against reproductive cloning no longer carried any weight?

One point not often acknowledged in this discussion is that, though it might be possible to estimate the risks in advance, we could not know for certain what the level of risk in human cloning was until we tried it.[17] Experiments on other animals might give some idea of the risks, but would not give unequivocal answers about the risks in humans, since the embryology of every mammal is different. Therefore the first clones would in a sense inevitably be 'experimental subjects', and, in the nature of the case, the experiment would be without their consent. Some years ago, Paul Ramsey made a similar observation about the birth of Louise Brown, the first IVF baby, arguing that it was wrong in principle to develop IVF, because it inevitably exposed children to some risk, however slight, that was not for their direct benefit and to which they could not give their consent.[18] This argument in itself, though, might not be decisive against reproductive technologies, or indeed against human cloning. For one thing, risk is not always as neatly

15 Harris, *On Cloning*, p. 144.

16 See, for example, Harris, *On Cloning*, pp. 22–33.

17 This paragraph is taken with modifications from Neil Messer, *The Ethics of Human Cloning* (Grove Ethical Studies no. 122), Cambridge: Grove Books, 2001, p. 9.

18 Paul Ramsey, 'On In Vitro Fertilization', reprinted in S. E. Lammers and A. Verhey (eds), *On Moral Medicine: Theological Voices in Medical Ethics*, Grand Rapids, MI: Eerdmans, 1987, pp. 339–45.

quantifiable as Ramsey's argument seems to require, particularly in the area of human procreation. For another, the only alternatives as far as Louise Brown was concerned were to be born as a result of IVF or never to exist, so it might not be straightforward to say in what sense she was exposed to risk by virtue of being conceived by IVF.[19] This is an instance of what Derek Parfit has called the 'non-identity problem',[20] which features from time to time in arguments about cloning.

Apart from these risks of gross physical harm, it is often argued that there are risks of other kinds of harm arising from cloning, and these risks justify prohibiting the practice. For example, as Onora O'Neill has argued, cloned children could suffer psychosocial harm from the '*confused* and *ambiguous* family relationships' created by cloning. She defines the kind of confusion and ambiguity she has in mind in this way: 'Family relationships are confused when *several individuals hold the role of one*; they are ambiguous when *one individual holds the roles of several*.'[21] It is worth noting that O'Neill's point is not only about the harm that confusion and ambiguity might do to clones, but also about the responsibility or otherwise of those who set out to bring a child into being with confused and ambiguous relationships: 'would responsible parents seek confused relationships for their children from the start?'[22] However, John Harris, who takes issue with O'Neill's objections to cloning, treats her point simply as an argument about harm. He appeals to both empirical research and anecdotal experience to call into question the claim that the confusion and ambiguity created by cloning would cause serious

19 For two views of these questions, see Noam J. Zohar, 'Prospects for 'Genetic Therapy' – Can a Person Benefit from Being Altered?', *Bioethics* 5.4 (1991), pp. 275–88, and Jeffrey Kahn, "Genetic Harm: Bitten by the Body that Keeps You?", *Bioethics* 5.4 (1991), pp. 289–308.

20 Derek Parfit, *Reasons and Persons*, Oxford: Clarendon Press, 1984, ch. 16.

21 Onora O'Neill, *Autonomy and Trust in Bioethics*, Cambridge: Cambridge University Press, 2002, p. 67, emphasis original.

22 O'Neill, *Autonomy and Trust*, p. 68.

harm,[23] and draws on Parfit's account of the non-identity problem to argue that '[a] rational would-be child of cloning ... would regard the slight risk of confusion as a price well worth paying for existence, unless of course such confusion made life very terrible indeed'.[24]

These exchanges serve to illustrate the scope and limits of arguments about consequences in relation to reproductive cloning. Claims about the risk of harms, physical or otherwise, that might be suffered by clones could support an argument for proceeding with caution, and perhaps a temporary ban or moratorium, but it is hard to see how they could support an absolute and permanent prohibition of reproductive cloning. Furthermore, arguments about harms suffered by individual clones, or the welfare of those clones, are complicated by the non-identity problem, namely that the choice for an individual clone would seem to be between an existence with certain harms and no existence at all. This does not rule out some kind of impersonal utilitarian calculus in which decisions about cloning should be made to minimize the total harm or maximize the total benefit, regardless of who experienced that harm or benefit, a mode of argument that Harris, for example, is quite prepared to endorse.[25] But a consequentialist framework is unlikely to accommodate claims that human cloning should be permanently and absolutely prohibited: within such a framework, Harris is most likely right to draw the permissive conclusions that he does. In Chapter 1, however, I argued that such a frame of reference omits, obscures and distorts important parts of the moral landscape. There is more to be said about the moral legitimacy or otherwise of human cloning.[26]

---

23 Harris, *On Cloning*, pp. 77–83.

24 Harris, *On Cloning*, pp. 86–8; quotation at p. 86.

25 Harris, *On Cloning*, pp. 87–8.

26 I am not suggesting, of course, that public moral discourse about cloning is framed entirely in consequentialist terms. Sometimes, for example, the debate is framed in terms of 'procreative liberty' or 'procreative autonomy', a concept articulated influentially by John A. Robertson, *Children of Choice: Freedom and the New Reproductive Technologies*, Princeton, NJ: Princeton University Press, 1994; see also Harris, *On Cloning*, pp. 57–66. According

Attempting a theological diagnosis

In Chapter 1, I argued that to be addressed satisfactorily from a Christian theological standpoint, bioethical questions must be located within the frame of reference in which we and the world we inhabit are understood as God's good creatures, in need of God's saving work accomplished in Christ, and heirs to God's promised good future. Within that frame of moral reference, the basic question to ask about any medical, scientific or technological project is whether it goes *with the grain* of God's creative, saving and eschatological purposes, is *opposed* to the good purposes of God, or is a would-be *substitute* for God's good purposes. I proposed a series of 'diagnostic questions' to help discern between these three possibilities: first, does the project reflect the *imago dei* or human action *sicut deus*? Second, what attitude does it express towards the material world (including our own bodies)? Third, what does it reveal about our attitudes to our neighbours? Fourth, is it good news for the poor? Finally, what attitude does it embody towards past failures? These questions can help inform a theological evaluation of human reproductive cloning that is able to go beyond the limited terms of much contemporary discussion.

Playing God or bearing God's image?

The language of 'playing God' and 'acting against nature' is frequently heard, from both religious and non-religious people,

---

to Robertson, some reproductive cloning scenarios are justified by a right to procreative liberty, and should not be prohibited if the technology were safe and reliable: John A. Robertson, 'Liberty, Identity, and Human Cloning', *Texas Law Review* 76 (1998), pp. 1371–456. Since the purpose of the present chapter is not to review every aspect of ethical and policy debates about cloning, but to develop a Christian ethical analysis framed by the theological perspective articulated in this volume, space does not permit an extended discussion of arguments from procreative liberty; but for a critique, see Brent Waters, 'One Flesh? Cloning, Procreation, and the Family', in Ronald Cole-Turner (ed.), *Human Cloning: Religious Responses*, Louisville, KY: Westminster John Knox Press, 1997, pp. 78–90, and Brent Waters, *Reproductive Technology: Towards a Theology of Procreative Stewardship*, London: Darton, Longman and Todd, 2001.

in discussions of human reproductive cloning. Of course, such language is often used in very imprecise ways, to express a general unease or repugnance, and partly for that reason, many theological commentators are wary of it.[27] However, even when it expresses a fairly inarticulate sense of repugnance, it should not on that account be dismissed too quickly. Of course, instinctive reactions of revulsion or repugnance can turn out to be baseless, and even reflect prejudices that are better abandoned. But as Leon Kass argued in the wake of Dolly's cloning, in an article frequently cited in subsequent debates, some such reactions turn out to indicate wise insights that might be hard to articulate but that we ignore at our peril.[28] It could be that the language of 'playing God' and 'acting against nature', and the sometimes inchoate concerns expressed by these phrases, draw attention to a serious question about the scope of the ambitions at work, implicitly or explicitly, in human cloning – the question that I have expressed by asking whether such a project reflects the *imago dei* or is an aspect of humanity *sicut deus*. At the heart of these concerns seems to be a sense that there is a 'givenness' about nature, which demands our respect. This does not necessarily mean a blanket objection to all attempts to manipulate natural processes or structures: empirical research on attitudes to other areas of biotechnology suggests that members of the public who reflect seriously along these lines are quite capable of discriminating between what they hold to be acceptable and unacceptable uses of new technologies.[29] The con-

27 For example Ted Peters, *Playing God? Genetic Determinism and Human Freedom*, New York: Routledge, 1997; Allen Verhey, *Reading the Bible in the Strange World of Medicine*, Grand Rapids, MI: Eerdmans, 2003, p. 286.

28 Leon R. Kass, 'The Wisdom of Repugnance', *New Republic* 216.22 (2 June 1997), pp. 17–26, online at http://www.catholiceducation.org/articles/medical_ethics/me0006.html (accessed 12 September 2010). In the theological perspective of this book, the kind of repugnance that Kass discusses could be considered a putative 'secular parable of the kingdom', to use Karl Barth's term: *Church Dogmatics*, vol. IV.3.1, p. 117; see above, pp. 73–4.

29 Celia Deane-Drummond, Robin Grove-White and Bronislaw Szerszynski, 'Genetically Modified Theology: The Religious Dimensions of Public Concerns about Agricultural Biotechnology', *Studies in Christian Ethics* 14.2 (2001), pp. 23–41.

cern often seems to be that in the technological changes we make, we ought not to assume that nature is manipulable without limit; rather, we ought to proceed circumspectly and in ways that go 'with the grain' of the natural world rather than against it.

One very interesting recent articulation of what I have called respect for the givenness of nature comes from the political philosopher Michael Sandel, reflecting in part his experience as a member of the US President's Council on Bioethics. [30] Sandel considers various projects of human enhancement, including cloning, genetic engineering, eugenics by a variety of means including the selection of donated gametes and pre-implantation genetic diagnosis, the use of drugs to enhance athletic or academic performance, and forms of 'hyper-parenting' in which parents go to extraordinary lengths to train their children for sporting, artistic or academic achievement. While the main focus of his discussion is on eugenics and genetic enhancement rather than cloning, the latter is one of the forms of enhancement that he has in view, and the arguments he develops are certainly of relevance to it. He discerns a widely held sense of unease with projects of human enhancement, unease that he believes cannot be adequately accounted for by fears of harmful consequences or worries that the autonomy of those who are enhanced will be undermined. Rather, he argues:

> The problem with eugenics and genetic engineering is that they represent the one-sided triumph of willfulness over giftedness, of dominion over reverence, of molding over beholding ... If the genetic revolution erodes our appreciation for the gifted character of human powers and achievements, it will transform three key features of our moral landscape – humility, responsibility, and solidarity. [31]

---

30 Sandel, *The Case against Perfection*.
31 Sandel, *The Case against Perfection*, pp. 85–6.

Both our inability to control how our children turn out, and the limits to our capacity for self-improvement, can teach us a kind of humility that enables us to be receptive to the unexpected and the unbidden. This in turn can relieve us of the burden of unlimited responsibility for the way we, and our children, are: 'The more we become masters of our genetic endowments, the greater the burden we bear for the talents we have and the way we perform.'[32] Already, high-level players of some sports who do not use performance-enhancing drugs are (it is said) thought to be letting their team-mates down, and some parents of children with inherited disabilities feel that they are blamed for bringing such children into the world. Furthermore, Sandel argues, if it becomes routine to take control over one's own genetic endowments, the practices of social solidarity by which resources are shared with those who suffer misfortune will be eroded. If screening out children with disabilities or predispositions to poor health becomes routine, it becomes easier for some to argue that those who have failed to do so should not be a drain on the resources of those who have acted more prudently.[33]

Sandel's argument is easily caricatured,[34] but this misses the point. If one is working within a consequentialist frame of reference, some of the points made by Sandel will seem weak or hard to support. But I have already argued that a consequentialist frame of reference is inadequate for the analysis of bioethical problems, in part because it supplies such a narrow moral canvas that the kind of concern to which Sandel draws attention is excluded from the picture.

Perhaps a more interesting question is whether Sandel's argu-

---

32 Sandel, *The Case against Perfection*, p. 87.

33 Sandel, writing in a US context, focuses particularly on how this could happen in a health insurance market, but the same could be true *mutatis mutandis* of a publicly funded health care system whose resources were under constant pressure.

34 There are, for example, elements of caricature in the critique offered by John Harris, *Enhancing Evolution: The Ethical Case for Making Better People*, Princeton, NJ: Princeton University Press, 2007, pp. 109–22.

ments will in the end require a theological context to sustain them. He thinks not, holding that many people use the language of 'sanctity' and 'gift' in respect of human life and abilities without attributing them to a divine Giver who sanctifies them. When we speak of an athlete's or musician's gift, for instance, we mean simply that 'whether he has nature, fortune or God to thank for it, [his] talent is an endowment that exceeds his control'.[35] By the same token, he enumerates a range of theological and non-theological meanings that could be borne by talk of the 'sanctity' of life or nature: that nature is 'enchanted, or inscribed with inherent meaning, or animated by divine purpose', or that its sanctity is derived 'from God's creation of the universe', or simply 'that it is not a mere object at our disposal'.[36]

However, this does not necessarily free Sandel's own understandings of sanctity and gift from implicit dependence on something like a Christian theological perspective. The range of understandings that he offers encompasses a wide variety of different, perhaps incommensurable, views of life and nature, which are likely to have different practical outworkings. It is not clear that the specific things Sandel wishes to say about life can simply be hitched up, willy-nilly, to just any of these understandings. They certainly seem closest to the more specifically theological ones, as is signalled by his use of the word 'talent' in articulating an allegedly non-theological notion of 'gift'. While 'talent' in everyday speech often means no more than 'ability', it of course has its origins in a parable of Jesus in which the 'talents' were sums of money entrusted to servants by a ruler, to whom the servants were accountable for the use of what they held in trust (Matt. 25.14–30). Perhaps, then when the language of 'gift' or 'talent' has the kind of resonance that Sandel wishes to ascribe to it, it is because of its origins in a specifically Christian narrative. Maybe the language

---

35 Sandel, *The Case against Perfection*, p. 93.
36 Sandel, *The Case against Perfection*, pp. 93–4.

of gift is not so easy to unhitch from its theological moorings as he thinks.[37]

Whether or not Sandel is in the end able to articulate his insights about humility, responsibility and solidarity coherently without reference to theology, a theologian working in the tradition articulated in this book can recognize them as genuine insights, congruent with what we know of God and the good in the light of Christ.[38] This could, however, prove to be one of those points in bioethical discourse and debate where the concepts and insights that make most sense of the truth of things turn out to have a theological ancestry; if so, the clarity and coherence of those debates might be best served by making that ancestry explicit.

Controlling identities and welcoming strangers

As has often been pointed out, an important feature of the moral meaning, as it were, implicit in the practice of human reproductive cloning is a drive towards greater control over our bodies and our identities: the 'triumph of willfulness over giftedness', in Sandel's apt phrase.[39] In theological perspective, the drive towards ever greater control over our bodies and identities, and the concomitant reluctance to acknowledge any limits in principle to that control, have every appearance of the attempt to be 'like God' in the way promised by the serpent (Gen. 3.5): striving after god-like knowledge and power in a way that has the tragic effect of alienating us *from* God.

This concern, that the control implicit in human cloning falls on the wrong side of the line between human action in conformity to the *imago dei* and humanity *sicut deus*, is intensified by some of my other diagnostic questions. In particular, the *attitude to the*

---

37 For a somewhat similar critique, see also Michael Banner, *Christian Ethics: A Brief History*, Chichester: Wiley-Blackwell, 2009, pp. 125–30.

38 Cf. Barth, *Church Dogmatics* IV.3.1, pp. 113–25.

39 Sandel, *The Case against Perfection*, p. 85.

material world explicit or implicit in the practice of reproductive cloning seems to be a fairly one-sided attempt at *mastery* over the material, particularly the bodies of the clones we produce. As Gerald McKenny and others have argued, this suggests an underlying assumption that the material world, including our own bodies and those of others, is at best morally neutral and at worst a potential enemy and threat to our well-being, to be bent to the control of our wills in the service of our needs and desires.[40] Regardless of the conscious attitudes and motivations of the would-be cloners, therefore, at some level the practice of reproductive cloning bespeaks a hatred of the material untenable by Christians who are committed to affirming that the physical world is God's good creation.

The first two questions, about the contrast between the *imago dei* and humanity *sicut deus* and our attitude to the material world, focus attention on the moral character of the practice of cloning, and its implications for character of the individuals and communities who might attempt such control over the genetic identities of others. But would the clones themselves be wronged by such an attempt to control their identities? Some Christian commentators have suggested that they would. For example, a statement drafted by Donald Bruce for the Church of Scotland's Society, Religion and Technology (SRT) Project, in the wake of Dolly's cloning, argued that

> to choose to replicate the genetic part of human make up technologically is a violation of a vital aspect of the basic dignity and uniqueness of each human. By definition, to clone is to exercise unprecedented control over the genetic dimension of another individual. This is quite different from the control parents exert in bringing up our children ... No one exerts the level of control involved in preselecting a

---

40 Gerald P. McKenny, *To Relieve the Human Condition: Bioethics, Technology and the Body*, Albany: State University of New York Press, 1997, pp. 17–24; see above, pp. 26–8.

child's entire genetic make up except by a very deliberate act. Moreover, a child can reject any aspect of its upbringing, but it could never reject the genes that were chosen for it. Such control by one human over another is incompatible with the ethical notion of human freedom, in the sense of [*sic*] that each individual's genetic identity should be inherently unpredictable and unplanned.[41]

Various distinct concerns can be discerned in this summary statement. One is, in effect, that the autonomy of the clone will be compromised: though the term 'autonomy' is not used, this is what seems to be in view in the worry that a cloned child would have no say in the genome chosen for him or her. To the standard objection that this is no different in principle from the control that parents and communities exercise over their children through upbringing, education and socialization, the SRT statement responds that 'a child can reject any aspect of its upbringing, but it could never reject the genes that were chosen for it'. This, I think, over-draws the contrast between genetic and social determinants of personal identity, both understating the profound influence of our close relationships, social environment and upbringing in shaping the persons we become, and perhaps, implicitly, overstating the extent and fixity of our genetic influences.[42] In any event, I have already noted Sandel's argument that concerns about autonomy, while perhaps valid and important, fail to capture what is most profoundly at issue in the prospect of genetic control. Later, in Chapter 8, I shall argue in a different context that autonomy might in any case turn out not to be a helpful category for the theological analysis of bioethical issues.[43]

---

41 Church of Scotland Society, Religion and Technology (SRT) Project, 'Should We Clone Humans?' (revised version, 19 November 1998), n.p. Online at http://www.srtp.org.uk/clonhum2.htm (accessed 4 June 2010). See also Donald M. Bruce, 'A View from Edinburgh', in Cole-Turner, *Human Cloning*, pp. 1–11 (pp. 8–9).

42 See, further, Neil Messer, 'Human Cloning and Genetic Manipulation: Some Theological and Ethical Issues', *Studies in Christian Ethics* 12.2 (1999), pp. 1–16.

43 See below, pp. 213–19.

Another dimension of the concern about cloning as control expressed in the SRT statement is that human dignity is in some way bound up with the uniqueness of each individual, and with his or her genetic identity's being 'inherently unpredictable and unplanned'. This relatively brief statement does not explain in any depth why dignity depends on uniqueness and unpredictability. As an earlier part of the statement acknowledges, identical twins also are not genetically unique; however, it is argued, '[t]winning is a random, unpredictable event, involving the duplicating of a genetic composition which … at that point is unknown. Cloning would choose the genetic composition of some existing person and make another individual with the same genes.'[44] So the crucial point seems to be the *choice* of an individual's genotype in cloning *versus* the unpredictable and unplanned genetic legacy of any naturally conceived human, twins included. Yet further explanation is required as to why it is so important that our genetic inheritance is unpredictable and unplanned. Not all forms of unpredictability are self-evidently a good thing, or conducive to human dignity: radical unpredictability in a person's behaviour, for example, would most likely be taken as a sign of psychological disturbance.

However, it seems to me that this part of the SRT statement does express an important theological insight, which can be clarified by reference to another of my diagnostic questions: *what does the practice of cloning reveal about our attitudes to our neighbours?* It is often observed that Christians are called to welcome strangers, including those strangers who come to them in the form of their own children. Stanley Hauerwas is one theologian who has made such a point: contrary to our usual intuitions, he writes, we do not *choose* to have children, but rather are called to receive them as gifts.

> [Children] are basic and perhaps the most essential gifts that we have because they teach us how to be. That is, they create

---

44 SRT Project, 'Should We Clone Humans?', n.p.

in us the proper need to want to love and regard another. For love born of need is always manipulative love unless it is based on the regard of the other as an entity that is not in my control but who is all the more valuable because I do not control him. Children are gifts exactly because they draw our love to them while refusing to be as we wish them to be.[45]

Similarly, Oliver O'Donovan has argued that there is a crucial distinction between those whom we *beget* and that which we *make*.[46] Those whom we beget are like us and can be in a relationship of equals with us. Things that we make, by contrast, are in a sense alienated from us, and our stance towards them is instrumental, in a way that our relationships with those whom we beget should never be. O'Donovan has developed this distinction into a critique of reproductive technologies: they tend to introduce an element of 'making' into the process of human 'begetting' or procreation. One thing that distinguishes 'begetting' from 'making', he argues, is the contingency of the former – it is never fully under our control, so we can never see our children as things designed and made by us. But if we develop techniques for selecting and controlling our children's genotype, we are in effect attempting to introduce an element of 'making' into our procreation. It could then become all too easy to see a child as an artefact or a commodity rather than one who commands our respect *as she is*, in all her stubborn otherness.

Whether or not O'Donovan is right to hold that reproductive technologies such as IVF tend to make the procreation of children more a matter of making and less of begetting,[47] his distinction does get to the heart of the issue about reproductive cloning: if

---

45 Stanley Hauerwas, *Truthfulness and Tragedy: Further Investigations into Christian Ethics*, Notre Dame, IN: University of Notre Dame Press, 1977, p. 153.

46 Oliver O'Donovan, *Begotten or Made?* Oxford: Clarendon Press, 1984, p. 1 and *passim*.

47 For a counter-argument about reproductive technologies, using many of O'Donovan's own theological presuppositions, see Waters, *Reproductive Technology*, esp. pp. 49–55.

near-total control is exerted over the genotype of a child, the welcome of the stranger commended by Hauerwas and others seems to be significantly undermined. In O'Donovan's terms, a cloned child would to a very significant extent be 'made' rather than 'begotten'. In theological perspective, this is one of the chief concerns about cloning as control: to the extent that we engage in attempts to take control over the genetic and physical identities of our children, we make ourselves (as Sandel puts it) 'inhospitable to the unbidden'.[48]

Whether the attempt to control children's identities through cloning would ever succeed is largely beside the point. It is generally acknowledged that a human person's identity is the product of such an irreducibly complex interaction of influences from the individual's genome, physical environment, social relationships, experiences and so forth that any attempt to replicate a personal identity by cloning would be futile.[49] It is doubtful whether this would stop some people trying, if the technology were available, reliable and safe. According to some reports, pet owners who have used commercial services to clone dead pets have quite explicitly been trying to replicate both the physical appearance and the 'personality' of the animals they have lost.[50] If people will go to these lengths in respect of 'companion animals' dear to them, then in a culture that is at times apt to regard bereavement as a failure of technological medicine, there is no particular reason to doubt that some, at least, would harbour

---

48 Sandel, *The Case against Perfection*, p. 86. For an earlier use of the distinction between 'begetting' and 'making' in relation to human cloning, see Kass, 'The Wisdom of Repugnance'.

49 See, for example, Ronald Cole-Turner, 'At the Beginning', in Cole-Turner (ed.), *Human Cloning*, pp. 119–30 (pp. 122–26); Harris, *On Cloning*, p. 47

50 For examples and discussion, see Sandel, *The Case against Perfection*, pp. 4–5 – though it should be noted that the demand for these services has proved more limited than providers initially expected, and the first commercial provider of pet cloning services subsequently withdrew from this market: Lou Hawthorne, 'Six Reasons We're No Longer Cloning Dogs', online at http://www.bioarts.com/press_release/ba09_09_09.htm (accessed 12 September 2010).

similar aspirations regarding their closest human companions and loved ones. Even if those trying to clone humans were not consciously or explicitly trying to determine or replicate a personal identity, however, concerns about cloning as control would remain. The point of the diagnostic questions is not just about the conscious intentions and motivations of those engaging in technological projects, but also about the moral logic, as it were, implicit in the practices themselves. Implicit in the practice of human reproductive cloning would be an attempt to determine the identity of the clone, whether or not those who commission him or her were consciously so motivated.

Good news for the poor?

The conscious motivation for some instances of reproductive cloning could, as I noted above (pp. 83–4), be quite other: the desire to have a genetically related child when all other means of doing so were closed off, or to have a child without the danger of passing on a terrible inherited disease. If cloning offered a way to satisfy these longings and aspirations, could it not be regarded as *good news for the poor* – or if not for the literally poor, then at any rate for some very vulnerable and suffering people?

There is good reason to doubt that reproductive cloning would rate very highly as good news for the vulnerable, marginalized or oppressed. For one thing, the costliness of the procedure makes it seem unlikely that those who were literally poor would share equitably with the wealthy in its benefits, if benefits there were.[51] These questions of access to the technique are, in a sense, extrinsic to the practice, and could in principle be addressed politically: publicly funded health care systems do sometimes succeed in

---

51 When attempts were first made to market commercial services for the cloning of pets, the prices quoted ran to tens of thousands of US dollars: Maggie Shiels, 'Carbon Kitty's $50,000 Dollar Price Tag', online at http://news.bbc.co.uk/1/hi/sci/tech/3663277.stm (accessed 12 September 2010).

reducing inequalities in access to expensive medical procedures. But other, less tractable, concerns are also prompted by the question about good news to the poor. For example, in the wake of Dolly's cloning in 1997, Peter J. Paris wrote of the danger that human cloning could be used to support a racist programme of eugenics:

> Since Europeans and Euro-Americans have never been able to affirm the value of the world's darker races as equals, there is little reason to believe that their scientists would not seek to rid the world of some of its racial diversity by combining the science of eugenics with that of human cloning.[52]

This specific concern seems overstated, not because it is inconceivable that a technological society might mount a racist programme of eugenics – the history of the past century shows that this is all too conceivable – but because there would almost certainly be easier, cheaper ways to do so. But there are other related concerns. As the history of eugenics also shows, a drive towards genetic control all too easily goes hand in hand with an intolerance of those whose genetic inheritance is considered undesirable. That could be an ethnic inheritance, but others too are vulnerable to such dynamics, in particular those with inherited disabilities or impairments.[53] If reproductive cloning were on offer, alongside pre-implantation genetic diagnosis and perhaps germ-line genetic modification, as part of a battery of techniques of genetic control that came to be used routinely in reproductive

---

52 Peter J. Paris, 'A View from the Underside', in Cole-Turner, *Human Cloning*, pp. 43–8 (p. 47).

53 For some examples, see Amos Yong, *Theology and Down Syndrome: Reimagining Disability in Late Modernity*, Waco, TX: Baylor University Press, 2007, pp. 51–5. Among his examples is the notorious *Buck v. Bell* case heard by the US Supreme Court in 1927, in which Justice Oliver Wendell Holmes, upholding the compulsory sterilization of Carrie Buck, remarked that '[t]hree generations of imbeciles are enough' (p. 53). He gives evidence that *Buck v. Bell* was cited as a precedent in the enactment of eugenics laws in the German Third Reich in the 1930s (p. 54).

medicine, it is not at all implausible that their availability would generate and foster the expectation that they would be used to eliminate 'abnormalities' from the population. If that is a real possibility, it suggests that technologies of genetic control, including reproductive cloning, could prove to be very *bad* news for the poor, the vulnerable or those who do not fit society's dominant norms.

My final diagnostic question asks about the *attitude to past failures* expressed or implicit in the project. Since the earlier history of human genetic control has such a terrible dark side, current projects of genetic control – including reproductive cloning – need to demonstrate a lively awareness of the dangers of abuse and a clear understanding of how such abuses are to be avoided: in this area, failure to be alert to this amounts to a dangerous naïvety about the evil that quite ordinary humans are capable of perpetrating. It is not always clear that enthusiasts for cloning and other forms of genetic control avoid this danger. One important contribution that a Christian theological tradition can make to debates about these matters might well prove to be its doctrine of sin. In the course of a highly illuminating and fruitful presentation of that doctrine, Alistair McFadyen has explored the dynamics of the Holocaust, showing how the Nazi 'Final Solution' involved the use of instrumental forms of bureaucratic and technical rationality in the service of atrocious social ends, coupled with the creation of distorted social structures and discourses that denied the victims (most notoriously Jews, but also others deemed unworthy of life, such as those with congenital disabilities) any possibility of articulating or choosing undistorted perspectives.[54] To introduce this comparison is not of course to equate twenty-first-century democracies with the Third Reich. Part of McFadyen's point is that a 'thick' description of the dynamics identifiable in the two particularly intense pathologies he examines in detail – child

---

54 Alistair McFadyen, *Bound to Sin: Abuse, Holocaust and the Christian Doctrine of Sin*, Cambridge: Cambridge University Press, 2000, pp. 80–104.

sexual abuse and the Holocaust – also draws attention to the more mundane and pervasive dynamics of the pathological in everyday human life.[55] The burden of his argument is that sin, if properly understood as a theological category rather than merely a synonym for moral transgression,[56] has real and indispensable explanatory power in relation to such pathologies. According to McFadyen, sin has at its heart the fundamental distortion that the Christian tradition names as idolatry: the basic refusal to let our lives be oriented toward the triune God in joy, faith and worship;[57] this is not unrelated to the dynamic that Bonhoeffer has in view in contrasting the *imago dei* with humanity *sicut deus*.[58] From this basic distortion in our relationship to God spring other forms of distortion in our relationships with ourselves, one another and the non-human creation. These forms of distortion can be characterized in various ways. Karl Barth, for example, identifies three basic aspects of sin: pride, sloth and falsehood.[59] It is not hard to see how the well-intentioned desire to address the human suffering caused by genetic disease or infertility could become distorted by the kind of pride that makes us want to be our own helpers, and thereby alienates us from the true help offered by God in Christ:[60] for example, by imagining that technological solutions will meet the social, moral and spiritual needs made evident by the experience of genetic disease, disability and difference.[61] If this kind of pride were to become coupled to the falsehood of a

55 McFadyen, *Bound to Sin*, pp. 49–50.

56 As it is treated, for example, by Mary Midgley, *Wickedness: A Philosophical Essay*, London: Routledge, 2001 (1984), pp. 6–7.

57 McFadyen, *Bound to Sin*, pp. 200–26.

58 Dietrich Bonhoeffer, *Creation and Fall: A Theological Exposition of Genesis 1–3* (Dietrich Bonhoeffer, *Works*, vol. 3), ET ed. John W. De Gruchy, trans. Douglas Stephen Bax, Minneapolis, MN: Fortress Press, 1997, pp. 111–14.

59 Barth, *Church Dogmatics*, vols. IV.1–3; for summary and discussion, see Messer, *Selfish Genes*, pp. 169–84.

60 Barth, *Church Dogmatics*, vol. IV.1, p. 458–78.

61 See, further, Mary Jo Iozzio, 'Genetic Anomaly or Genetic Diversity: Thinking in the Key of Disability on the Human Genome', *Theological Studies* 66 (2005), pp. 862–81.

discourse that labelled those with inherited impairments as fundamentally abnormal and problematic – so that preventing their existence could be represented as an act of compassion to the 'abnormal' themselves, as well as the 'normal' people around them – then a compassionate and well-intentioned beginning could end in a rather toxic form of social and cultural dynamic.[62] More broadly, some envisaged applications of reproductive cloning raise other questions about the attitude to the past – in particular, the attitude to past losses and misfortunes – implicit in them. The attempt to replace a loved one who had died by means of cloning, for example, would suggest a desire for another form of control: to use technology in an attempt (most likely futile) to undo past losses and tragedies rather than seeking the moral and spiritual resources to face them and live with them.

In short, examination of the prospect of human reproductive cloning through the lens of my diagnostic questions suggests that there are good reasons to doubt whether, in theological perspective, it could ever be considered morally justified. There is no reason to deny that projects of reproductive cloning would typically be prompted by innocent and even laudable motives, but the analysis offered here suggests that those motives would all too likely be betrayed by the moral logic implicit in the practice of cloning. The benefits it promises are more plausibly regarded as counterfeits or parodies of God's saving work in Christ than as forms of human action that 'go with the grain' of God's work. And in some respects, the project of human cloning seems hospitable to a spirit more blatantly at odds with God's good and loving purposes, one serving rather the ends of chaos and destruction.

---

62 See Yong, *Theology and Down Syndrome*, p. 54.

4

Embryonic Stem Cells and Human Admixed Embryos

In Chapter 3 I offered a theological analysis of the ethical issues raised by the prospect of human reproductive cloning, and concluded that there are powerful reasons to doubt that it could ever be morally justified in the perspective of a Reformed Christian tradition. However, as I noted in that chapter, the somatic cell nuclear transfer (SCNT) technique used for mammalian cloning since the 1990s also has a range of other applications, often collectively referred to as 'therapeutic cloning', some of which are much nearer in prospect than the reproductive cloning of humans. The present chapter offers a moral analysis of these and related activities through the same theological lens used in Chapter 3, followed by a discussion of a more recent development: research and therapy using human-animal hybrid embryos, or 'human admixed embryos', as they are called in current UK legislation.

Stem cells and admixed embryos: the technologies and their uses

Human embryonic stem cells

Many, though not all, applications of the nuclear transfer technique envisaged under the heading of 'therapeutic cloning' would combine that technique with *embryonic stem cell technology*.[1] The

---

1 One that would not is another possible approach to avoiding the inheritance of mito-

human body contains many thousands of specialized types of cells, all with structures and properties adapted to the specific functions that they perform in the various tissues and organs, such as blood, brain, liver, muscle, skin and so on. All of these specialized cell types are descended from the undifferentiated cells of the early embryo by way of complex and precisely controlled processes of differentiation during the growth and development of the individual from embryo to adult. 'Stem cells' are relatively undifferentiated cells with the potential to differentiate into a range of more specialized cell types. There are many types of stem cells, some found in children and adults; for example, bone marrow contains stem cells capable of giving rise to the various types of blood cell. The cells of the early embryo, however, are stem cells with the special property of being *totipotent*: that is, they have the potential to differentiate into any type of cell found in the foetus, the placenta (which is derived from embryonic cells), the child or the adult.[2] This makes them particularly attractive to biomedical researchers for two main reasons. First, culturing human embryonic stem cells (hESCs) in the laboratory could enable researchers to gain a greater understanding of the mechanisms and processes of embryonic and foetal development, which in turn could give insight into the disorders that arise when these processes go wrong.

---

chondrial genetic diseases. If the female partner of a couple suffered from a mitochondrial disease, an egg cell could be donated from a third party, its nucleus removed and replaced with the nucleus from one of the woman's own *egg* cells (not somatic cells). This hybrid egg would have the healthy mitochondria from the donor, but the recipient's nuclear DNA. It would be fertilized *in vitro* by the male partner's sperm. Unlike clones, children conceived in this way would be the true genetic offspring of the couple. See Philippa Brice, 'Step Towards Therapeutic Cloning for Mitochondrial Diseases' (28 August 2009), online at www.phgfoundation.org/news/4775/ (accessed 10 September 2010).

2 Stem cells are often classified as totipotent (having the capacity to differentiate into any cell type in the body, plus all of the cell types in extra-embryonic tissues such as the components of the placenta), pluripotent (able to differentiate into any of the cell types in the body, but not extra-embryonic tissues such as those of the placenta, and therefore not able to give rise to a new individual) and multipotent (able to differentiate into a more limited number of cell types): see Anon., 'Glossary', in *Stem Cell Information*, Bethesda, MD: National Institutes of Health, US Department of Health and Human Services, 2010, online at http://stemcells.nih.gov/info/glossary.asp (accessed 13 September 2010).

Second, because hESCs can differentiate into any cell type found in the human body, they could potentially be used therapeutically to replace cells or tissues lost by disease or injury. Examples often discussed include the replacement of damaged skin in burn victims and the replacement of dead brain cells in neurological conditions such as Parkinson's disease.[3]

Stem cells could be obtained from 'spare' embryos created during *in vitro* fertilization or from embryos created for research. For therapeutic applications, these would have the disadvantage that they would be recognized by the patient's immune system as foreign, and would be vulnerable to rejection in a similar way to transplanted donor organs. In principle, this problem could be circumvented if an embryo were cloned from one of the patient's own cells, and that cloned embryo used to make hESCs, since these cells would be to all intents and purposes genetically identical to the patient's own. It has thus far proved technically difficult to produce hESCs from cloned human embryos, but there is no reason to think that it cannot be done.[4]

A major source of controversy over the use of hESCs for research and therapy is that their preparation usually involves the destruction of human embryos, an issue that will be discussed later in the chapter.[5] Because of this, the question arises whether

---

3 See, for example, Anon, 'Stem Cells and Diseases', in *Stem Cell Information*, online at http://stemcells.nih.gov/info/health.asp (accessed 13 September 2010).

4 The first authenticated cloning of a human embryo from a skin cell was reported in 2008: Andrew J. French et al., 'Development of Human Cloned Blastocysts Following Somatic Cell Nuclear Transfer with Adult Fibroblasts', *Stem Cells* 26.2 (2008), pp. 485–93. However, at the time of writing, hESCs have not yet been successfully produced from cloned human embryos. Earlier claims of the cloning of human embryos and extraction of stem cells from them were subsequently found to be fraudulent and retracted: Donald Kennedy, 'Editorial Retraction of Hwang *et al.* Papers', *Science* 311 (2006), p. 355.

5 It was reported in 2006 that human embryonic stem cell lines had been successfully cultivated from single cells removed from embryos by a technique similar to that used in pre-implantation genetic diagnosis, so that the embryos were not destroyed: Irina Kilmanskaya et al., 'Human Embryonic Stem Cell Lines Derived from Single Blastomeres', *Nature* 444 (2006), pp. 481–5. However, media comment by specialists in the field suggested that this technique was unlikely to replace destructive methods of obtaining hESCs: Ian Sample, 'Scientists Make Human Stem Cells Without Destroying the Embryo', *Guardian*,

stem cells obtained from any other source could be used for the same therapeutic applications. For example, adult stem cells taken from the patient being treated would also be invulnerable to immune rejection. There have been recent examples of novel therapies using adult stem cells, such as the successful treatment in 2008 of a woman suffering from collapsed airways, who was given a replacement bronchus made from a deceased donor's trachea stripped of its original cells and seeded with cells derived from the patient's own bone marrow.[6] However, the difficulty for many potential therapeutic uses is that adult stem cells usually only have the potential to differentiate into a relatively small range of more specialized cells. If ways could be found to make pluripotent stem cells from adult cells (so-called 'induced pluripotent stem cells', or iPSCs), this would in principle allow the development of stem cell therapies without the destruction of human embryos. In recent years, significant progress has been made in this direction.[7] Biomedical researchers, though, usually argue that embryonic as well as adult stem cell research is still needed, not least because the understanding of developmental biology needed to 'reprogramme' adult cells successfully to become pluripotent is likely to come from the study of embryonic stem cells.[8] Current UK legislation reflects this argument, allowing the creation of embryos, including cloned embryos, for hESC research, and the harvesting of hESCs from 'spare' embryos created by IVF for

24 August 2006, online at http://www.guardian.co.uk/science/2006/aug/24/stemcells.genetics (accessed 21 July 2010).

6 Paolo Maccherini et al., 'Clinical Transplantation of a Tissue-engineered Airway', *Lancet* 372 (13 December 2008), pp. 2023–30.

7 James F. Battey, Jr, et al., 'Alternate Methods for Preparing Pluripotent Stem Cells', in *Stem Cell Information*, online at http://stemcells.nih.gov/info/2006report/2006chapter8.htm (accessed 26 August 2009).

8 See, for example, Chief Medical Officer's Expert Group on Therapeutic Cloning, *Stem Cell Research: Medical Progress with Responsibility*, London: Department of Health, 2000, paras. 2.11–2.14, online at http://www.dh.gov.uk/prod_consum_dh/groups/dh_digital assets/@dh/@en/documents/digitalasset/dh_4065085.pdf (accessed 13 September 2010).

fertility treatment.[9] In other industrialized countries, legislation and regulation vary widely: within Europe, the UK's is among the most permissive.[10] In the USA, the severe restriction on Federal funding of hESC research introduced during the Bush administration was revoked in 2009 by President Obama, but at the time of writing, the Obama administration's guidelines on stem cell research funding are the subject of an ongoing legal dispute.[11]

Human admixed embryos

A related area that has more recently entered public consciousness is the creation of various kinds of human-animal hybrid embryos, or *human admixed embryos*, as they are called in recent UK legislation.[12] The term 'human admixed embryo' refers to various kinds of modified or artificially constructed embryo that incorporate both human and animal genetic material. Various kinds have been envisaged and are mentioned in the 2008 Act; some have been possible for some time, others are more recent developments or speculative possibilities:

- *Transgenic human embryos* are human embryos that have had animal DNA sequences inserted into their genomes using recombinant DNA ('genetic engineering') technology.

---

9 See UK Stem Cell Initiative, *Report and Recommendations*, London: Department of Health, 2005, p. 43, online at http://www.dh.gov.uk/prod_consum_dh/groups/dh_digital assets/@dh/@en/documents/digitalasset/dh_4124088.pdf (accessed 13 September 2010).

10 For an overview, see UK Stem Cell Initiative, *Global Positions in Stem cell Research*, online at http://www.dh.gov.uk/ab/UKSCI/DH_098510 (accessed 13 September 2010).

11 Presidential EO 13505, 'Removing Barriers to Responsible Scientific Research Involving Human Stem Cells', 9 March 2009, online at http://www.whitehouse.gov/the_press_office/ Removing-Barriers-to-Responsible-Scientific-Research-Involving-Human-Stem-cells/ (accessed 13 September 2010); Jeremy Pelofsky and Maggie Fox, 'US Court Rules Against Obama's Stem Cell Policy', online at http://www.reuters.com/article/idUSTRE67M4 HA20100823 (accessed 29 August 2010); Peter Aldhous, 'US Stem Cell Funding Freeze Lifted – For Now', *New Scientist*, 9 September 2010, online at http://www.newscientist.com/ article/dn19437-us-stem-cell-funding-freeze-lifted—for-now.html (accessed 13 September 2010).

12 Human Fertilisation and Embryology (hereafter HFE) Act (2008).

- *Chimaeras* are made by introducing some animal cells into human embryos, so that the resultant embryo is a 'mosaic' of human and animal cells.

- *Cytoplasmic hybrids* or *'cybrids'* are constructed by using the nuclear transfer technique to insert a human nucleus into an animal egg cell. This is seen as a way of overcoming the shortage of donated human eggs available to create cloned hESC lines. Since the nuclear DNA of cybrids would be entirely human, the resultant cells could be expected to behave very much like human stem cells and therefore to be usable for research and perhaps therapy, though much of their mitochondrial DNA would come from the animal egg cell mitochondria, which could make some difference to their functioning.[13]

- The products of combining human with animal gametes (egg and sperm cells) are referred to as *true hybrids*. It is not clear what research or therapeutic uses these might have, and they were excluded from an earlier draft of the UK legislation, but are permitted in the version that has become law. This was the result of pressure from the biomedical research community and the biotechnology industry lobby, who argued that within limits, the legislation should be as flexible as possible in order to leave researchers free to respond quickly to new developments and promising lines of research in a fast-moving area of science.[14]

- The legislation also contains a 'catch-all' provision to include other forms of admixed embryo that might become possible in the future.

---

13 Academy of Medical Sciences, *Inter-Species Embryos*, London: Academy of Medical Sciences, 2007, section 8.1.

14 For example Report of the Joint Committee on the Human Tissue and Embryos (Draft) Bill, Vol. II: Evidence, HL 169-II (2006–07), pp. 4, 239–40, 265, 404. Hereafter: Report on the HTE (Draft) Bill.

The 2008 Act permits the creation of these forms of admixed embryo within broadly the same limits first proposed for human embryo research in the Warnock Report in the 1980s and enshrined in UK law since 1990:[15] they may be used for research for certain specified purposes under licence from a regulatory authority, maintained in the laboratory until they are 14 days old, after which they must be destroyed, and may not be implanted in a woman or an animal.[16]

Theological diagnoses

Embryonic stem cell research

As in other areas of bioethical debate, arguments about consequences have played a prominent role in public debates about therapeutic cloning and stem cell research. In these debates the emphasis tends to be on the great benefits, particularly treatments for serious diseases and injuries, to be expected from these areas of research. As so often, John Harris expresses the point with particular pungency in relation to therapeutic cloning, concluding that it

> is ethical, permissible and indeed mandatory ... there are overwhelmingly powerful reasons to pursue therapeutic cloning, stem cell research and other research which therapeutic cloning will augment and probably make much more effective. The reasons for pursuing this research are so strong that it would be unethical not to pursue this research.[17]

However, Harris does no more than express more sharply and clearly what is by far the dominant mode of argument in these

---

15 Report of the Committee of Inquiry into Human Fertilisation and Embryology (Cmnd 9314, 1984), ch. 11; Human Fertilisation and Embryology Act (1990).

16 HFE Act (2008), section 4.

17 Harris, *On Cloning*, p. 143.

debates from the biomedical research community and patient support groups: that there are no moral principles that would prohibit such research, and the benefits it promises are so great as to offer a compelling case in its favour.

In Chapter 1 I argued that while the relief of suffering is – of course – a proper and important goal of health care in Christian perspective, Christians should resist forms of argument or rhetoric that present it as the *over-riding* goal, the one that trumps all others. Such argument or rhetoric represents a distorted and diminished kind of moral discourse. Therefore appeals to the great medical benefits expected of stem cell research, such as therapies for awful and debilitating diseases, cannot simply be taken as discussion-stoppers, closing off the expression of other moral and theological concerns. Other theological and ethical questions can and should be asked, and should not simply be dismissed as self-indulgent scruples. The five diagnostic questions set out in Chapter 1 offer one way of articulating these more expansive moral and theological concerns.[18] In terms of attitudes to the material world and the body, for example, it can properly be asked whether the practice of stem cell research displays a tendency to regard human embryos – and by extension, human bodies – as un-problematically manipulable in the service of human needs, desires and goals. Is there a tendency, in other words, to regard the human body as raw material available for any kind of use that will relieve suffering and meet human needs? Such an attitude would reflect what, following Gerald McKenny, I referred to in Chapter 1 as a 'Baconian' mindset: a reluctance to acknowledge that the material world (including our own bodies) is God's good creation, with its own proper ends and goals that should be respected in our human activities and projects. If human embryos did come to be seen as little more than raw material for research and therapy, this would amount to a kind of hatred of the material creation,

---

18 See above, pp. 37–42.

an unwillingness, in Dietrich Bonhoeffer's words, to 'forgive God for having created what is'.[19]

This concern by itself, however, amounts to a cautionary note rather than a knock-down objection to stem cell research. The theological perspective that informs my diagnostic questions does provide a strong mandate for both medicine and medical research. It would be wrong-headed to regard all biomedical research and high-tech medicine as the kind of overweening desire for knowledge and power that Bonhoeffer calls the attempt to be 'like God' (*sicut deus*). Much medical research, and the therapies to which it gives rise, can quite properly be regarded as legitimate and important human action reflecting the *imago dei*, expressive of a proper care and regard for the 'penultimate' realm of this world in which we have the task of responding to God's call and promise of the 'ultimate'. A wholesale suspicion of biomedical research could itself amount to a kind of contempt for the material creation, a theological form of what Bonhoeffer calls the 'radicalism' that would sweep away the penultimate in the light of the ultimate.[20]

The stated aims and goals of at least some stem cell research, to develop therapies for serious injuries (such as burns and spinal injuries) and diseases (such as Parkinson's and Alzheimer's) are undoubtedly serious and worthwhile. Other considerations aside, those aims and goals *could* be understood as consistent with a properly Christian mandate to heal, in line with a proper respect for the material creation: neither regarding it as an enemy to be subdued nor making it bear the burden of our ultimate human hopes. Activity directed towards those aims and goals *could* be regarded as responsible human action in conformity to the *imago dei*, expressive of a proper concern for those who suffer among our neighbours. However, the use of human embryonic stem cells

---

19 Dietrich Bonhoeffer, *Ethics* (*Dietrich Bonhoeffer Works*, vol. 6), ET ed. Clifford J. Green, trans Reinhard Krauss, Charles C. West and Douglas W. Stott, Minneapolis: Fortress Press, 2005, p. 155.

20 Bonhoeffer, *Ethics*, p. 153.

to achieve those goals of course entails the destruction of embryonic human life. Does this mean that even if the ends are good in themselves, the means must always be considered opposed to God's good purposes?

Many (though by no means all) Christian commentators on human embryo research argue that they must, because human life has a distinctive kind of value that forbids this kind of destructive use of it to meet others' needs. Such appeals to the distinctive value of human life are sometimes couched in explicitly biblical or theological terms, grounded for example in the command 'You shall not murder' (Exod. 20.13) or the affirmation that all humans bear the image of God (Gen. 1.27), but are sometimes justified more generally on the claim that intentionally taking innocent human lives (that is, the lives of human beings who have done nothing to justify their being killed) is simply wrong. Do human embryos, though, count as the kind of human life that it is wrong intentionally to kill?

This question is habitually set up in terms of arguments about 'personhood', so that 'persons' – human or not – are a class of beings with a distinctive kind of value that (*inter alia*) makes it wrong to kill them intentionally, unless there are specific reasons to justify their killing. If the discussion is set up in this way, the question becomes whether or not human embryos count as persons. Standard approaches to this discussion identify persons by means of criteria or 'indicators' such as consciousness, self-awareness, awareness of one's identity over time, the capacity for rationality, the possession of interests and moral agency. Such understandings of personhood have their roots in the thought of early modern philosophers such as Locke,[21] but their deployment in bioethical debates began more recently with authors such as Mary Ann Warren, Michael Tooley and Joseph Fletcher.[22] Ac-

---

21 John Locke, *An Essay Concerning Human Understanding*, Book II, ch. 27, section 9. Everyman edn, 2 vols., London: J. M. Dent, 1961, vol. 1, pp. 280–1.

22 For example Joseph Fletcher, 'Indicators of Humanhood: A Tentative Profile of Man', *Hastings Center Report* 2.5 (1972), pp. 1–4; Michael Tooley, 'Abortion and Infanticide',

cording to such approaches, most humans meet enough of the chosen criteria to be clearly counted as persons, but those that meet few or none of them – such as embryos, at least some foetuses, anencephalic infants, adults in persistent vegetative state and those with severe dementia – are not persons.[23] While there may still be good reasons not to kill such humans, killing them will not be wrong for the distinctive reasons or in the distinctive sense in which it is wrong to kill persons. Conversely, if a non-human (say an ape, a dolphin, an alien or a highly advanced computer) met enough of these criteria, that being would be a person, whose life commanded the same degree of respect as most human life.[24]

According to Tooley, '[t]hat certain clusters of properties are sufficient [to make something a person] is almost universally accepted among philosophers.'[25] However, this approach to identifying persons is not as uncontroversial as he implies. It is perceived by some critics as a device for identifying classes of human being whose lives need not be protected, or at least protected as rigorously

---

Philosophy and Public Affairs 2 (1972), pp. 37–65; Mary Ann Warren, 'On the Moral and Legal Status of Abortion', *The Monist* 57 (1973), pp. 43–61.

23 Such 'criterial' approaches are found among theologians as well as philosophers: for example, Ronald Cole-Turner's claim that the embryo before the 14-day limit 'is so profoundly unlike us that it cannot be one of us' is in effect a criterial approach to identifying personhood (albeit with criteria – deliberately – less precisely stated than in the philosophical treatments cited above): 'Beyond the Impasse over the Embryo', in Brent Waters and Ronald Cole-Turner (eds), *God and the Embryo: Religious Voices on Stem Cells and Cloning*, Washington, DC: Georgetown University Press, 2003, pp. 88–97 (p. 91).

24 It should be noted that a criterial approach is not the only way in which embryos can be denied the status of person. For example, Michael Sandel deploys the 'sorites' paradox (often expressed as a puzzle about how many grains of sand make a heap, and whether there is a point at which the addition of one further grain will make a heap) and various *reductio ad absurdum* arguments to deny that embryos or blastocysts count as persons. He argues that this does not mean they have no moral importance or significance, but that they do lack the distinctive significance ascribed to persons, and therefore may be destroyed for a sufficiently weighty purpose, such as the creation of stem cells to treat serious diseases: Michael J. Sandel, *The Case against Perfection: Ethics in the Age of Genetic Engineering*, Cambridge, MA: Harvard University Press, 2007, pp. 101–28.

25 Michael Tooley, 'Personhood', in Helga Kuhse and Peter Singer (eds), *A Companion to Bioethics*, Oxford: Blackwell, 1998, pp. 117–26 (p. 120).

as most human lives should be. Christian theologians sometimes compare the question 'Who is a person?' to the lawyer's question to Jesus in Luke's Gospel, 'Who is my neighbour?': an unwarranted attempt to set boundaries on our moral concern and our obligations to others.[26]

A dissatisfaction with 'criterial' approaches to personhood and suspicion of the motivation of such approaches can lead arguments about embryo research in various directions. It might lead to a robust assertion that embryos are not to be considered as non-persons, or even potential persons, but quite simply as human persons that have the properties and capacities proper to their stage of development. It might also prompt the thought that the moral consequences of wrongly excluding individuals from the status of person are so grave that *any* reasonable doubt about the status of embryos calls for a strong presumption in favour of treating them as persons. Both of these lines of thought are expressed in official Roman Catholic teaching:

> Even if the presence of a spiritual soul cannot be ascertained by empirical data, the results themselves of scientific research on the human embryo provide 'a valuable indication for discerning by the use of reason a personal presence at the moment of the first appearance of a human life: how could a human individual not be a human person?'
>
> Furthermore, what is at stake is so important that, from the standpoint of moral obligation, the mere probability that a human person is involved would suffice to justify an absolutely clear prohibition of any intervention aimed at killing a human embryo.[27]

---

26 Oliver O'Donovan, *Resurrection and Moral Order: An Outline for Evangelical Ethics*, 2nd edn, Leicester: Apollos, 1994, pp. 239–40; Richard B. Hays, *The Moral Vision of the New Testament*, Edinburgh: T & T Clark, 1997, p. 461; Ian A. McFarland, 'Who is my Neighbor? The Good Samaritan as a Source for Theological Anthropology', *Modern Theology* 17.1 (2001), pp. 57–66.

27 John Paul II, *Evangelium Vitae* (25 March 1995), 60, online at http://www.vatican.va/

The latter thought is taken up by Robert Song, quoting the Catholic philosopher and theologian Germain Grisez: 'to be willing to kill what for all one knows is a person is to be willing to kill a person'.[28] It is worth noting that this formulation of the argument refers not just to the *act* of killing an embryo as an action that might transgress a gravely important moral principle, but also points to the intention and the character of the agent who does the killing. It is morally wrong to *intend* to kill an innocent person, whether or not one carries out that intention, and it is a serious matter to become the *kind of person* who is willing to kill persons.

However, theological suspicion of criterial approaches to identifying persons, motivated in part by the readings of the parable of the Good Samaritan alluded to earlier, could lead in another direction: to the conclusion that arguing about the personhood of embryos is the wrong way to settle ethical questions about embryo research. Since the language of personhood originated in Christian theology as a way of speaking of the Trinity and the person of Christ, it might simply not be suited to the kind of conceptual and ethical work that it is made to do in modern bioethical controversies.[29] In particular, arguments about whether or not human embryos are persons are likely to prove interminable, because the language of personhood was not developed within Christian theology to do that kind of work. This might help explain the observation made by various critics, that arguments about the personhood of embryos couched in the terms of

---

holy_father/john_paul_ii/encyclicals/documents/hf_jp-ii_enc_25031995_evangelium-vitae_en.html (accessed 18 March 2010), quoting Congregation for the Doctrine of the Faith, *Donum Vitae* (22 February 1987), I, no. 1.

28 Robert Song, 'To Be Willing to Kill What for All One Knows is a Person is to Be Willing to Kill a Person', in Waters and Cole-Turner (eds), *God and the Embryo*, pp. 98–107 (p. 102), quoting Germain Grisez, *The Way of the Lord Jesus*, vol. 2, Quincy, IL: Franciscan Herald Press, 1983, p. 497.

29 Cf. McFarland, '"Who is My Neighbor?"' As is well known, the *term* 'person' (*persona* in Latin, *prosopon* in Greek) originally referred to the mask worn by an actor, and by extension, to a part played in a drama, but before the term was taken up by Christian theologians, it had no great philosophical or ethical significance.

modern philosophical ethics often prove circular, relying on stipulative definitions of 'person' that will produce the desired conclusion – whether of a 'conservative' or 'liberal' stamp.[30]

If arguments about personhood fail to settle the question of the moral status of human embryos, the doctrine of the *imago dei* might be thought a better starting point. The conviction, based on biblical texts such as Genesis 1.26–28, that humans are made in the image of God is sometimes said to underpin the *intrinsic* dignity of all human life.[31] Some of these appeals, at least, seem to assume what is sometimes called a 'substantialist' understanding of the *imago*, according to which it is (in Paul Sands' words) 'an endowment given by God at creation – an inalienable component of human nature',[32] such as reason or morality, which confers intrinsic dignity. If it is understood in this way, then the grounds for attributing dignity to human beings are not so very different from those in view in 'criterial' understandings of personhood, though such appeals to the *imago dei* tend to assume that dignity is conferred on all individuals by virtue of their membership of the species created with this 'endowment', and cannot be denied to those who temporarily or permanently lack capacities associated with the *imago*.

However, there is a widespread consensus that 'substantialist' readings of the *imago dei* are exegetically and hermeneutically un-tenable.[33] Instead, many systematic theologians favour 'relational' interpretations, following Barth's reading of Genesis 1.26–28, in

---

30 See, for example, Michael Banner, *Christian Ethics and Contemporary Moral Problems*, Cambridge: Cambridge University Press, 1999, pp. 101–14; Maureen Junker-Kenny, 'Embryos *in vitro*, Personhood, and Rights', in Maureen Junker-Kenny (ed.), *Designing Life? Genetics, Procreation and Ethics*, Aldershot: Ashgate, 1999, pp. 130–58 (pp. 133–5).

31 See, for example, Report on the HTE (Draft) Bill, vol. II, pp. 281–2, 316, 328–9, 396.

32 Paul Sands, 'The *Imago Dei* as Vocation', *Evangelical Quarterly* 82.1 (2010), pp. 28–41 (pp. 31–2).

33 Nathan MacDonald, 'The *Imago Dei* and Election: Reading Genesis 1:26–28 and Old Testament Scholarship with Karl Barth', *International Journal of Systematic Theology* 10.3 (2008), pp. 303–27 (p. 304), citing Francis Watson, 'In the Image of God', in *Text and Truth: Redefining Biblical Theology*, Edinburgh: T & T Clark, 1997, pp. 277–304.

which he connects creation in the divine image with creation as male and female, and associates the *imago* with the 'I–Thou' relationship.[34] Biblical scholars, on the other hand, often reject Barth's reading on the grounds that it is exegetically implausible and projects a particular set of philosophical presuppositions – essentially those of Martin Buber's personalism – back onto the text of Genesis 1.[35] Many prefer 'functionalist' readings, based on parallels with other ancient Near Eastern texts, in which the *imago dei* denotes the task, assigned to humanity, of being God's representatives and agents in the world.[36] However, according to Nathan MacDonald, when critics claim that a functionalist reading of the *imago* is preferable on exegetical grounds to Barth's allegedly implausible relational reading, they miss their target in so far as their exegesis depends on hermeneutical presuppositions that Barth sees no need to share. In particular, functionalist readings tend to depend on ancient Near Eastern parallels to support a reading of the *imago* for which there is little evidence in the biblical texts themselves.[37]

MacDonald argues plausibly that the *impasse* between relational and functionalist readings can be overcome – using Barth's hermeneutical method against Barth's own, admittedly problematic, equation of the *imago* with the male–female relation – by understanding the image of God as 'a relationship to God and the world analogous to Israel's election',[38] a distinctive relationship that *implies* a particular role. This can do justice to the christological focus of the *imago dei* in New Testament texts such as Colossians 1.15,

---

34 Barth, *Church Dogmatics*, vol. III.1, pp. 182–206. For one example of a contemporary systematic theological treatment that follows this line of thought, see Alistair I. McFadyen, *The Call to Personhood: A Christian Theory of the Individual in Social Relationships*, Cambridge: Cambridge University Press, 1990, ch. 1.

35 James Barr, *Biblical Faith and Natural Theology*, Oxford: Clarendon Press, 1993, ch. 8; J. Richard Middleton, *The Liberating Image: The* Imago Dei *in Genesis 1*, Grand Rapids, MI: Brazos, 2005, pp. 21–4.

36 Middleton, *Liberating Image*; Sands, 'The *Imago Dei* as Vocation'.

37 MacDonald, 'The *Imago Dei* and Election'.

38 MacDonald, 'The *Imago Dei* and Election', p. 303.

because '[f]or Barth *the* elect one and *the* image of God are one and the same, Jesus Christ'.[39] It has the additional virtue of connecting the creation stories with the history of Israel as the covenant people narrated in the Hebrew Scriptures, thus preventing 'a disembodiment of the image under the old covenant and a loss of Israelite identity with the fullness of the christological image'.[40]

If substantialist readings of the *imago dei* must be abandoned, and more specifically if MacDonald is right to discern an analogy between the *imago* and election, this shifts the focus of the doctrine's ethical implications away from the claims about intrinsic human dignity that it is sometimes used to support in bioethical debate.[41] To be sure, Genesis 9.6 does link a prohibition of the shedding of human blood with the image of God, but this is a rather slight foundation on which to construct a whole ethical edifice of inviolable human dignity. This prohibition of unlawful killing is perhaps better read as following from the call to live as those made in God's image, a way of life in which, as MacDonald puts it, 'the role of bearing God's grace to others ... flows out of a unique relationship [with God]'.[42]

One aspect of this calling is to exercise power and authority in the world as God's vice-regents. However, the contrast drawn by Bonhoeffer between the *imago dei* and humanity *sicut deus* ('like God', Gen. 3.5) suggests that the power and authority in view here are of a distinctive kind, not to be confused with our ordinary notions.[43] It is all too common for sinful humans, alienated from

---

39 MacDonald, 'The *Imago Dei* and Election', p. 326.

40 MacDonald, 'The *Imago Dei* and Election', p. 326.

41 *Contra* Sands, 'The *Imago Dei* as Vocation', pp. 39–40. Sands develops a functionalist reading of the *imago* as divine vocation, heavily influenced by Middleton, *Liberating Image*. However, when he comes to draw out the ethical implications of his account, he begins with respect for the inalienable dignity of human beings and the protection of human life. While I am largely in agreement with his practical conclusions, I am not persuaded that his reading of the *imago* supports them as securely as he believes.

42 MacDonald, 'The *Imago Dei* and Election', p. 327.

43 Dietrich Bonhoeffer, *Creation and Fall: A Theological Exposition of Genesis 1–3* (Dietrich Bonhoeffer, *Works*, vol. 3), ET ed. John W. De Gruchy, trans. Douglas Stephen Bax,

God, one another, ourselves and the creation, to seek essentiall, violent and coercive ways of exercising godlike power over one another and the world. But the power and authority that conform to the *imago dei* are not of this kind. If we wish to understand the kind of power and authority consistent with the calling expressed in the *imago*, we must look to Jesus Christ, who is 'the image of the invisible God' (Col. 1.15) and, in Bonhoeffer's words, 'agnus dei – the human being who is God incarnate, who was sacrificed for humankind sicut deus, in true divinity slaying its false divinity and restoring the imago dei'.[44] By suffering the violent power of humanity *sicut deus* on the cross, Jesus the Lamb of God puts an end to violence, showing and making possible a new way to live together in the world before God. Such a reading of the *imago dei* certainly implies a good deal about the quality of relationships we should have with one another, including the least and most vulnerable,[45] but what it implies is not best articulated in terms of claims about intrinsic human dignity. If we wish to know why and how we should value other human beings, the reply 'because they are made in God's image' is not the best place to *start*.

Why are human beings valuable – or more precisely, why should we value other human beings? Among the diagnostic questions set out in Chapter 1, the question about our attitudes to our neighbours points to the beginning of a Christian answer: we should value other human beings because they are neighbours whom God has given us to love.[46] Furthermore, the neighbours whom God calls us to love are those for whom Christ died, and in our love for our neighbours we are called to reflect God's love for them and us, shown in the death of Christ. The 'vertical' dimension

---

Minneapolis: Fortress Press, 1997, pp. 111–14. In this respect I do concur with Middleton: see *Liberating Image*, esp. Part 3.

44 Bonhoeffer, *Creation and Fall*, p. 113.

45 It also implies a good deal about the relationship of humans with non-human creatures, a theme taken up below in Chapter 6.

46 For a similar approach, albeit with different practical conclusions, see Brent Waters, 'Does the Human Embryo Have a Moral Status?', in Waters and Cole-Turner (eds), *God and the Embryo*, pp. 67–76.

of our response to God's love for us is inseparable from the 'horizontal': 'those who do not love a brother or sister whom they have seen, cannot love God whom they have not seen' (1 John 4.20b). And since it is God who gives us neighbours to love, it is not up to us to decide who does or does not count as a neighbour. That insight is part of the subversive effect that Jesus' parable of the Good Samaritan has on the lawyer's attempt to 'justify himself' by asking, 'Who is my neighbour?' (Luke 10.25–37). Famously, the parable does not answer the question, instead refocusing attention on the questioner by concluding with a counter-question ('Which of these three, do you think, was a neighbour to the man …?') and a command ('Go and do likewise').[47] It seems fairly obvious that the patients whose diseases stem cell therapies are intended to treat are neighbours whom God has given us to love, and love for our neighbours is a proper and powerful motivation for both health care and biomedical research.[48] But if it is true that 'neighbour', properly understood in theological perspective, is not a bounded category from which we are entitled to exclude some, then we must reckon with the possibility that the embryos who might be destroyed, to make stem cells for the research and therapy aimed at treating those patients, are our neighbours too.

What will it entail to love the neighbours whom God has given us? A good deal of ink has been spilled over the content of neighbour-love, and it is in any case almost certainly true that the ethical significance of the call to love our neighbours cannot be adequately captured by broad generalizations about universal principles or moral requirements entailed by the love command. As McFarland puts it, 'the crucial ethical judgment in my behavior toward those I meet on the road is not primarily the determination of the general category under which they fall ... but rather the way in which I define my relationship to them in their par-

---

47 See, further, McFarland, 'Who Is my Neighbor?'
48 On neighbour-love, medicine and medical research, see further below, Chapter 5.

ticularity.'[49] Nonetheless, it seems uncontroversial that one minimal requirement is to obey the command 'You shall not murder' (Exod. 20.13): as Barth puts it, to respect and protect the human life that 'is [God's] loan and blessing', the life that 'God has unequivocally and fully accepted ... in Jesus Christ, in the incarnation of His Word'.[50] We are commanded unconditionally, then, to protect human life. But as Barth shows, care is needed in elucidating what forms that command might take. The life we are called to protect, he observes, 'is not the eternal life promised to man, but temporal.'[51] This means that while the command most obviously and commonly requires us to preserve and defend life, we are not entitled to assume that this is the only form it can ever take: 'we cannot deny the possibility that God as the Lord of life may further its protection even in the strange form of its conclusion and termination rather than its preservation and enhancement.'[52] God, who is sovereign, *could* permit or command the ending of a human life. It is important to recognize that if there are situations where the ending of a life is permitted or commanded, these are not arbitrary exceptions to, or suspensions of, the command 'You shall not murder', but (as Nigel Biggar puts it) 'unusual mode[s] of keeping it'.[53] Barth emphasizes that while exceptional cases of this sort 'cannot be completely excluded', they 'can and should be envisaged ... only as highly exceptional, and therefore with the greatest reserve, on the exhaustion of all other possibilities'.[54]

---

49 'Who Is my Neighbor?', p. 64. This implies that Ted Peters and Gaymon Bennett ('A Plea for Beneficence: Reframing the Embryo Debate', in Waters and Cole-Turner (eds), *God and the Embryo*, pp. 111–30) miss the full significance of the ethic of neighbour-love articulated by the parable of the Good Samaritan when they use it, along with other rich biblical and theological themes, to ground what ends up as a rather thin ethic of beneficence, permitting the use and destruction of embryos to relieve the suffering caused by serious diseases and injuries.

50 Barth, *Church Dogmatics*, vol. III.4, p. 397.

51 Barth, *Church Dogmatics*, vol. III.4, p. 397.

52 Barth, *Church Dogmatics*, vol. III.4, p. 398.

53 Nigel Biggar, *The Hastening that Waits: Karl Barth's Ethics*, Oxford: Clarendon Press, 1993, p. 34.

54 Barth, *Church Dogmatics*, vol. III.4, p. 398.

Thus, for example, in relation to abortion, he holds that 'a definite No must be the presupposition of all further discussion'.[55] Yet it is not an exceptionless No. There could be cases – highly exceptional, as he emphasizes again – in which abortion is permitted or commanded by God. Such situations will be recognizable by the fact that the pregnancy threatens the life or health of the mother, so that 'one life [is] balanced against another ... the sacrifice of one or the other being unavoidable'.[56] We are not entitled to state as a general rule that abortion is permitted or commanded even in those circumstances, but it could be. By contrast, when Barth turns his attention to euthanasia, he rules out any possibility that there could be such exceptional cases in which it is permitted or commanded, on the grounds that it does not present situations of the 'life against life' kind, in which the protection of life also requires the taking of life and the sacrifice of one or other life is unavoidable.[57]

Presumably the first thing to be said about the destruction of human embryos for treatment or research is, in Barth's phrase, 'a definite No'. But once that 'No' has been said, should stem cell research be regarded in the way Barth regards abortion – as a practice that could, in highly exceptional cases, turn out to be permitted or commanded as an unusual way to protect life – or, as he argues of euthanasia, as an activity that could not possibly give rise to such exceptions?

The truly exceptional character of the 'exceptional cases' envisaged by Barth would seem to require that only those situations should be considered in which patients' lives could only be preserved from terrible and life-threatening diseases by using embryonic stem cells for research or treatment. Even if we conclude that the use of embryonic stem cells could exceptionally be permitted or commanded, in any concrete situation it should not

---

55 Barth, *Church Dogmatics*, vol. III.4, p. 417.
56 Barth, *Church Dogmatics*, vol. III.4, p. 421.
57 Barth, *Church Dogmatics*, vol. III.4, pp. 423–7.

be contemplated until all other avenues for research and treatment have been exhausted. Some critics of embryonic stem cell research argue that the claims made for the benefits of embryonic stem cell research are overstated and that other more promising avenues of research tend to be neglected by comparison,[58] which could raise the question of how likely such extreme cases truly are. However, allowing for the sake of argument that they do occur, could the use of embryonic stem cells be permitted or commanded in these situations?

One important disanalogy with abortion – and other forms of killing, such as war, where Barth allows the possibility of exceptional cases – is that in those situations, there is in some sense a conflict between the life that may be taken and the life that is thereby protected. In war, lethal force is to be used against hostile combatants. In the case of abortion, the unborn child is of course unwitting and innocent; but in the tragic exceptional cases envisaged by Barth, the pregnancy threatens the mother's life or health, so it is the life of *this* foetus, and not some other, that must be balanced against that of the mother. By contrast, the embryos that might be used as sources of stem cells are not parties to this kind of tragic conflict. They are more in the position of bystanders, uninvolved until they are co-opted to be sacrificed for the preservation of others' lives. So the question then is whether this kind of 'co-option' of embryonic human life could ever be permitted or commanded as a way to protect other human lives.[59]

---

58 Cf. David Jones, 'A Submission to The House of Lords Select Committee on Stem Cell Research', London: Linacre Centre, 2000, online at http://www.linacre.org/stemcell.html (accessed 13 September 2010).

59 It is sometimes argued that embryos created for research in the laboratory have a different (and lower) moral status by virtue of their having been made for this purpose. But this is unpersuasive: if it were possible to make an artificial womb in which human babies could be brought to term for the purpose of being used in experiments and then killed, it is not obvious that the circumstances of their origins would alter their moral status and lead us morally to evaluate their destruction any differently to the same treatment of babies born naturally. So if such an argument is used of embryos, it presumably rests on an assumption that their moral standing is negotiable and can be determined by context in a

Within a utilitarian frame of reference, the answer would seem simple: the number and quality of lives saved by embryonic stem cell research would far outweigh the value of embryonic life lost.[60] However, I have argued that in theological perspective, utilitarian and other consequentialist frames of reference produce a bio-ethical picture that is not only incomplete but distorted. It is hard to see how a Christian ethic that regards others as valuable because they are neighbours whom God has given us to love could countenance the purely instrumental use of some neighbours for the sake of others, particularly when the instrumental use in question involves the destruction – we might say *sacrifice* – of the co-opted lives for the sake of others.

A Christian theological vision formed by the Scriptures would seem to point in a different direction. For example, in the Fourth Gospel's ironic portrayal of an exchange between the High Priest Caiaphas and the Sanhedrin, Caiaphas tells his hearers, 'it is better for you to have one man die for the people than to have the whole nation destroyed' (John 11.50). This remark seems on the surface to express a *Realpolitik* not so very different from the kind of utilitarian calculus that would weigh the number and quality of lives saved by stem cell research against the embryonic lives destroyed.[61] But of course the point is that there is a good deal more to Caiaphas' comment than meets the eye: 'He did not say this on his own, but being high priest that year he prophesied that Jesus was about to die for the nation, and not for the nation only, but to gather into one the dispersed children of God' (John 11.51–52). Caiaphas speaks more truly than he knows, just as Abraham, in

---

way in which that of babies or children is not and cannot, perhaps because a ball of cells is thought to be, in Cole-Turner's words, 'so profoundly unlike us that it cannot be one of us' ('Beyond the Impasse over the Embryo', p. 91) – a line of argument that I have already criticized on theological grounds.

60 Cf. Harris, *On Cloning*, p. 143.

61 I leave aside the question of whether John's narrative accurately reflects something that the High Priest could be expected to have said, or whether it is a polemical story reflecting a particularly bitter conflict between one community of Christians and their Jewish compatriots: cf. Hays, *Moral Vision*, pp. 146–7, 424–8.

one of the most terrible and mysterious stories in the canon, speaks more truly than he knows when he tells his son Isaac that 'God himself will provide the lamb for a burnt-offering' (Gen. 22.8).[62] Christian readers of the 'binding of Isaac' have often taken it to point towards Jesus Christ, 'both the substituted lamb of sacrifice and the beloved son of the promise'.[63] Jesus' willing acceptance of death on the cross is the sacrifice that puts an end to sacrifice and wins for humanity the ultimate hope of eternal life (cf. Heb. 10.19–25). In the light of this, it is possible to read God's command to Abraham, 'Do not lay your hand on the boy or do anything to him' (Gen. 22.12), as signalling an end to the project of saving human life by sacrificing human life. As I have repeatedly emphasized, this does not make the protection of mortal human life in this world unimportant, nor does it belittle the vocations of those (such as health care professionals) whose business it is to protect human life.[64] To think that it does would be to fall prey to what Bonhoeffer calls 'radicalism', collapsing the tension between the ultimate and the penultimate in favour of the ultimate. It does, however, mean that we no longer need to invest our *ultimate* hopes in this mortal life,[65] and so are freed from the compulsion to ward off threats to this life by any means necessary. All of this at any rate intensifies the doubt that the co-option of uninvolved bystanders is the kind of killing to protect life that could ever be permitted or commanded – even if the 'bystanders' in question are human embryos. At the very least, the burden of proof is on those who would argue that such a situation *can* provide such 'exceptional cases'.[66]

---

62 For the echo of Abraham's unwitting prophecy in Caiaphas', see R. R. Reno, *Genesis* (Brazos Theological Commentary on the Bible), Grand Rapids, MI: Brazos, 2010, p. 198.

63 Reno, *Genesis*, p. 206.

64 Nor does it deny that tragic conflicts of life against life sometimes occur in a finite and broken world, as I have noted with reference to Barth's discussion of abortion. But it is one thing to face those conflicts when we are confronted by them; quite another to create choices of life against life by our own initiative.

65 So Allen Verhey, *Reading the Bible in the Strange World of Medicine*, Grand Rapids, MI: Eerdmans, 2003, p. 144.

66 This conclusion represents a shift of emphasis from my discussion in *Selfish Genes and*

Human admixed embryos

If one agrees with John Paul II that 'the mere probability that a human person is involved would suffice to justify an absolutely clear prohibition of any intervention aimed at killing a human embryo',[67] might the moral problem be sidestepped by using human admixed embryos, which are not unambiguously human, as a source of stem cells?

One of the questions raised by this suggestion is whether admixed embryos should be counted as human or not. Some perplexity about this was evident in debates about UK legislation on admixed embryos.[68] The answers that are intuitively attractive differ for the various types of admixed embryo. A transgenic embryo with a small amount of inserted non-human DNA cannot plausibly be regarded as anything other than human, whereas a human-animal chimaera made by introducing animal cells into a human embryo could be much more ambiguous.[69] The kind of admixed embryo most likely to be used in stem cell research and therapy is the cybrid, in which the nuclear DNA is human but the cytoplasm of the egg cell and the mitochondrial DNA of the embryo that develops from it are non-human. To all intents and purposes, cybrid cells would be genetically human, though it is possible that the presence of non-human mitochondria would affect the functioning of the cells.[70] Presumably cybrid-derived stem cells would be useful for most of the research and treatment applications envisaged for them just to the extent that they behaved like human stem cells: the point would be to make something as much like a human embryo as possible. If that is the

---

Christian Ethics: Theological and Ethical Reflections on Evolutionary Biology (London: SCM Press, 2007), pp. 238–41.

67 See above, n. 27.

68 This was evident, for example, in a consultation with faith groups and 'others with particular ethical perspectives' held by the Parliamentary Select Committee on the draft bill: Report on the HTE (Draft) Bill, vol. I, pp. 96–8.

69 As David Jones observes: Report on the HTE (Draft) Bill, vol. II, pp. 386–7.

70 Academy of Medical Sciences, Inter-Species Embryos, pp. 25–6.

case, then perhaps we are once more confronted by at least the 'probability that a human person is involved', in the words of John Paul II, in which case the use of cybrids would at any rate not offer an easy way to side-step the moral problems associated with human embryonic stem cells.

The very ambiguity about the humanness of admixed embryos was a major ethical concern for many of those involved in recent UK debates. For example, the philosopher Søren Holm observed, in evidence to the Joint Committee on the Human Tissue and Embryos (Draft) Bill, that the various forms of admixed embryos under consideration 'are all problematic ... for the reason that they are blurring a species boundary'.[71] A report from the bioethics network BioCentre develops a similar claim more fully, arguing at some length that the mixing of various kinds of human and non-human material creates ambiguities about human identity, which

> may begin to undermine the whole distinction between humans and animals. And, as a result, this may then undermine the whole concept of dignity and human rights. This is because uncertainty exists towards the embryo's moral status and whether it is even entitled to full dignity.[72]

However, it often remains unclear in such arguments just *how* ambiguity about species identity undermines human dignity. In his submission to the Joint Committee, David Jones addressed this point more fully and clearly than most: first, humans, as 'animals of a particular kind ... have a particular character and flourish in particular ways'.[73] Transgressing the species boundary amounts to a failure to respect 'the dignity of our own specific animal nature'.[74]

---

71 Report on the HTE (Draft) Bill, vol. II, p. 219.
72 BioCentre: The Centre for Bioethics and Public Policy, *The New Inter-Species Future? An Ethical Discussion of Embryonic, Fetal and Post-Natal Human-Nonhuman Combinations*, London: BioCentre, 2007, p. 38.
73 Report on the HTE (Draft) Bill, vol. II, p. 385.
74 Report on the HTE (Draft) Bill, vol. II, p. 386.

Second, 'human community, human solidarity and human equality are hugely important for our moral understanding': while there is a proper kind of community between humans and other living beings, 'the relations between human beings are and ought to be different from those between human and nonhuman animals'.[75] To bring a human-nonhuman hybrid into the world would create a situation of 'moral perplexity' in which it would not be clear whether we should relate to the hybrid as a human or a non-human animal.[76] Finally, Jones argues that if the wrongness of creating hybrids lies in the crossing of the species boundary, this wrongness applies just as much to the creation of hybrid embryos, even if there is no intention of bringing them to term.[77]

Jones does succeed in fleshing out somewhat the intuition that crossing or blurring the species boundary would undermine human dignity. He acknowledges that this concern is hard to articulate, but warns that in exploring it, 'we should be careful not to demand a level of clarity greater than that we demand when giving an account of other fundamental beliefs – such as rejection of murder, of slavery, or of torture.'[78] The point is well taken, but nonetheless, the connection between transgression of the species boundary and the violation of human dignity remains somewhat elusive, rendering these expressions of ethical concern vulnerable to the rather reductive treatment of critics such as the Academy of Medical Sciences:

> We judge it unlikely that 'human dignity' ... derives simply from species membership. If the concept of 'human dignity' has content, it is because there are factors of form, function or behaviour that confer such dignity or command respect. Either hybrid creatures would possess these factors or they

---

75 Report on the HTE (Draft) Bill, vol. II, p. 385.
76 Report on the HTE (Draft) Bill, vol. II, p. 385.
77 Report on the HTE (Draft) Bill, vol. II, p. 386–7.
78 Report on the HTE (Draft) Bill, vol. II, p. 384.

would not. If they do possess these factors, they would also have a specific type of dignity analogous or identical to human dignity that other creatures lack; if not, they would not.[79]

Perhaps part of the difficulty is the rather protean and elusive character of the concept of human dignity itself. Among the contributors to this debate, we find in the Academy of Medical Sciences report what I earlier described as a 'criterial' notion of human dignity, set against an account from BioCentre which owes a good deal (though not everything) to Kant, and one from David Jones, grounded in the notion of a species with a particular character and ways of flourishing, which suggests an Aristotelian-Thomist perspective. It is not clear that when the same words are used in these different philosophical contexts, they mean the same thing at all.

A further difficulty has to do with the widespread assumption that '[h]uman rights and human dignity are dependent upon the distinctness of humanity from non-humanity'.[80] What this remark from the Christian Institute's submission puts rather baldly, others such as David Jones also claim, in a more nuanced fashion.[81] However, there are various difficulties with using our differentness from other species to underwrite human dignity. One is that biologically, the boundaries between species are nothing like as clear-cut as commonsensical concepts would suggest, a point recognized by Calum MacKellar in a briefing paper for the Christian Medical Fellowship, submitted along with their evidence to the Joint Committee.[82] Among other things, the high level of genetic

---

79 Academy of Medical Sciences, *Inter-Species Embryos*, p. 29.

80 Report on the HTE (Draft) Bill, vol. II, p. 311.

81 Report on the HTE (Draft) Bill, vol. II, pp. 383–7.

82 Calum MacKellar, *Chimeras, Hybrids and 'Cybrids'*, CMF File no. 34, London: Christian Medical Fellowship, 2007, n.p., online at http://www.cmf.org.uk/publications/content. asp?context=article&id=1939 (accessed 13 July 2010); Report on the HTE (Draft) Bill, vol. II, p. 316. The fuzziness of species boundaries is acknowledged, but its significance for this debate downplayed, by David Jones: Report on the HTE (Draft) Bill, vol. II, p. 386.

homology between species (the presence of very similar DNA sequences, often with the same function, derived from a common ancestor) and the prevalence of 'horizontal gene transfer' (the transfer of DNA sequences between species by retroviruses capable of infecting both) make species boundaries more fuzzy than is often assumed. A related problem is that the concept of a biological species itself is contested and far from straightforward – a point to which I shall return later.

More important, though, are theological reasons to question the assumption that it is our differentness from non-humans that underwrites human dignity. Michael Northcott has traced to Kant the attempt to safeguard the moral status of human persons and ensure that they 'could not be instrumentalized like objects' by asserting the distinctiveness and absolute value of rational nature.[83] By implication at least, animals are non-rational and may be treated as objects. But this move, as Northcott argues, failed to take proper account of human sociability and embodiment: 'If humans are embodied, and acquire their knowledge of the world through embodied engagements with other bodies, and with other beings in their environment, then an account of moral reasoning that neglects this is also likely to be inadequate.'[84]

It is often assumed by friends and foes of the Christian tradition alike that this kind of sharp separation between humans and non-humans is deeply rooted in that tradition.[85] Yet a number of recent authors have questioned that claim. For example, John Berkman, Celia Deane-Drummond and others have argued that in the thought of Thomas Aquinas – long held to be a villain of the piece by critics of Christianity's treatment of animals[86] – such a sharp

---

83 Michael Northcott, '"They shall not hurt or destroy in all my holy mountain" (Isaiah 65.25): Killing for Philosophy and a Creaturely Theology of Non-violence', in Celia Deane-Drummond and David Clough (eds), *Creaturely Theology: On God, Humans and Other Animals*, London: SCM Press, 2009, pp. 235–48 (quotation at p. 239).

84 Northcott, 'They shall not hurt or destroy', p. 241.

85 For example John Gray, *Straw Dogs: Thoughts on Humans and Other Animals*, London: Granta, 2002.

86 See, for example, Andrew Linzey, *Animal Theology*, London: SCM Press, 1995, pp. 12–19.

separation is by no means unequivocally found.[87] According to Michael Northcott, parts of the history of Christian monasticism came close to realizing the vision of just and peaceable relations between humans and non-humans expressed in Isaiah 65.25 ('They shall not hurt or destroy on all my holy mountain, says the LORD'). David Clough finds tensions in Martin Luther between, on the one hand, strongly anthropocentric perspectives, and on the other, a recognition of the deep commonalities between humans and non-humans and of God's care for non-human creatures.[88] Among modern Christian thinkers, Karl Barth is one who emphasizes our closeness to non-human animals, 'created with [human beings] on the sixth day', which for example means that 'when man kills a beast he does something which is at least very similar to homicide'.[89] To be sure, none of this is to deny that the Christian tradition does understand humanity as distinctive, particularly in its relationship with God and its God-given vocation within the created world, but to imagine that human worth and dignity depend on our *not being like* God's other creatures is perhaps a peculiarly modern reading of that tradition.

A different kind of theological critique is suggested by Elaine Graham, who observes that '[n]ew technologies have complicated the question of what it means to be human in a number of ways',[90] including – importantly for the present discussion – the blurring of species boundaries. Graham characterizes this uncertainty about human identity as 'a dissolution of the "ontological hygiene"

---

87 John Berkman, 'Towards a Thomistic Theology of Animality', in Deane-Drummond and Clough (eds), *Creaturely Theology*, pp. 21–40; Celia Deane-Drummond, *The Ethics of Nature*, Oxford: Blackwell, 2004, pp. 65–77, and 'Are Animals Moral? Taking Soundings through Vice, Virtue, Conscience and *Imago Dei*', in Deane-Drummond and Clough (eds), *Creaturely Theology*, pp. 190–210.

88 David Clough, 'The Anxiety of the Human Animal: Martin Luther on Non-Human Animals and Human Animality', in Deane-Drummond and Clough (eds), *Creaturely Theology*, pp. 41–60.

89 Karl Barth, *Church Dogmatics*, III.4, p. 352. On Barth and non-human animals, see further Chapter 6, below.

90 Elaine L. Graham, *Representations of the Post/human: Monsters, Aliens and Others in Popular Culture*, Manchester: Manchester University Press, 2002, p. 2.

by which for the past three hundred years Western culture has drawn the fault-lines that separate humans, nature and machines'.[91] In somewhat Foucauldian vein, she investigates the drawing of these fault-lines by tracing genealogies of 'boundary-creatures' such as monsters and other almost-human beings who 'feature as indicators of the limits of the normatively human'.[92]

Thus, in the long history of teratology (the study of monsters) in Western thought, monsters have been understood in a complex mix of ways. According to Augustine they bore witness to God's power to create and to transform creaturely natures, and served as portents of divine judgement on a disordered world.[93] As David Williams shows, however, another perspective also discernible in Augustine was developed in the Middle Ages, particularly through the apophatic thought of Pseudo-Dionysius and John Scotus Eriugena: the monstrous could serve as a sign that pointed beyond itself to God, its very monstrosity helping to avert the danger of confusing the sign with the transcendent divine reality to which it pointed.[94]

The work of the sixteenth-century French surgeon Ambroise Paré marks a transition between mediaeval and early modern views of monstrosity. Like many of his predecessors, he regarded monstrous and prodigious beings as indications of moral disorder and signs of divine judgement on such disorder.[95] For example, he held that half-human and half-animal creatures result from the unnatural mixing of seed between species. But he also sought naturalistic explanations, an approach taken up by early modern scientists and philosophers such as Francis Bacon, for whom

---

91 Graham, *Representations of the Post/human*, p. 11.

92 Graham, *Representations of the Post/human*, pp. 11, 13.

93 Augustine, *The City of God*, 21.8, trans. Marcus Dods, in Philip Schaff (ed.), *Nicene and Post-Nicene Fathers*, vol. 2, Edinburgh: T & T Clark, 1887. Online at http://www.ccel. org/ccel/schaff/npnf102.iv.XXI.8.html (accessed 19 July 2010).

94 David Williams, *Deformed Discourse: The Function of the Monster in Mediaeval Thought and Literature*, Exeter: University of Exeter Press, 1996.

95 Ambroise Paré, *On Monsters and Marvels*, trans. Janis L. Pallister, Chicago, IL: University of Chicago Press, 1982 (1573).

monsters were to be treated as natural phenomena whose study could yield insights into natural processes.[96] Yet, as Elaine Graham argues, modernity's rationalistic approach to monstrosity did not mean that the latter ceased to serve as a moral boundary-marker: in the work of Enlightenment thinkers such as d'Alembert, Hume and Hobbes, '[t]he limits of morality, represented by the monster, indicated in an inverted form the qualities of reason and benevolence by which the quintessentially human could be recognised'.[97]

Drawing attention to the political aspects of this long and complex history of teratology, Graham observes that '[m]onsters stand at the entrance to the unknown, acting as gatekeepers to the acceptable ... the horror of monsters may be sufficient to deter their audience from encroaching upon their repellent territory'.[98] One troubling aspect of this is the danger that 'monstrous' beings themselves become scapegoats for the moral disorder that they are held to signify. While the work of an author such as Paré does not display such scapegoating, Graham argues that it is all too easy for those whose physical characteristics differ from the norm to be regarded as deviants and pathologized.[99] More generally, she argues that monsters have a paradoxical function, neither totally beyond the bounds of the human nor conforming completely to norms of humanity. As such they both mark and destabilize the boundaries of humanity:

Their otherness to the norm of the human, the natural and

---

96 Francis Bacon, *The New Organon, or: True Directions Concerning the Interpretation of Nature*, trans. James Spedding, Robert Leslie Ellis and Douglas Denon Heath, Boston, MA: Taggard and Thompson, 1863, 2.29. Online at http://www.constitution.org/bacon/nov_org.htm (accessed 19 July 2010).

97 Graham, *Representations of the Post/human*, p. 50.

98 Graham, *Representations of the Post/human*, p. 53.

99 As Graham points out (*Representations of the Post/human*, ch. 3), Mary Shelley's *Frankenstein: Or the Modern Prometheus* (ed. Johanna M. Smith, London: Macmillan, 1992 [1818]) – perhaps the best-known of all modern monster narratives – implicitly criticizes this process of scapegoating and pathologization by giving Victor's creature his own voice within the narrative, a voice that is cultured, sensitive and expresses a longing for human relationship.

the moral, is as that which must be repressed in order to secure the boundaries of the same. Yet at the same time, by showing forth the fault-lines of binary opposition – between human/non-human, natural/unnatural, virtue/vice – monsters bear the trace of difference that destabilizes the distinction.[100]

Aspects of this long tradition of teratology find striking parallels in some of what is proposed for research on human admixed embryos. The term for a construct made by mixing human and animal cells, a chimaera, is itself borrowed from the classical myth of a monstrous creature that was part lion, part goat and part serpent,[101] and the construction of a true hybrid, made by combining human and animal gametes, bears analogy to the 'mixing of seed' envisaged by Paré and others.[102] As such, it is not surprising if some of the anxieties and concerns that were associated with monsters in earlier teratological literature re-emerge in relation to these hybrids. This is not to say that all concerns about crossing the species boundary can be written off as unwarranted anxieties about 'ontological hygiene': as I shall argue later, there are proper theological concerns about what it means to be a creature of a particular, human, kind. However, Graham's account at any rate raises a critical question about the bald assertion made by some contributors to recent debates that human dignity is 'dependent upon the distinctness of humanity from non-humanity',[103] an assertion that the Christian tradition, on closer examination, might not turn out to warrant as straightforwardly as those contributors believe.

Graham draws attention to the ways in which new biotechnological developments have complicated our understanding of

---

100 Graham, *Representations of the Post/human*, p. 54.

101 Homer, *Iliad*, Book 6.

102 Indeed, some contributors to ethical and policy debates have referred to the construction of admixed embryos as 'an in vitro version of bestiality': Report on the HTE (Draft) Bill, vol. II, p. 311; cf. p. 328.

103 Report on the HTE (Draft) Bill, vol. II, p. 311.

what it is to be human, arguing that what we have taken to be fixed natural boundaries between the human and the non-human are in fact contingent and fluid. An implication of this is that new ways must be found of understanding what it means to be human in an age when technology opens up all kinds of 'post/human' possibilities.[104] Clearly, the question of what it is to be human is a central concern of theological ethics, and must be addressed anew in the new context created by new biotechnological developments (though, as I suggest below, a Christian theological ethic should go about that task in quite distinctive ways).

There is a sense, however, in which a Christian ethical response to human admixed embryos needs to be even more radical than this. It would be easy to assume that the significance of what it means to be human consists in knowing where to draw the boundary of the special moral concern that we are required to show to one another: in other words, that 'human' in this context functions rather as 'person' does in other bioethical discussions. If that were so, Graham's critique of 'ontological hygiene' could be read simply as questioning ways of drawing that boundary which exclude the marginalized and vulnerable. I argued earlier, however, that the use of bounded categories like 'person' or 'human' to mark out the limits of our moral concern is subverted by a Christian moral vision informed by New Testament texts such as the parable of the Good Samaritan (Luke 10.25–37). Putting this in the terms of David Jones' thought-experiment about the successful birth of a human-chimpanzee hybrid, 'Holly',[105] if we wish to understand our moral obligations in respect of Holly, then 'Is it human?' is the *wrong* question to ask. We would be nearer the mark if we asked, 'Is she my neighbour?', but even this question implies an attempt to draw a boundary around the category of 'neighbour' in a way

---

104 Graham, *Representations of the Post/human*, ch. 10. Her coining of the term 'post/ human' signals this ambiguity: the beings produced by the technological innovations now in prospect will not unambiguously be either 'human' or 'posthuman'.

105 Report on the HTE (Draft) Bill, vol. II, pp. 383–7.

that is undermined by Jesus' response to the lawyer: better still would be the question, 'How am I called to be a neighbour to Holly?' Furthermore, if (as McFarland argues) the parable can be read christologically and the Samaritan identified with Jesus, this suggests that we become 'neighbours' by virtue of Jesus' compassion in his death for us all.[106] If that is so, then perhaps it would be even more illuminating to imagine how we would respond were Holly, echoing Acts 8.36, to ask us, 'What is to prevent me from being baptized?'

I have argued, then, that in theological perspective, the concern that human dignity is undermined by crossing the species boundary fails to settle the ethical question about admixed embryos. However, alongside this argument, another more overtly theological line of thought has been evident in recent debates. In the words of the conservative evangelical group Affinity, '[i]n creating inter-species embryos man would be making something which God has not made, and to those whose lives are bound up with the ways of God, such a step represents a defiance of God's benign providence in the life of man and society.'[107]

Affinity's formulation of this argument is overly simplistic in various ways. For one thing, it appears to speak univocally of divine and human making, failing to take account of the qualitative difference between the two. God is the Creator who has called into being, out of nothing, all that is; without God's sustaining work, all that is would simply not be. Human creativity might be better described as 'sub-creation':[108] we are creatures, whose creativity consists only in fashioning what has been given us into new constructs and artefacts. (This is as true of, say, intellectual, verbal or musical creativity as of the making of material things.) There is analogy between such 'sub-creation' and God's

106 McFarland, 'Who Is My Neighbor?', pp. 62–3.

107 Report on the HTE (Draft) Bill, vol. II, p. 251.

108 Colin E. Gunton, *The Triune Creator: A Historical and Systematic Study*, Grand Rapids, MI: Eerdmans, 1998, p. 1, citing J. R. R. Tolkien, 'On Fairy Stories', in *Tree and Leaf*, London: HarperCollins, 2001, pp. 3–81, esp. pp. 46–56, 70–3.

work of creation: human making is genuine creativity, an aspect of what it means to bear God's image, but is derivative of and dependent upon God's creative work.[109]

It is perfectly possible, of course, for humans to put their 'sub-creative' abilities to use in ways that go against God's good purposes in creation. Fashioning minerals, chemicals, bacteria or viruses into weapons of mass destruction, or fashioning ideas and words into tracts that incite ethnic hatred and violence, are examples that come easily to mind. All too often we reject the invitation expressed in the *imago dei*, to be 'sub-creators' whose work reflects the creative work of God. We grasp instead for the ultimately self-defeating ways of being 'like God' to which the serpent tempts the humans in Genesis 3: our activity in the world becomes an attempted substitute for God's creative work, or we even put our skills and abilities to use in ways that invite chaos and destruction (what Barth calls 'nothingness', *das Nichtige*) into the world.[110] So it is *possible* that in making embryonic constructs that cross and blur the boundaries of the human species, we are making what God did not will should be made, producing arte-facts that parody God's good creation or contribute to the chaos and destruction of the world, rather than reflect the image of the Creator in us. The question is how we might know whether or not human admixed embryos *were* constructs that God did not will. The Affinity submission answers that question by identifying the species that exist in the world with 'God's benign providence'. This gives the impression of a somewhat naïve theological-ethical

---

109 The language of 'co-creation' is often used, particularly in reflections on science and theology, to express this relationship, describing humans as 'created co-creators': see, for example, Ted Peters, *Playing God: Genetic Determinism and Human Freedom*, London: Routledge, 1997, p. 15 and *passim*. However, I am uneasy about this language, since I am not convinced that (even with the qualifier 'created') it adequately conveys the difference between divine creation and human making. See, further, Michael S. Northcott, 'Concept Art, Clones, and Co-Creators: The Theology of Making', *Modern Theology* 21.2 (2005), pp. 219–36.

110 Barth, *Church Dogmatics*, vol. III.3, pp. 289–368. On Barth's concept of *das Nichtige*, see further Neil Messer, 'Natural Evil after Darwin', in Michael Northcott and R. J. Berry (eds), *Theology after Darwin*, Carlisle: Paternoster Press, 2009, pp. 139–54.

naturalism, an assumption that the will or purposes of God can straightforwardly be read off an empirical investigation of the way things are. From the standpoint of a Christian theological ethic, there are many well-known difficulties with such a naturalistic approach. One is that it fails to reckon adequately with the complex ways in which good and evil are entangled in the world disclosed to us by the natural sciences.[111] This amounts to an expectation that biology can tell us about the purposes of God, something that by virtue of its methods, it is simply not equipped to do.[112]

Calum MacKellar develops a similar line of thought in a more nuanced way. Recognizing that Christian moral norms cannot simply be read off nature, he turns to biblical sources, particularly the first creation narrative (Gen. 1.1—2.4a), in which God creates living things 'according to their kinds', or 'of every kind' (*min*, vv. 11, 12, 21, 24, 25) and the Holiness Code, which prohibits various activities that would mix different kinds (e.g. Lev. 19.19). Commentators have long discerned in these texts a concern for the ordering of the world by the maintenance of cosmic boundaries (the separation of light from darkness, dry land from water, different kinds of plants and animals, the Sabbath from the rest of the week),[113] which might appear to reflect the same preoccupations later evident in what Graham calls the 'ontological hygiene' of the modern West. However, it would be premature to write off a theological concern with the 'kinds' of living creatures

---

111 An excellent survey of one aspect of this problem, and a serious and creative – though in my view not ultimately successful – attempt to address it, can be found in Christopher Southgate, *The Groaning of Creation: God, Evolution and the Problem of Evil*, Louisville, KY: Westminster John Knox Press, 2008. For my critique of Southgate's approach, see Messer, 'Natural Evil and Theodicy after Darwin', and for his response, Christopher Southgate, 'Natural Theology and Ecology', in Fraser Watts and Russell Re Manning (eds), *The Oxford Companion to Natural Theology*, Oxford: Oxford University Press, forthcoming. My thanks to Chris Southgate for an advance copy of the last of these.

112 See further below, pp. 172–4, and Neil Messer, *Selfish Genes and Christian Ethics: Theological and Ethical Reflections on Evolutionary Biology*, London: SCM Press, 2007, Ch. 5.

113 See, for example, Claus Westermann, *Genesis 1—11: A Commentary*, trans. John J. Scullion, London: SPCK, 1984, pp. 74–177.

as nothing more than an unhealthy obsession with the policing of ontological boundaries. Since creaturely life is finite and particular, to be a creature who is *like this* is also to be a creature who is *not like that*. This finitude and particularity are not, in themselves, a cause for regret: the same creation narrative which relates how God created living things 'according to their kinds' also affirms that 'God saw everything that he had made, and indeed, it was very good' (Gen. 1.31). The different 'kinds' of living creature created by God can be regarded as different expressions of God's creative love, each – as David Jones observes of humans particularly – with its own distinctive good, its own way of flourishing and praising God. The sheer variety of God's creatures has long been recognized as a cause to praise God, as in Basil of Caesarea's *Hexaemeron*:

> What language can attain to the marvels of the Creator? What ear could understand them? And what time would be sufficient to relate them? Let us say, then, with the prophet, 'O Lord, how manifold are thy works! in wisdom hast thou made them all.'[114]

Furthermore, the creation in all its variety is destined for ultimate fulfilment in God's good future, so the distinctive goods of the different 'kinds' of creature God has made can be recognized as destined for eschatological completion.[115] In short, then, there are reasons to think that the 'kinds' in which living creatures come have some theological importance.

It appears from recent debates that particular concern is attached to *human* admixed embryos as distinct from biotechnological constructs that mix different non-human species (which

---

114 Basil of Caesarea, *Hexaemeron* 9.3, trans. Blomfield Jackson, in Philip Schaff and Henry Wace (eds), *Nicene and Post-Nicene Fathers*, second series, vol. 8, Edinburgh: T & T Clark, 1895, online at http://www.ccel.org/ccel/schaff/npnf208.viii.x.html (accessed 21 July 2010). See also, for example, 5.7, 7.2.
115 See further Gunton, *The Triune Creator*, ch. 10.

is not to say that the latter cause no anxiety).[116] It might be tempting to regard this emphasis as an unwarranted kind of anthropocentrism, but in theological perspective, that would be premature. There is a proper priority to be given to reflection on the *human* species and on human identity, simply because humans are the kind of creature we are. Our primary business is to respond to the 'command of God the Creator' to *us*, one aspect of which is God's liberating call 'quite simply ... to exist as a living being of this particular, i.e. human, structure'[117] (though, of course, it may well be that this divine calling *includes* a distinctive responsibility for the integrity and flourishing of other living species). There is, then, a proper theological concern for the identity of 'kinds' of living creatures, particularly for human identity: there are reasons for thinking that in the loving purposes of a good Creator, living things are made in particular kinds, and God's good purposes are honoured by our being creatures of the kind God has made us. There is therefore also a theologically legitimate ethical concern about human activities that seem to make the identity of 'kinds', particularly human kind, ambiguous.

MacKellar articulates this concern, proposing that '[i]t would ... be acceptable to try mixing animals within a kind, such as generating different breeds of dogs, but not to try mixing between different kinds'.[118] However, he still has trouble explaining how we might identify the 'kinds' beyond which mixing would be theologically and ethically unacceptable. Biological species identity, as he recognizes, cannot answer that question. As I have already noted, the concept of the species is contested and unstable. Different working definitions of species are used by biologists for different purposes, and there is no consensus among biologists or philosophers of biology on how species should be understood, or

---

116 For example, Animal Procedures Committee, 'Animal Procedures Committee Report on Biotechnology', June 2001, paras. 52–7. Online at http://apc.homeoffice.gov.uk/reference/biorec.pdf (accessed 9 September 2010).

117 Barth, *Church Dogmatics*, vol. III.4, p. 324.

118 MacKellar, *Chimeras, Hybrids and 'Cybrids'*, n.p.

even whether they are real entities.[119] But even if there were no biological and philosophical 'species problem', biological taxonomy in and of itself could not identify the 'kinds' that have theological and ethical significance, since the methods of the biological sciences bracket out the relevant considerations of purpose, the good and theology.[120] MacKellar acknowledges this difficulty, arguing that 'in the biblical perspective, species integrity is ultimately defined by God, rather than by physical features'.[121] So far so good; but the conclusion he then draws from this, that '[t]he fusion of human and nonhuman genomes may therefore be perceived as running counter to the sacredness of human life and humanity created in the image of God',[122] appears to beg the question by assuming that the biological taxon *Homo sapiens* (identified by 'physical features', broadly understood) can be equated with the human kind called into a distinctive relationship with God. To be sure, texts such as Genesis 1.26–28 might suggest this identification, but since they are not preoccupied with modern scientific concerns,[123] it is not clear that these texts can settle the question definitively. In short, the importance attached in Genesis 1 and elsewhere to the creation of living beings 'according to their kinds' gives theological grounds for suspicion that to make some types of admixed embryo is a form of sub-creative activity that goes against against God's good purposes in creation; but the persistent difficulty of equating biblical 'kinds' with modern biologically defined species means that this suspicion falls short of certainty.

If concerns about the mixing of kinds cannot settle the question definitively, it might be helpful to shift the focus away from what

---

119 For an extensive recent discussion, see David N. Stamos, *The Species Problem: Biological Species, Ontology, and the Metaphysics of Biology*, Lanham, MD: Lexington, 2003.

120 See further below, Chapter 6.

121 MacKellar, *Chimeras, Hybrids and 'Cybrids'*, n.p.

122 *Chimeras, Hybrids and 'Cybrids'*, n.p.

123 Walter Brueggemann, *Genesis* (Interpretation: A Bible Commentary for Teaching and Preaching), Atlanta, GA: John Knox, 1982, pp. 25–6.

is made to the *character of the making*. The 'command of God the Creator', in Barth's terms, is directed to us in our particular kind of creaturely existence, summoning us and setting us free to be the particular (human) kind of creatures that God has made us to be. If we want to know what it means, in God's purposes, to be that kind of creature, biological data in and of themselves will not tell us,[124] but we do have theological 'data' that point us towards an answer: the biblical witness to Jesus Christ, who is both the Word of God incarnate and the true human, our representative. The five 'diagnostic questions' deployed in this chapter and elsewhere are heuristic devices for helping us to discern what forms of action are consistent with that vocation to live in the world as human creatures whose lives conform to the image of God revealed in Christ (cf. Col. 1.15).

In particular, the first of these questions – does the practice reflect the *imago dei* or human action *sicut deus*? – contrasts the vocation of authority and responsible care that God has given humanity in relation to other creatures (cf. Gen. 1.28; 2.15) with the parody of that role that the humans, incited by the serpent, seize (Gen. 3.5–7). Conformity to the image of God could be expected to give rise to acts of 'making' with a rather different character from those that were aspects of human activity *sicut deus*. God's creative activity is characterized by an expansive, generous love. God does not create as a matter of necessity or in order to meet any divine need: the creation is, in a sense, contingent, the outcome of God's free will. But this does not mean that it is the product of an *arbitrary* divine decision, as, for example, some forms of late mediaeval voluntarism could suggest.[125] Rather, as Barth puts it:

> [God] wills and posits the creature neither out of caprice nor

---

124 Though biological data, critically appropriated, might very well help to 'flesh out' a theologically formed understanding of what it means 'to exist as a living being of this particular, that is human, structure': see further Messer, *Selfish Genes*, pp. 125–6.

125 In particular, that of William of Ockham: see Gunton, *The Triune Creator*, pp. 121–5.

> necessity, but because He has loved it from eternity, because He wills to demonstrate His love for it, and because He wills, not to limit His glory by its existence and being, but to reveal and manifest it in His own co-existence with it.[126]

There are acts of human 'sub-creation' that, thanks to God's grace at work in the world, reflect this expansive, generous love of God. For example, the creation of a work of art, a garden, a work of scholarship, a human community, and (in a distinctive way) the *pro*-creation of children, can all have this character – which is not to say, of course, that they always do. The making of hybrid embryos, however, has a rather different character. In doing this, we are making a new kind of living creature – new to human experience, at any rate – simply and solely in order to serve human needs. It might be destroyed in the course of meeting those needs, as when a cybrid is used to make embryonic stem cells. If our use of it does not destroy it, then by law (at any rate in the UK) we must destroy it when we have finished using it, in order to avoid any risk of its being let loose in the world.

It is worth emphasizing again that this is a reflection about the character of the practice, not necessarily the character or motivations of those engaging in it. Those engaging in admixed embryo research might very well be motivated overwhelmingly by simple compassion for their sick and suffering neighbours. But we must ask whether the moral trajectory, as it were, of the practice itself points in a different direction. Does the making of admixed embryos manifest human action *sicut deus* or reflect the *imago dei*? As I suggested earlier, to distinguish between these two possibilities, we must refer to Jesus Christ, 'the image of the invisible God' (Col. 1.15). He demonstrates a radically different way of using power: not using others instrumentally to meet his own or others' needs, but instead, as the 'lamb of God' (*agnus dei*), laying

---

126 Barth, *Church Dogmatics*, vol. III.1, p. 95. See further Gunton, *The Triune Creator*, pp. 162–5.

down his own life for the lives of others, even his enemies.[127] In the light of this, we might suspect that the kind of making involved in the production of human admixed embryos is a form of human action *sicut deus*, rather than reflecting the *imago dei*. This suspicion is reinforced by raising some of the other diagnostic questions, in particular what attitude to the neighbour is expressed by the practice and whether it represents good news for the poor, marginalized and oppressed. Now of course, those patients whom admixed embryo research is intended to help are our neighbours, and suffering and vulnerable neighbours at that. It goes without saying that the love of neighbour would support the use of any means legitimately at our disposal to address the plight of such patients. But, as I argued earlier, we are not entitled to exclude from the category of 'neighbour' those human-nonhuman hybrid constructs that we make. The parable of the Good Samaritan suggests that 'neighbour' is not the kind of category around which we can draw boundaries in order to exclude some. Moreover, as David Jones' thought-experiment about a human-animal hybrid child implies, if we are not entitled to exclude such a child from the category of 'neighbour', neither are we entitled to exclude hybrid embryonic constructs. The mere fact that they are very small and lack the capacities that they might acquire later in their development is not sufficient reason to say that they are not our neighbours. And if they *are*, then they could hardly be more marginalized neighbours, being placed by our design on the very margins of humanity itself. The practice of bringing into being such a marginal neighbour for the sole purpose of meeting the needs of others, and destroying that neighbour either in the course of meeting those needs or once we have no further use for him or her, seems the antithesis of the hospitality, welcome and love that we are called to show our neighbours.

Considerations that arose from examining other practices, particularly human embryo research, through the lens of the

---

127 Cf. Bonhoeffer, *Creation and Fall*, p. 113.

diagnostic questions are also relevant to human admixed embryos. The question about our attitude to the material world (including our own bodies), for example, prompted a concern about the drive for mastery over the matter of human bodies implicit in embryo research and various forms of genetic control. This concern also emerges in relation to the making of admixed embryos, and serves to intensify the theological doubts already expressed about that practice. In short, examining the practice of human admixed embryo research through the lens of my diagnostic questions suggests that there are powerful reasons to doubt that it can be regarded as conforming to God's saving work in the world: there is as yet no convincing reason to think that it could be mandated by the theological ethic being articulated in this book.

5

Medicine, Science and Virtue

The last chapter dealt with two particularly controversial and ethically problematic areas of biomedical research, namely human embryonic stem cells and human admixed embryos. The first of these is problematic because it entails the destruction of embryonic human life; the second because it involves the making of embryos that are not unambiguously either human or non-human. In discussing these issues I remarked in passing that Christians have good reason in general to support biomedical research directed towards the treatment of serious disease, as a form of 'penultimate' activity that can be expressive of a proper care for embodied human life in this world. This does not mean, however, that no theological and ethical reflection is needed on medical research more generally or that no ethical concerns are raised by it. In this chapter I shall explore one particular ethical problem that arises from the quite routine practice of clinical research involving human participants. In this chapter (as also in Chapter 7), the theological-ethical analysis is focused in particular on questions of virtue and character, and my conversation partners include Thomas Aquinas and some contemporary authors influenced by him. Although this represents a somewhat different focus from other chapters, it is nonetheless of a piece with the overall theological approach articulated in this book, as I have claimed in the Introduction.

The problem and a popular solution: clinical research and clinical equipoise

In the modern era, medicine has had a close and reciprocal – if somewhat ambiguous – relationship with the natural sciences. In recent years that relationship has taken the form of an increasing emphasis upon 'evidence-based medicine', by which is meant, among other things, that 'clinical decisions should be based on the best available scientific evidence'.[1] It is obvious that much of this evidence concerns the effects that treatments have on human beings. Evidence-based medicine therefore requires the use of human participants in scientific experimentation that inevitably involves some level of risk, burden and harm (however slight) with the aim of benefiting patients in the future by improving medical care. A situation in which some human beings are subjected to risk, burden or harm for the benefit of others brings with it particular dangers of exploitation, which is of course why a large ethical literature has grown up around clinical research, and why heavyweight frameworks of ethical regulation exist to police such research in Western countries.

The central moral dilemma of clinical research can be seen most clearly in the case of those clinical trials in which clinical investigators, who are also health care professionals, recruit their own patients as research participants. These cases appear to involve a conflict of roles on the part of the clinical investigator. As clinician, she has an obligation to do the best for each of her patients, including offering them the most effective and appropriate treatments to which she has access. As investigator, she has an obligation to obtain the best possible data about the effectiveness of the treatments. This typically requires a randomized controlled trial

---

1 F. Davidoff et al., 'Evidence Based Medicine: A New Journal to Help Doctors Identify the Information They Need', *British Medical Journal* 310 (1995), pp. 1085–6, quoted in Tony Hope, 'Evidence Based Medicine and Ethics', *Journal of Medical Ethics* 21.5 (1995), pp. 259–60 (p. 259).

(RCT) in which participants are assigned at random to groups receiving different treatments. For example, in a clinical trial designed to assess the effectiveness of a newly developed treatment, one group will receive the new treatment. This group might be compared with another that receives an established treatment for the same condition, with a group that receives an inert placebo, or with both. Where possible, such trials are double-blind (neither investigators nor participants know which group each participant is in) to avoid the distortion of results by psychological factors.

In such a trial, if the investigator recruits participants from among those of her patients who have the condition in question, it appears that she is *not* doing her best for all of her patients. In order to compare the effects of different regimes, she is placing her patient-participants in a situation where some of them will receive a less effective treatment than others. Some are therefore being subjected to some measure of risk or harm (albeit, in many cases, very slight) for the benefit of others: future patients who will benefit from the scientific knowledge gained from the trial.[2]

During the 1970s and 1980s, an apparently promising way of resolving this dilemma was developed: the concept of 'clinical equipoise', or genuine uncertainty within the professional community as to which of the different treatments being compared in an RCT offers the greatest therapeutic benefit. If equipoise exists, then an investigator can be considered as doing her best, in good faith, for all of the patients whom she enlists as trial participants, since she is offering each of them a treatment regime which, for all that she and her colleagues know, could be the best for them.

However, the concept of clinical equipoise has been attacked in various ways. One critique has been developed by Franklin Miller and Howard Brody, who argue that the concept expresses a funda-

---

2 Participants may benefit in various ways from their participation in trials, but this does not resolve the dilemma, which arises because trials are not conducted with the *aim* of benefiting participants.

mental confusion about the ethics of clinical research.[3] Clinical equipoise is an aspect of what they call the 'similarity position': the view that clinical research must be located within the same ethical framework that governs clinical medicine. Against this view, they advocate the 'difference position': that clinical research is a fundamentally different kind of activity from clinical medicine, and must be evaluated by means of a different ethical framework. To argue that research and therapy are different activities, of course, invites the questions whether, and why, both should continue to be done. Miller and Brody make it clear that they believe clinical research to be a valuable and ethically justifiable activity because it has the potential to improve medical care in the future. In other words, they locate its value within what Gerald McKenny and others have called the 'Baconian project': science and technology are valuable because they allow mastery over nature (which, of course, includes human bodies) in order to relieve suffering and maximize individual choice.[4]

Testing the critique: practices, virtues and clinical research

While it would be possible to question various aspects of Miller and Brody's argument, their central claim – that clinical medicine and clinical research are fundamentally different activities that must be assessed by means of different ethical frameworks – is an interesting and provocative one that merits serious investigation. One way of exploring this claim (albeit probably not a way that would commend itself to Miller and Brody) is to consider clinical medicine and clinical research as 'practices' in something like Alasdair MacIntyre's sense of the term, to compare the two and to ask how they are related to one another. In what follows, I shall

---

3 Franklin G. Miller and Howard Brody, 'A Critique of Clinical Equipoise: Therapeutic Misconception in the Ethics of Clinical Trials', *Hastings Center Report* 33.3 (2003), pp. 19–28.
4 Gerald P. McKenny, *To Relieve the Human Condition: Bioethics, Technology and the Body*, Albany, NY: State University of New York Press, 1997, pp. 17–21. See further above, pp. 26–8.

attempt to do so, and shall thereby argue that Miller and Brody are wrong to make a sharp separation between the ethics of medicine and the ethics of clinical research: the two are more closely related than Miller and Brody allow, though the relationship between them is not exactly that described or implied by standard accounts of equipoise.

MacIntyre's definition of a practice is well known:

> any coherent and complex form of socially established human activity through which goods internal to that form of activity are realized in the course of trying to achieve those standards of excellence which are appropriate to, and partially definitive of, that form of activity, with the result that human powers to achieve excellence, and human conceptions of the ends and goods involved, are systematically extended.[5]

It is clear from MacIntyre's account that practices do not lend themselves to simple, one-line definitions. To understand the nature of a particular practice, its internal goods and standards of excellence, one must be part of the community of those who participate in it. Furthermore, that community's understanding of the practice is constantly subject to argument, extension and renegotiation. If this is so, then the task of comparing medicine and clinical research is likely to be more difficult than Miller and Brody's account would suggest: an adequate account of each will not be supplied by a thumbnail sketch of its aims and goals,[6] but will have to emerge from within the relevant community of practitioners. However, it may be possible to discern the outlines of such an account by thinking about each practice in terms of the *virtues*.

According to MacIntyre, the virtues are qualities that we need

---

5 Alasdair MacIntyre, *After Virtue: A Study in Moral Theory*, 2nd edn., London: Duckworth, 1985, p. 187.

6 As offered in 'A Critique of Clinical Equipoise', p. 21.

in order to achieve the goods internal to practices; some virtues at least, including courage, justice and truthfulness, are essential to sustain any practice. Furthermore, not all qualities that sustain practices can be called virtues, but only those that also contribute to the good of a 'whole human life' and are connected to an 'ongoing tradition'.[7] But it seems likely that any practice will have its own characteristic 'map' of virtues that are particularly important for it, or that work out in particular ways in it. Sketching the maps of virtues characteristic of clinical medicine and of clinical research may enable us to characterize these two practices and their relationship with one another in a more richly textured way than Miller and Brody's rather thin description allows.

Clinical medicine[8]

William F. May draws attention to three distinctive 'marks' of the profession of clinical medicine, each of which requires a correlative virtue.[9] First, there is the *intellectual* mark: doctors can be expected to have command of a body of specialist knowledge that guides and informs their practice. Some of this specialist knowledge is scientific knowledge of the sort that could be gained from clinical research. However, the specialist knowledge expected of doctors is not limited to scientific knowledge, since medicine is

---

7 MacIntyre, *After Virtue*, pp. 191–2, 275.

8 I begin with medicine for two reasons. First, there is already a well-established body of virtue-ethical reflection on the practice of medicine, but not on the practice of scientific research, and it seems easier and clearer to begin with the better-mapped territory and move from there to the less well charted. Second, and more importantly, even on Miller and Brody's account, medicine provides the context within which clinical research has its value and importance, and without which there would be little need to discuss it.

9 William F. May, 'The Medical Covenant: An Ethics of Obligation or Virtue?', in Gerald P. McKenny and Jonathan R. Sande (eds), *Theological Analyses of the Clinical Encounter*, Dordrecht: Kluwer Academic Press, 1994, pp. 29–44. There is obviously much more that could be said about the virtues characteristic of the medical profession, and of other health care professions such as nursing. However, within the confines of this chapter, the account derived from May suffices to outline some of the most significant virtues associated with the practices of health care and to offer points of contact and comparison with the practice of clinical research.

not merely a technology but also an art. The virtue that is required to sustain the 'healer's art' is *prudence*, in the Aristotelian-Thomist sense of a kind of practical wisdom that can see the patient as a whole, but also as a particular patient, and can discern the action required to care for him or her. The second mark identified by May is the *moral* mark: while professionals, by definition, make a living from their profession and accordingly have an interest in it, they are not expected simply to be self-interested, but to place their patients' interests before their own. (May, like Miller and Brody, notes a potential conflict here between the priorities of clinical medicine, which place the individual patient's interests first, and those of clinical research, which has other aims than the needs of this particular patient.) To support the trustworthiness that is expected of doctors, the virtue of *fidelity* is required. Third, there is the *organizational* mark: modern health care often demands large resources (and therefore a political and economic system for making those resources available), it takes place in institutions with complex organizational structures, and is delivered by professionals who are members of professional organizations. The practice of medicine is inescapably a corporate activity, and professionals require the virtue that May calls '*public-spiritedness*' to support their co-operation with others in this enterprise. He defines public-spiritedness as 'the art of acting in concert with others for the common good',[10] and it includes professional discipline and a concern for justice in the distribution of health care resources.[11]

An obvious point, implicit in May's account, is that all of these virtues are located in the context of a practice that is directed to the *good* of suffering people. In other words, the prudence, fidelity and public-spiritedness of medical professionals are all in the service of another virtue, *benevolence*: prudence can be understood as the practical wisdom that helps the doctor to discern in

---

10 May, 'The Medical Covenant', pp. 164–5.
11 For further discussion of health care resource allocation, see below, Chapter 7.

what the patient's true good consists, fidelity as a steadfast commitment to the patient's good, and public-spiritedness as a disposition to act for the common good, recognizing that in any health care institution or political community, there are many patients whose good must be considered and sought. As we shall see, this is an obvious point of contact with clinical research, for which benevolence is also said to be central. However, benevolence alone is insufficient to sustain either clinical medicine or (as I shall suggest later) clinical research. Clinical medicine motivated by nothing richer than benevolence would be susceptible to various kinds of distortion. For example, the prudence needed to discern the patient's true good could collapse into mere paternalism or, paradoxically, into an unbalanced 'respect for autonomy' in which acting for the patient's good is reduced to respecting her wishes.[12] Or again, the public-spiritedness that looks to the common good and the wise use of resources could be reduced to a merely utilitarian form of cost–benefit analysis.[13] I shall argue later that if practices motivated by benevolence are to be protected from such distortions, benevolence in its turn must be placed in the context of the virtue of which it is a part, *charity*. This will also entail the claim that the account of the virtues needed to sustain the practices of medicine and clinical research, and protect them from the kinds of distortion to which I draw attention, turns out to be a theological one.

---

12 If McKenny and others are right to argue that the Baconian project (see above, n. 7) frames much modern bioethical discourse, then the latter is likely to be a particular concern in relation to many of the issues with which this book engages: the expansion of individual choice is one of the overriding aims attributed by McKenny to that project, the other being the relief of suffering (see above, pp. 26–8). Thus, for example, public debates about assisted dying are dominated by arguments about respect for patients' autonomous choices and compassion in the face of their suffering (see below, Chapter 8). In an ethic framed by the Baconian project, it becomes difficult, perhaps impossible, to ask whether there are some things that are, and others that are not, *good* for humans to desire or prefer. As we shall see, the approach that I propose in this chapter as a way of framing the ethics of medicine and clinical research suggests a way of asking and answering that question.

13 An obvious example is the widespread use of the quality-adjusted life year (QALY) concept in decisions about health care resource allocation; for a critique, see below, Chapter 7.

Clinical research

There are various ways in which one could attempt to define the virtues particularly important in clinical research; the following discussion will proceed by thinking in general terms about the nature of the practice of clinical research and identifying some of the virtues whose absence from all practitioners would render that practice unsustainable.

Truthfulness

As I observed earlier, MacIntyre holds that truthfulness is one of those virtues that is essential to any practice. It would appear particularly, and distinctively, important for the practice of clinical research. In science generally, it seems that few things disturb the research community so much as scientific fraud and related forms of misconduct such as fabrication, falsification and plagiarism.[14] The popular image is that such misconduct is rare and is severely punished when it does occur.

Fraud illustrates very well MacIntyre's distinction between goods internal and external to a practice.[15] The external goods of scientific research are those (such as career advancement, reputation, power and prestige) that one might hope to gain by doing good research, but that could conceivably sometimes be gained more effectively by falsifying one's results. By contrast, internal goods, such as discovering interesting and valuable things about the world that we did not know before, can only be gained by

---

14 The UK Research Integrity Office (UKRIO) offers a definition of research misconduct that includes fabrication, falsification, '[m]isrepresentation of data and/or interests and or [sic] involvement', plagiarism and '[f]ailures to follow accepted procedures or to exercise due care' for humans, animals used in the research, the environment and information on individuals: UKRIO, *Procedure for the Investigation of Misconduct in Research*, London: UKRIO, 2008, p. 27. Online at http://www.ukrio.org/resources/UKRIO%20Procedure %20for%20the%20Investigation%20of%20Misconduct%20in%20Research.pdf (accessed 15 August 2010).
15 MacIntyre, *After Virtue*, pp. 188–9.

doing good research, not by falsely pretending to. Fraud radically undermines the internal goods of research, and this is particularly evident in clinical research, where the goal is not merely knowledge for knowledge's sake, but an understanding of disease processes and treatments that is directed towards more effective patient care. The virtue of *truthfulness* would seem to be essential for the practice of clinical research.

This simple account of truthfulness as a scientific virtue, though, is open to various kinds of challenge. First, the standard view of scientific fraud – that it is rare, and subject to severe sanctions – is called into question by sociological studies of scientific misconduct. Empirical evidence from the United States has suggested that, while fabrication, falsification and plagiarism are indeed rare, other forms of questionable scientific behaviour are much more widespread: one-third of the scientists surveyed reported that they had engaged in at least one form of scientific behaviour that, if discovered, would get them into trouble with their institutions or with government regulators.[16] The standard view has been challenged more seriously still by radical critic Brian Martin. He argues that a sharp distinction tends to be maintained within the scientific establishment between fraud, which is held to be a rare aberration and is severely denounced, and other, supposedly less serious, forms of dubious activity, which are accepted or tolerated, because such a distinction serves the interests of those social groups that have most power over scientific research and most to gain from it.[17]

Evidence of widespread dubious behaviour, in and of itself, does not seriously undermine the claim that truthfulness is needed to

---

16 Brian C. Martinson, Melissa S. Anderson and Raymond de Vries, 'Scientists Behaving Badly', *Nature* 435 (2005), pp. 737–8. Examples of such conduct include the failure to present data that would contradict the researcher's own previous research, and altering the design, methodology or results of a piece of research in response to pressure from a sponsor.

17 Brian Martin, 'Scientific Fraud and the Power Structure of Science', *Prometheus* 10.1 (1992), pp. 83–98. Online at http://www.bmartin.cc/pubs/92prom.html (accessed 15 August 2010).

sustain the internal goods of scientific research. It simply unsettles any complacent assumption that most scientists successfully exhibit the virtue of truthfulness most of the time, suggesting that truthfulness may be a harder virtue to practise, and the vices opposed to it more subtle and complex, than we tend to suspect. Even Brian Martin's more radical claim about the relationship between dubious behaviour and power structures *could* be understood as simply adding two things to this picture: drawing attention to the social and structural as well as individual aspects of untruthfulness, and demonstrating that subtle as well as blatant forms of it can be effective means of gaining external goods from research while at the same time compromising its internal goods. Martin's critique, though, could be read in a more radical way, as supporting the kind of sociological perspective which would emphasize the constructed character of scientific knowledge and the social processes of negotiation involved in the formation of scientific beliefs about the world.[18] Strong forms of this view would at least invite suspicion of the claim that truthfulness should be considered a virtue central to the practice of science.

Critics of strong social-constructivist accounts often point out that the latter have problems with self-reference, appearing to deconstruct their own claims as well as those of the scientific discourses to which they refer.[19] However, it is not necessary to be a strong social-constructivist to recognize the importance of personal and social factors in influencing and sometimes distorting what is discovered in scientific research. The perspectives of researchers, and the wider social, cultural and economic context in which the research takes place, undoubtedly influence what research questions are asked, what data are noticed or ignored and

---

18 See, for example, Bruno Latour, *Science in Action: How to Follow Scientists and Engineers Through Society*, Cambridge, MA: Harvard University Press, 1987.

19 For example Jarrett Leplin, *A Novel Defense of Scientific Realism*, New York: Oxford University Press, 1997, pp. 3–5; John L. Taylor, 'The Postmodern Attack on Scientific Realism', *Science and Christian Belief* 14.2 (2002), pp. 99–106 (pp. 100–1).

the way they are interpreted.[20] In clinical research, particular risks of distortion arise from the fact that much of it is commercially sponsored: the interests of commercial sponsors may shape the clinical research agenda in general, influence particular decisions about which trials are or are not conducted, and determine decisions about publication or non-publication of results.[21] To acknowledge the importance of these influences and potential distortions is (once again) not to deny the possibility or importance of truthfulness as a scientific virtue, but to recognize the range and severity of threats to it.

My claim about truthfulness might seem to be undermined in another way if the ontological and epistemological claims of scientific realism – that theories can be either true or false, depending on whether they make true claims about the way the world really is, and that it is possible, at least in principle, to have warranted belief in scientific theories[22] – are called into question by instrumentalist claims that theories cannot be true or false (or, in more modest versions, that nothing can be known about their truth or falsity) and must be regarded merely as useful instruments for organizing observations and directing future research. Space does not permit any detailed engagement with the complex, often highly technical and perhaps interminable debates between scientific realists and instrumentalists.[23] However, the theological

---

20 To give just one example, the gender bias of male sociobiologists is said to have had a distorting effect on their observations and theories of human behaviour: Sarah Blaffer Hrdy, *Mother Nature: A History of Mothers, Infants and Natural Selection*, New York: Pantheon, 1999, pp. 3–117.

21 See, for example, Trudo Lemmens, 'Piercing the Veil of Corporate Secrecy about Clinical Trials', *Hastings Center Report* 34.5 (2004), pp. 14–18; Carl Elliott, 'Pharma Goes to the Laundry: Public Relations and the Business of Medical Education', *Hastings Center Report* 34.5 (2004), pp. 18–23.

22 Ian Hacking, *Representing and Intervening: Introductory Topics in the Philosophy of Science*, Cambridge: Cambridge University Press, 1983, pp. 28–9.

23 For a brief survey, not over-optimistic about resolving the disagreement, see Jarrett Leplin, 'Realism and Instrumentalism', in W. H. Newton-Smith (ed.), *A Companion to the Philosophy of Science*, Oxford: Blackwell, 2000, pp. 393–401; and for more extensive treatments by realists, Leplin, *A Novel Defense*, and Christopher Norris, *Truth Matters: Realism, Anti-Realism, and Response-Dependence*, Edinburgh: Edinburgh University Press, 2005.

commitments espoused in this chapter and elsewhere in this book do seem to sit most comfortably with some chastened form of realism: there is a created world to be discovered, however much our investigation of it is limited by the finitude of our intellects and distorted by individual and corporate sin.[24]

The desire for knowledge

Without a desire for knowledge, clinical research, like other areas of science, would be unsustainable. If clinicians had no desire to understand disease mechanisms better, to seek new treatments that worked better than the existing ones, and so forth, there would be no clinical research. Yet in the Christian tradition, the desire for knowledge is an ambiguous thing. Thomas Aquinas, for example, draws an analogy with physical desires: just as our bodies naturally desire food and sex, so our minds naturally desire knowledge.[25] Like our physical desires, our desire for knowledge can be rightly or wrongly ordered. Aquinas calls the rightly ordered desire for knowledge *studiositas*, 'studiousness', and relates it to the cardinal virtue of *temperance* or self-restraint.

The vice of having a disordered desire for knowledge is *curiositas*, 'curiosity', and Aquinas says that this disordered desire can take various forms: we can become distracted from the knowledge that we should be pursuing, concentrating instead on 'less profitable' matters; we can seek knowledge from illicit sources; we can seek knowledge of created things without referring that knowledge to God; and we can seek knowledge beyond our capabilities.[26] This typology of *curiositas* offers interesting insights into some of

---

24 See Colin E. Gunton, *The Triune Creator: A Historical and Systematic Study*, Grand Rapids, MI: Eerdmans, 1998, ch. 5. For two recent essays defending scientific realism within a theological frame of reference, see Taylor, 'The Postmodern Attack', and Edward L Schoen, 'Clocks, God, and Scientific Realism', *Zygon*, 37.3 (2002), pp. 555–79.

25 Thomas Aquinas, *Summa Theologiae*, ET ed. Thomas Gilby, London: Eyre and Spottiswode, 1964–76, II-II.166.

26 Aquinas, *Summa Theologiae*, II-II.167.1.

the ways in which medical research might be distorted. A good example of the first type of disorder, being distracted from the more important knowledge by the less profitable, is that the diseases of the wealthy populations of the world attract a disproportionate amount of research effort and funding, and that many diseases of poor populations are neglected by comparison.[27] The reasons are not hard to imagine: the diseases of the wealthy are those most likely to bring commercial research sponsors a return on their investment, are of the greatest concern to the electorates of those governments with the resources to sponsor publicly funded research, and are the ones most likely to worry people wealthy enough to give to medical research charities. This form of *curiositas*, then, is related to the economic distortion of research agendas to which I drew attention under the heading of truthfulness.

It is worth noting that in identifying this type of *curiositas*, Aquinas need not be taken to mean that all learning and research should be directed towards topics that are 'useful' in a narrow sense: research that simply enhances our understanding of the created world, without any obvious or immediate practical application, may be worth doing.[28] But where research is aimed directly at meeting human needs, as clinical research is, Aquinas' analysis of *curiositas* is a reminder that its priorities must be set by a properly proportioned understanding of the needs that exist. May's medical virtues of prudence and public-spiritedness could help to maintain this proper proportion; this is one way in which a close connection between the practices of clinical medicine and clinical research could help save the latter from some forms of distortion.

Aquinas' second type of *curiositas* is to seek knowledge from

---

27 See further the website of the Campaign for Access to Essential Medicines, sponsored by the NGO Médecins sans Frontières, online at http://www.accessmed-msf.org/ (accessed 30 August 2010).

28 So Margaret Atkins, 'For Gain, for Curiosity or for Edification: Why Do We Teach and Learn?', *Studies in Christian Ethics* 17.1 (2004), pp. 104–17 (pp. 111–15).

illicit sources. One way in which this might be done in clinical research would be to use research participants in exploitative or abusive ways; I shall return to this theme later, when discussing benevolence and charity. The third type involves seeking knowledge of created things without referring our knowledge to God. Now the thought that scientific research, if it is to be properly ordered, must make reference to God is unusual in the modern world, to say the least. Indeed, we tend to assume that the extraordinary success and power of science are the result of its *refusal* to refer to God in seeking explanations of natural phenomena, and some scientists and philosophers make much of the stultifying effect that attempts to refer to God are supposed to have had on science in the past.[29] To be sure, it is perfectly possible that inadequate *ways* of making reference to God (for example, treating the Christian doctrine of creation as a rival explanatory hypothesis to neo-Darwinian evolution) can indeed distort the scientific enterprise; it may also be true, as Margaret Atkins argues, that it is not so much the research itself as the character of the researcher that is at risk of distortion by a failure to attend to God.[30] But it is also possible that there are ways in which proper reference to God can safeguard the integrity of the *research* as well as the researcher. Atkins herself points towards one such way when she observes that a defence of scientific research as worth doing, in and of itself, seems to require some notion that the world is both good and ordered, and that this is precisely the understanding articulated by the Christian doctrine of creation.[31] Certainly it is frequently argued that, historically, the Christian doctrine of creation was

---

29 For example Daniel C. Dennett, *Darwin's Dangerous Idea: Evolution and the Meanings of Life*, London: Penguin, 1996.

30 Atkins, 'For Gain, for Curiosity or for Edification', p. 111.

31 Atkins, 'For Gain, for Curiosity or for Edification', p. 113. Of course, as her account makes clear, this only amounts to a claim that a Christian understanding of the world as created is *sufficient* to support the attitude that is required in order for science to flourish; it does not (yet) amount to an argument that such a Christian understanding is a *necessary* condition of such an attitude.

part of the soil in which modern science took root and flourished in the West.[32]

The fourth form of *curiositas* described by Aquinas is to seek knowledge beyond our capabilities. Again, this may not initially seem like a welcome thought to most scientists, since science seems to have flourished in modern times precisely by *refusing* to accept that there are any problems that will always remain insoluble, or that there are fixed limits to the knowledge of the world of which humans are capable.[33] But at least one form of humility about our knowledge and abilities is familiar to scientists: the honest acknowledgement of the *current* limits to our knowledge and technical capabilities at any given time. Without such an honest admission of how little we know, and how little we are able to do, it would be easy for researchers to attempt to go too far too fast, which could lead to all kinds of failures and false starts, and in the case of clinical research, to unjustifiable treatment of participants.

Benevolence

Doing good to others is central to the standard ethical justification of clinical research: that it will improve patient care in the future. A measure of suspicion may be in order: this justification might sometimes be a cover for other motivations, such as corporate profit, career advancement or even an inordinate desire for scientific knowledge. But there is no reason to doubt that the desire to benefit patients is a genuine motivation for many, perhaps most, clinical researchers.

According to Miller and Brody, clinical research has the 'frankly utilitarian purpose' of seeking the good of future patients by means of experimentation on present research participants. This

---

32 See further Gunton, *The Triune Creator*, pp. 102–16.

33 See, for example, Francis Bacon, *The New Organon* 1.92, online at http://www.constitution.org/bacon/nov_org.htm (accessed 30 August 2010).

leads them to insist that it is fundamentally different from clinical medicine in that it does not directly aim for the good of the research participants. The view that clinical research should benefit research participants, they argue, is a widespread misconception; it is prevalent perhaps because it meets the 'psychological needs' of clinical researchers who feel uncomfortable about exposing research participants to risk, burden and harm.[34]

But perhaps what Miller and Brody represent as a kind of psychological weakness on the part of investigators is actually a trace of a virtue without which neither clinical medicine nor clinical research would be sustainable in the long run. According to Aquinas, willing and doing good to others are aspects of the supernatural virtue of *charity*, which directs our lives towards love of God and neighbour.[35] But they are only part of it, and if the virtue of benevolence becomes detached from its wider context in charity, it could be at risk of various forms of distortion: for example, into a 'frankly utilitarian' willingness to use some individuals merely instrumentally for the benefit of others. A disposition to treat one's neighbour instrumentally would seem to be contrary to the virtue of charity, and in the long term, this erosion of charity would be likely to undermine the internal goods of both clinical medicine and clinical research. That is to say, a disposition to use human beings instrumentally could not sustain either medical practice or research that were genuinely directed towards relieving suffering and benefiting the needy, though it could sustain (for example) medical practice directed towards earning a large salary and clinical research directed towards enhancing the investigator's academic reputation or selling more drugs.

---

34 Miller and Brody, 'A Critique of Clinical Equipoise', pp. 20–1.
35 Aquinas, *Summa Theologiae*, II-II.25.1.

Conclusion: relocating clinical research in a theological context

My attempt to map the practices of clinical medicine and clinical research in terms of the virtues characteristic of each has suggested that they are more closely related to one another than Miller and Brody allow, and that the most basic connection between them is that they both depend crucially on the virtue of charity as it has in view the needs of sick and suffering people. This suggests a way of characterizing the relationship between them. I have already suggested that Miller and Brody characterize the relationship in terms of the 'Baconian project', but if what I have said about charity is right, then the Baconian project as applied to clinical research will tend to undermine itself. Thanks to a thin conception of the human good that owes much to early utilitarianism, a Baconian approach tends to emphasize some aspects of charity (especially benevolence) but neglect others; I have claimed that benevolence, isolated from its larger context in charity, is in danger of turning into a disposition to seek the welfare of *some* at the expense of *others*.

A related point is made by Allen Verhey: by disparaging the 'speculative sciences' of mediaeval scholasticism, Bacon and his successors cut themselves off from resources that are indispensable for guiding the wise and right use of the 'practical sciences', resources that the latter themselves cannot supply.[36] Setting clinical medicine and clinical research in a framework of the virtues gives us access to those resources and offers a way of understanding what it might mean to use the 'practical sciences' wisely and rightly. What this framework offers is a teleological understanding in which human life (in common with the whole created world) is ordered to an ultimate good. Both clinical medicine and clinical research are morally justified in so far as they are oriented towards

---

36 Allen Verhey, *Reading the Bible in the Strange World of Medicine*, Grand Rapids, MI: Eerdmans, 2003, pp. 151–3.

that good, and they should be practised in such a way as to contribute to its fulfilment.

But it should be clear from what I have already said that the ultimate good towards which these practices are to be oriented must be understood in theological terms: humans and the world are to be understood as created, loved, redeemed and destined for ultimate fulfilment by the triune God. In this perspective, both clinical medicine and clinical research should be practised in a way that enables our lives to be directed towards that ultimate fulfilment. Clinical research, for example, should be practised so as to enable research participants to display genuine, uncoerced neighbour-love by participating in research, and so as to rule out their merely instrumental use and exploitation by researchers.

I have argued, in short, that to sustain the practices of clinical medicine and clinical research requires a number of virtues – supremely, the virtue of charity – that must be understood theologically. But how are these virtues to be cultivated and supported? In *After Virtue*, MacIntyre famously argued that modern Western societies have largely lost the language of virtue from their moral understanding and practice, and that the best hope for the survival and recovery of this moral language is the creation of forms of community in which it can flourish.[37] Thanks to Stanley Hauerwas and others, the thought that Christian churches are called to be such 'communities of character' has become very familiar. Hauerwas is well known for arguing that a community very like the Church is needed to sustain the practice of medicine. This may also be true of the practice of clinical research, if I am right that the latter also depends for its coherence and integrity on virtues that must be understood theologically.[38] To scientists brought up on over-mythologized accounts of past conflicts between science and the Church, this might seem a sur-

---

37 MacIntyre, *After Virtue*, p. 263.
38 Stanley Hauerwas, *Suffering Presence: Theological Reflections on Medicine, the Mentally Handicapped and the Church*, Edinburgh: T & T Clark, 1988, pp. 63–83.

prising and unwelcome thought.[39] But, as I observed earlier, it is widely held that the Church and its theological traditions provided the intellectual soil in which modern science took root and grew in the West. It might turn out that the scientific enterprise is less able to flourish without the intellectual and moral context hitherto supplied by the Christian tradition than present-day 'cultured despisers' of Christianity sometimes imagine.

---

39 John Hedley Brooke has argued persuasively that such mythologized conflict narratives fail to do justice to the rich and complex relation between science and religion: *Science and Religion: Some Historical Perspectives*, Cambridge: Cambridge University Press, 1991.

6

Humans, Animals, Evolution and Ends

Modern medicine depends heavily not only on clinical research involving human participants, but also on the use of non-human animals in laboratory research. This, of course, is just one of the many ways in which humans make use of non-human animals, many of which involve killing them: for example, for food, clothing or sport. But are there limits to the use that humans ought to make of non-human animals, and if so, where are the limits to be drawn? Some limits would be harder to draw than others: in affluent Western contexts, it involves no great hardship, for example, to be vegetarian, and thus to avoid benefiting – directly, at any rate – from the killing of animals for food. In the same contexts, though, it is much harder to avoid benefiting directly from the killing of animals in medical research, since that would mean refusing much or most of what is on offer whenever one goes to the doctor or is admitted to hospital. But which, if any, of these uses of non-human animals is a theologically and morally acceptable way to treat our fellow-creatures? The present chapter is an attempt to locate these questions within the framework of the theological tradition articulated in this book, and to show how they might be constructively addressed within that tradition. The discussion of such practical questions, however, depends on answers to prior questions about how we understand ourselves and non-human animals, our and their places in the scheme of things, and so forth. So the two linked questions in view in this chapter are along the following lines: first, how ought we to understand the relationship between humans and non-human animals? Second, what does this understanding imply about how humans should treat non-human animals? The burden of my argument is that the kind of answer that proves theologically satisfactory will be in some sense teleological, and that the kind of teleology we need must be learned first and foremost through God's revelation in Christ.

On the need to learn about ends

How, then, is a theologically satisfactory account of the relationship between humans and non-human animals, and of the proper human treatment of animals, to be developed? What might such an account look like? Two approaches frequently taken in the literature on animals and ethics are unlikely to be satisfactory. The first is an ethic of non-maleficence and beneficence towards animals based on Jeremy Bentham's famous dictum that 'the question is not, Can they *reason?* nor, Can they *talk?* but, Can they *suffer?*'[1] It is not that such an ethic would necessarily be wrong, but that it would be radically incomplete and thin. The problem is that Bentham's dictum is rooted in his version of utilitarianism, in which the pursuit of the good is reduced without remainder to the maximization of happiness, the latter understood as pleasure and the absence of pain. But the maximization of happiness is widely held by theological critics to be an over-thin account of the *human* good;[2] and if we say that, it would seem a little odd if we were prepared to settle for such an account when attempting to speak theologically about the good in respect of God's other earthly creatures.[3]

---

1 Jeremy Bentham, *An Introduction to the Principles of Morals and Legislation*, ed. J. H. Burns and H. L. A. Hart, London: Athlone, 1970 (1789), p. 283.

2 See, for example, Gerald P. McKenny, *To Relieve the Human Condition: Bioethics, Technology and the Body*, Albany, NY: State University of New York Press, 1997, pp. 17–21.

3 Many utilitarians, of course, have attempted to develop richer accounts of utility than Bentham's. One recent example, influential in discussions of animals and ethics, is Singer's account of utility as preference satisfaction: Peter Singer, *Practical Ethics*, 2nd edn, Cambridge: Cambridge University Press, 1993. However, even such elaborations of utilitarian

The second approach that is unlikely to prove satisfactory is to set the discussion up in terms of the *rights* of animals. Apart from the philosophical problems associated with the use of rights language in relation to non-human animals, there is an important question as to how an ethic of animal rights might be located within a theological frame of reference. This problem was acknowledged and a solution attempted in Andrew Linzey's account of 'theos-rights', in which the rights of creatures are derivative of God's rights in the creation.[4] But what is required by the Creator's right must then be filled out with some content. If this is not to be simply a matter of divine *fiat* that lapses into the worst kind of voluntarism (certainly not what Linzey intends), this account must depend on some understanding of what kinds of treatment are congruent with God's good purposes in creating these kinds of creature. Accordingly, in Linzey's account, the proper treatment of animals is determined by God's good purposes for them, which are directed towards an eschatologically realized *telos*. The account for which I shall argue will have a good deal in common with Linzey's. The difference between us is at least partly an argument about language: I am not convinced that rights language is the most helpful for giving this kind of account of the proper human treatment of animals, nor that it is secure against the kinds of confusion and misunderstanding well rehearsed by its critics.[5]

In introducing Linzey's account of animal rights, I have hinted at one of the central claims of this chapter, which bears repeating and emphasizing: a theologically satisfactory account of proper

---

theory, whatever their other merits, offer too reduced a conception of the good to be *theologically* satisfactory accounts (see, further, Andrew Sloane, 'Singer, Preference Utilitarianism and Infanticide', *Studies in Christian Ethics* 12.2 (1999), pp. 47–73, esp. pp. 62–72), and I would think that the critique suggested above applies *mutatis mutandis* to them as well.

4 Andrew Linzey, *Christianity and the Rights of Animals*, London: SPCK, 1987, pp. 68–98; *Animal Theology*, London: SCM Press, 1994, pp. 19–27; *Creatures of the Same God: Explorations in Animal Theology*, Winchester: Winchester University Press, 2007, pp. 35–46, 82–8.

5 See, for example, Mary Midgley, *Animals and Why They Matter*, Athens, GA: University of Georgia Press, 1984, pp. 61–4.

human conduct in respect of non-human animals will have to be *teleological* in character. It must be shaped and guided by an understanding of our, and their, proper ends: what we, and they, are *for*.

How (not) to learn about ends

If that is so, how might we learn what those ends are? One obvious source of a Christian teleological account would seem to be Thomas Aquinas, whose account of natural law is based on a threefold scheme of natural ends: first, those common to all beings, for example existing and maintaining their existence; second, those common to all animals, such as procreation and the raising of offspring; third, those peculiar to humans as *rational* animals, such as living in ordered societies and knowing the truth about God.[6] Over and above this threefold scheme of natural ends, of course, humans have the *ultimate* end of eternal life in God's presence.

Aquinas, influenced by both his reading of Scripture and Aristotelian biology, gives a fairly clear answer to the question of the proper relation between humans and animals – an answer that has been influential on the subsequent Christian tradition and for which he is frequently taken to task by both Christian and secular critics. '[T]he order of things is such that the imperfect are for the perfect', and it is in keeping with this ordering of nature that we kill plants for the benefit of animals and animals for our benefit.[7] Non-human animals are 'devoid of the life of reason whereby to set themselves in motion'.[8] This means that they are 'not competent, properly speaking, to possess good', which is one of three reasons given by Aquinas for holding that 'we cannot have the friendship of charity towards an irrational creature', though we

---

6 Thomas Aquinas, *Summa Theologiae*, I-II.94.2, ET ed. Thomas Gilby, 60 vols, London: Eyre and Spottiswoode, 1964–76.

7 Aquinas, *Summa Theologiae*, II-II.64.1, citing Aristotle, *Politics*, I.3.

8 Aquinas, *Summa Theologiae*, II-II.64.1 ad 2; cf. Aristotle, *Politics*, I.8.

can love such creatures in so far as they glorify God and are of use to our (human) neighbours; God too, according to Aquinas, loves non-human animals for these indirect reasons.[9]

The best science available to Aquinas was Aristotelian, and as already noted, Aquinas' view of animals depends significantly upon appeals to Aristotelian biology. This seems to make his account vulnerable to the extent that it depends on empirical or theoretical Aristotelian claims discredited by more recent biology. For example, the clear distinction between human and non-human animals, consisting in humans' being rational creatures and non-humans' being irrational, is called into question both theoretically and empirically by contemporary evolutionary biology.[10]

One possible way of addressing such difficulties might be to develop an updated version of Natural Law theory in which modern science does the work that Aristotelian biology did for Aquinas.[11] Two crucial and related modern developments, however, make this way of proceeding problematic. One is that whereas

---

9 Aquinas, *Summa Theologiae*, II-II.25.3.

10 See, for example, Frans B. M. de Waal, *Good Natured: The Origins of Right and Wrong in Humans and Other Animals*, Cambridge, MA: Harvard University Press, 1996. This distinction has sometimes been overstated: Aquinas of course recognizes that humans have much in common with non-human animals, as is clear from his presentation of the natural law in *Summa Theologiae*, I-II.94.2, and from his frequent use of the term 'rational animal' to describe human beings. It has also recently been argued that for Aquinas, the 'rationality' which distinguishes humans from other animals is not to be seen as an all-or-nothing characteristic, but a matter of degree; such a reading could tend to reduce the distance between Aquinas and modern authors such as de Waal. See Celia Deane-Drummond, *The Ethics of Nature*, Oxford: Blackwell, 2004, pp. 65–77, and John Berkman, 'Towards a Thomistic Theology of Animality', in Celia Deane-Drummond and David Clough (eds), *Creaturely Theology: On God, Humans and Other Animals*, London: SCM Press, 2009, pp. 21–40.

11 For example, in his early book *The Evolution of Altruism and the Ordering of Love* (Washington, DC: Georgetown University Press, 1994), Stephen J. Pope argued for a critical appropriation of evolutionary biology into a Christian natural law framework, and proposed that Christian moralists ought to be more cautious about asserting the universal and indiscriminate claims of neighbour-love, in the light of sociobiological arguments that humans have evolved a disposition to show greater love to kin than to unrelated strangers. In an extensive recent treatment of evolution and Christian ethics, Pope takes a more ex-

Aristotelian science was teleological in character, there was a powerful move in early modernity to exclude teleological thinking from the natural sciences. This non-teleological programme was more easily implemented in the physical than the biological sciences, and even after Darwin, opinion has been divided as to whether the theory of natural selection supports or disposes of teleological thinking in biology.[12] However, even if – as Michael Ruse argues – neo-Darwinian evolutionary theory *is* teleological in something like an Aristotelian sense,[13] a second problem comes into play: the problem of 'is' and 'ought'. This problem has bedevilled attempts to draw ethical conclusions from evolutionary biology ever since T. H. Huxley, under the influence of Hume, used it to discredit the evolutionary ethics of Herbert Spencer.[14] Even if neo-Darwinian evolution can be said to give an account of final causes, those final causes are survival and reproductive success. Whereas Aquinas could define the *good* as 'what all things seek after',[15] all that modern biology can say is that 'what all [living] things seek after' is survival and reproductive success. Biology *qua* biology gives no grounds for equating these ends with the *good*, in any morally informative sense, or for concluding that they are

---

plicitly critical stance towards sociobiology, making clear that while natural law reasoning can be informed by evolutionary insights, biology in and of itself cannot tell us what does or does not conform to 'nature' in a morally significant sense: 'The normative ideal of natural law identifies certain human capacities from within the larger conglomeration of traits that constitute our evolved human nature, but it is selected on theological and moral rather than on biological grounds.' Stephen J. Pope, *Human Evolution and Christian Ethics*, Cambridge: Cambridge University Press, 2007, p. 292. This seems quite close to the position that I develop in what follows, with reference to Eugene Rogers and others: see below, n. 18.

12 See, further, Michael Ruse, *Darwin and Design: Does Evolution Have a Purpose?*, Cambridge, MA: Harvard University Press, 2003.

13 Ruse, *Darwin and Design*, pp. 273–89.

14 Thomas Henry Huxley, 'Evolution and Ethics' (The Romanes Lecture, 1893), in *Evolution and Ethics and Other Essays*, Collected Essays, vol. 9, London: Macmillan, 1894, pp. 46–116 (p. 80). Hume's formulation of the problem is in David Hume, *A Treatise of Human Nature*, ed. L. A. Selby-Bigge, rev. P. H. Nidditch, Oxford: Clarendon Press, 1978 (1739–1740), p. 469. See, further, Neil Messer, *Selfish Genes and Christian Ethics: Theological and Ethical Reflections on Evolutionary Biology*, London: SCM Press, 2007, pp. 97–104.

15 Aquinas, *Summa Theologiae*, I-II.94.2.

proper ends. They may be, but biology cannot tell us that they are. This difficulty is intensified by theoretical and empirical claims that forms of behaviour which no credible ethic would call good have in some circumstances proved conducive to the survival and reproductive success of humans and our evolutionary relatives.[16]

Christian attempts to incorporate modern biology into a natural law theory are often motivated by the Thomist dictum that 'grace does not destroy nature but perfects it'.[17] I have no quarrel with that motivation, but a good deal hangs on what we mean by 'nature' and how we know it when we see it. For the reasons I have given, it seems clear that an understanding of 'nature' in a morally or theologically significant sense cannot straightforwardly be had from a scientific inspection of the world alone. As Eugene Rogers argues, a more satisfactory understanding of Aquinas' dictum will recognize that we cannot understand what nature is apart from its end, which is graciously given by God and made known in Jesus Christ: 'We ought to define nature in terms of grace because it takes Jesus Christ to tell us what nature is.'[18] Rogers explicitly connects Aquinas' understanding of the relation of nature and grace, so understood, with Karl Barth's principle that creation is the external basis of the covenant and the covenant is the internal basis of creation.[19] This link forms part of his argument that Aquinas' and Barth's theological projects had much more in common than is customarily recognized either by Thomists or by Barthians.

If Rogers is right, there is more common ground between Thomist natural law and Barthian divine command ethics than

16 See, for example, Sarah Blaffer Hrdy, *Mother Nature: A History of Mothers, Infants and Natural Selection*, New York: Pantheon, 1999; and Richard Wrangham and Dale Peterson, *Demonic Males: Apes and the Origins of Human Violence*, London: Bloomsbury, 1997.

17 Aquinas, *Summa Theologiae*, I.1.8 ad 2.

18 Eugene F. Rogers, Jr., *Thomas Aquinas and Karl Barth: Sacred Doctrine and the Natural Knowledge of God*, Notre Dame, IN: University of Notre Dame Press, 1995, p. 190.

19 Karl Barth, *Church Dogmatics*, ET ed. Geoffrey W. Bromiley and Thomas F. Torrance, 13 vols, Edinburgh: T & T Clark, 1956–75, vol. III.1, §41.2, 3.

might at first sight appear.[20] And that will have significant implications for the present project to give a teleological account of the proper human treatment of non-human animals. For Barth, theological ethics is a part of Christian doctrine, with the task of '[understanding] the Word of God as the Command of God'.[21] Thus Barth's ethics, like all his theology, is radically Christocentric: it is first and foremost 'Jesus Christ, as he is attested for us in holy scripture' who is 'the one Word of God which we have to hear and which we have to trust and obey in life and in death'.[22] In the three-fold scheme sketched in Barth's *Ethics*,[23] and whose full exposition was begun but left unfinished in his *Dogmatics*,[24] the divine command comes to us as the command of the Creator, the Reconciler and the Redeemer. If so, then a theological account of the proper ends of humans and non-human animals, and the proper relation between them, must get its bearings from God's good purposes in creating, reconciling and redeeming the world, as those purposes are disclosed to us in Christ.

It might seem that in this approach, there is no room for any sort of constructive conversation with the natural sciences; Darwin and his successors, for example, might play the role of 'masters of suspicion', destabilizing unsatisfactory approaches to the theological and ethical questions at issue, but no more than that. However, this would be an over-hasty conclusion, as a comparison with Barth's theological anthropology shows. If we ask what it is to be human, our answer must, of course, be determined from first to last by what is disclosed to us in 'Jesus Christ, as witnessed to in

---

20 So also Nigel Biggar, *The Hastening that Waits: Karl Barth's Ethics*, Oxford: Clarendon Press, 1993, pp. 41–2, 49; but for a counter-argument, see David Clough, *Ethics in Crisis: Interpreting Barth's Ethics*, Aldershot: Ashgate, pp. 2005, pp. 114–18.

21 Barth, *Church Dogmatics*, vol. III.4, p. 4.

22 *Theological Declaration of Barmen* (1934), ET online at http://www.creeds.net/reform ed/barmen.htm (accessed 30 August 2010).

23 Karl Barth, *Ethics*, ed. Dietrich Braun, trans. Geoffrey W. Bromiley, Edinburgh: T & T Clark, 1981.

24 Barth, *Church Dogmatics*, vol. II.2, §§36–39, vol. III.4, and *The Christian Life*, ET Geoffrey W. Bromiley, new edn, London: T & T Clark, 2004 (1981).

Holy Scripture'. Empirical investigations can, by contrast, only yield at best what Barth calls 'working hypotheses of human self-understanding'.[25] But, critically appropriated to a christologically determined understanding of the human, these 'working hypotheses' have their place. As Nigel Biggar puts it:

> Barth insists that a properly theological anthropology will not simply repudiate 'the phenomena of the human recognizable to every human eye and every thinking mind'. But it will qualify and order such 'general knowledge' with a necessarily theological account of real human being – that is, human being as creature, pardoned sinner, and child of the Father.[26]

By analogy – and as Barth emphasizes, we can *only* speak of our responsibilities in respect of animals cautiously and by analogy[27] – in a christologically determined account of God's good purposes in respect of non-human animals, it may be that critically appropriated insights from the biological sciences have their own contribution to make, for example in (almost literally) fleshing out our notions about what kinds of creature we are discussing and in what their good consists. The point is that no area of human understanding can give us knowledge of God, or of ourselves and our fellow creatures in relation to God, that is in principle independent of God's self-disclosure in Christ.

---

25 Barth, *Church Dogmatics*, vol. III.4, p. 44.

26 Biggar, *Hastening*, p. 156, quoting Barth, *Church Dogmatics*, vol. III.2, p. 199.

27 Barth, *Church Dogmatics*, vol. III.4, p. 348. This suggests that the charge of anthropocentrism frequently levelled at Barth might be partly misplaced. To be sure, he gives relatively little theological or ethical attention to non-human animals, but part of his reticence on this score is because he thinks that there is relatively little that we have been told about them, and therefore that we are not entitled to say very much. Perhaps unexamined anthropocentric assumptions lead him to be more reticent than he need be; in any event, the argument of this chapter is that his theological method offers resources for going well beyond what he himself says about the human treatment of non-human animals.

Diagnostic questions and ethical conclusions

I have argued that a theological account of the proper ends of human and non-human animals, and the proper relation between those ends, must be shaped by an understanding of God's good purposes in creation, reconciliation and redemption, as those purposes are made known in Christ. If this is so, then the practical questions in view in this chapter may be theologically addressed by asking whether our treatment of non-human animals goes with the grain of those good purposes of God. In Chapter 1 I argued that human activity that conforms to God's purposes must be distinguished not only from that which blatantly opposes God's good purposes, but also from attempts, however well intentioned, to *substitute* for God's work in Christ in and for the world. To discriminate between these three forms of human activity, I proposed five diagnostic questions: first, does the activity we are assessing conform to the *imago dei*, or is it an attempt to be 'like God' (*sicut deus*) in the initially appealing but ultimately destructive way offered by the serpent in the Fall narrative (Gen. 3.5)? Second, what attitude does it demonstrate towards the material world: does it avoid the opposite dangers of a 'Baconian' hatred of the material world and the kind of idolatry that would look to the material creation for the fulfilment of ultimate human hopes? Third, what attitude does it embody towards our neighbours? Fourth, is it good news for the poor, powerless, oppressed and marginalized? Finally, what attitude does it manifest towards past failures? In the remainder of this chapter I shall return to two of the concrete questions to which I alluded at the start, meat-eating and the use of animals in biomedical research. I shall try to show how this theological approach might guide a particular reading of the Scriptures and the Christian tradition, and how that in turn might suggest specific practical conclusions.

A key text in theological and ethical discussions of non-human animals is the Isaianic vision of the peaceable kingdom (Isa. 11.6–9), one of the texts cited by Barth in his discussion of the human use of animals.[28] Barth describes the history of the world as an 'interim' between the 'pre-historical realm' of creation depicted in Genesis 1 and 2 and the promised eschatological consummation. In the pre-historical realm, creation was in a state of peace in which there was no necessity for humans to kill animals, or animals to kill one another, for food or for any other purpose. By contrast, in the historical realm that we inhabit, this 'peace of creation' is broken by human sin. In this new situation, characterized by the 'struggle for existence',[29] the killing of animals became a possibility 'permitted and even commanded' by God. But the peace of creation depicted in Genesis 1 and 2 is a constant reminder that the present state of affairs 'does not correspond with the true and original creative will of God, and that it therefore stands under a *caveat*'. Texts such as Isaiah 11 are reminders of the promised 'last time ... when there will be no more question of the struggle for existence and therefore of slaughter between man and beast'.

This, according to Barth, is the perspective in which every practical question about the human use and killing of animals should be considered. On the detailed practical questions themselves he says little. Of vegetarianism, he allows the objection that 'it represents a wanton anticipation' of the new age promised in Isaiah's prophecy, but nonetheless acknowledges its value as a 'radical protest' against the routine exploitation of animals: 'for all its weaknesses we must be careful not to put ourselves in the wrong in the face of it by our own thoughtlessness and hardness of heart.'[30]

Taking his cue in part from Barth, Andrew Linzey has also

---

28 Barth, *Church Dogmatics*, vol. III.4, pp. 348–56. All the quotations in the present paragraph are from p. 356.

29 This seems to be a deliberate echo of Darwin: in German, Barth's phrase is '*der Kampf ums Dasein*', the same phrase used in German translations of the *Origin of Species*. See Barth, *Die Kirchliche Dogmatik*, III.4, Zollikon-Zürich: Evangelischer Verlag A. G., 1951, p. 402; cf. Charles Darwin, *Über die Entstehung der Arten im Thier- und Pflanzen-Reich durch natürliche Züchtung*, German trans. H. G. Bronn, Stuttgart: Schweizerbart, 1860, p. 65, online at: http://darwin-online.org.uk/contents.html (accessed 15 January 2008).

30 Barth, *Church Dogmatics*, vol. III.4, pp. 355–6.

drawn on Isaiah's vision of the peaceable kingdom. However, he is less reticent than Barth in drawing ethical inferences from it, calling on his readers to '[approximate] the Peaceable Kingdom', or seek 'to realize what can be realized in our own time and space of the Messianic Age'.[31] This line of thought leads him to advocate vegetarianism unequivocally, and informs his critique of animal experiments as 'un-godly sacrifices'.[32] Linzey is significantly influenced by Barth's method and shares many of his presuppositions, yet comes to rather different practical conclusions. Might the diagnostic questions that I proposed earlier help evaluate their differences?

The question about our attitude to the material world suggests the context in which our practical questions should be considered. One way of acting out a hatred of the material creation would be what could be called a pseudo-ascetic flight from it. This suggests, at any rate, that there could be bad reasons for being a vegetarian or refusing the benefits of scientific medicine. If we do conclude that either eating meat or animal experimentation represents unacceptable exploitation of non-human animals, our conclusion must not be motivated by a general disposition to reject the good gifts that God gives us to sustain our creaturely life in the world, gifts such as 'food from the earth, and wine to gladden the human heart, oil to make the face shine, and bread to strengthen the human heart' (Ps. 104.14–15).

Another way of expressing a kind of hatred of the material world would be to treat it as an adversary, a threat to human well-being, which must be subdued for our own protection. Something like this attitude is identified by Gerald McKenny in his analysis of the 'Baconian project', to which I have referred at various points: seeking mastery over the material world to the ends of relieving suffering and expanding individual choice.[33] But this drive to

---

31 Linzey, *Animal Theology*, pp. 134, 136.
32 Linzey, *Animal Theology*, pp. 95–113.
33 McKenny, *To Relieve the Human Condition*, pp. 17–24.

subdue the world in the service of our own needs and goals comes to seem more urgent if we believe that there is nothing more to human life or the life of the world than the present material reality that we inhabit. If this is all there is, then all human goals and aspirations depend solely on human action in this world. No-one will heal or save us if we do not do it for ourselves. Paradoxically, therefore, the second of the erroneous attitudes to the material creation that I identified – the reduction of everything to the material – reinforces the first. There could be elements both of 'radicalism' and 'compromise' (to use Bonhoeffer's terms) at work in much of our human action in the world, including many of our scientific, technological and medical projects.[34]

Another of the diagnostic questions makes use of Bonhoeffer's contrast between the *imago dei* and the attempt to be 'like God', *sicut deus*. Bonhoeffer associates the latter with knowledge that does indeed make us (in a sense) like God, but in so doing alienates us *from* God. In alienating ourselves from God, of course, we also become alienated from ourselves, one another and our fellow creatures. Bearing in mind the close and complex relationship between knowledge and power, and the analogy drawn by Nathan MacDonald between the *imago dei* and election – that is to say, a distinctive relationship with God that also implies a distinctive role in the world – the contrast between *sicut deus* and *imago dei* can be drawn as a contrast between two opposed ways of exercising power or authority in the created world.[35] Bonhoeffer points to the kind of power or authority consistent with God's good purposes when he introduces a third term into his discussion: 'Imago dei, sicut deus, agnus dei – the human being who is God incarnate, who was sacrificed for humankind sicut deus, in true divinity slaying its false divinity and restoring the imago

---

34 See, further, Messer, *Selfish Genes*, pp. 235–6.

35 See above, pp. 118–21, and Nathan MacDonald, 'The *Imago Dei* and Election: Reading Genesis 1:26–28 and Old Testament Scholarship with Karl Barth', *International Journal of Systematic Theology* 10.3 (2008), pp. 303–27.

dei.'[36] The sacrifice of Jesus, the Lamb of God, for our sakes is a complete inversion of the structures of domination by which alienated humans *sicut deus* exercise power over one another and the world. *Inter alia*, the sacrifice of the Lamb of God has put an end to animal sacrifices: in God's good future, there will be no need for humans to sacrifice non-human animals in order to heal their own ills or the ills of the world. Andrew Linzey understands this point very well, and infers from it that animal experiments are 'un-godly sacrifices' – in my terms, opposed to God's good purposes, or at best a parody of them.[37] Is he right to draw this inference?

It has to be said that much present human use of non-human animals has the appearance of humanity *sicut deus*: an exercise of raw power that hardly seems to reflect the *imago dei*. It also has to be acknowledged that much of what the Christian tradition has in the past taken to be proper dominion reflecting the *imago dei* looks, with hindsight, much more like the kind of domination characteristic of humanity *sicut deus*. We might say that the tradition has often failed to appreciate the difference made by the *agnus dei* in this sphere.

However, Barth's diagnosis of the pride that wants to be its own helper reminds us that it is possible to act *sicut deus* not only in ways that are blatantly opposed to God's good purposes – such as the exercise of raw, dominating and destructive power – but also in more subtle and well-intentioned ways, by confusing the kind of thing that is given to us to do in the world with what can only be done by God: in Bonhoeffer's terms, confusing the penultimate with the ultimate. We are called to live in ways that are congruent with what has been disclosed to us of God's good and loving purposes, and that witness to those purposes – specifically, in this case, to the promise of the peaceable kingdom. But we are *not* called to inaugurate or establish that kingdom; attempts to do so

36 Bonhoeffer, *Creation and Fall*, p. 113.
37 Linzey, *Animal Theology*, pp. 103–6.

risk lapsing into dangerous and potentially inhumane kinds of utopianism or fanaticism. Linzey's language of 'approximating' the peaceable kingdom has its dangers, because it tends to obscure this distinction between witnessing to and establishing the kingdom.[38]

In this connection, one useful piece of work that evolutionary biology can do for us is to remind us how distant God's promise of the peaceable kingdom is from our present experience of the world. As Barth says, we learn from the Bible that the 'struggle for existence' is a feature of this fallen world, and is no part of the peace depicted in the creation narratives and promised for the age to come.[39] But life as we know it in the present age has been profoundly shaped by the 'struggle for existence': in this world, lions would not *be* lions if they ate straw like oxen. So if we wish to take seriously the Isaianic promise of a coming age in which lions live at peace with cattle, we shall also have to acknowledge that it is quite beyond our power to imagine what such an age will look like, much less to bring it in or to 'approximate' it.[40]

Another way of putting this is to say that the life of the world is distorted in subtle and complex ways, the product of (*inter alia*) the contingent course of evolutionary history, the choices and actions made by our predecessors and the choices we ourselves make. Elsewhere, I have argued that the traditional Western Christian language of fallenness and original sin powerfully articulates this condition of distortion and brokenness.[41] If I am right, then the diagnostic question about our attitude to human failure should remind us that we cannot avoid this complex entanglement in human sin and the fallenness of the world. If we think we can save ourselves from this predicament, we are – again – guilty of

---

38 Linzey, *Animal Theology*, p. 134.

39 Barth, *Church Dogmatics*, vol. III.4, pp. 353–4.

40 See further Neil Messer, 'Natural Evil after Darwin', in Michael Northcott and R. J. Berry (eds), *Theology after Darwin*, Carlisle: Paternoster Press, 2009, pp. 139–54.

41 Messer, *Selfish Genes*, pp. 133–215. My understanding of sin is heavily indebted to Alistair I. McFadyen, *Bound to Sin: Abuse, Holocaust and the Doctrine of Sin*, Cambridge: Cambridge University Press, 2000.

the self-defeating pride that wants to be its own helper. We can only live in the world in dependence on God's mercy and forgiveness, and this has been so since the very beginning of our history.

According to Barth, one way in which God's mercy is manifested in this situation is in divine permission to use non-human animals – even, sometimes, to kill them – to meet human needs.[42] But as I have already noted, this permission is subject to the *caveat* that such use is no part of God's original good purpose or promised good future. Even in the present age, the permission is strictly limited: no easy compromise with a fallen world is in view. A properly repentant attitude to human sin and the brokenness of the world should lead us to avoid the violent exploitation of non-human animals whenever we can.

Barth, as we have seen, holds that vegetarianism risks being a 'wanton anticipation' of the peaceable kingdom. Stephen Clark remarks, 'the case would be more convincing if it were not so easy for us (I say nothing about lions, nor yet the Inuit) to be vegetarian.'[43] In many Western contexts, Clark's retort to Barth is telling – though as he suggests, there may well be other contexts in today's world in which it is hard enough to get an adequate diet as it is, and would be more or less impossible without eating meat or fish. In such contexts, vegetarianism would hardly be 'good news to the poor'. But for affluent Westerners, it is harder to see why we should *not* be vegetarian.

However, even in relation to this question, and more in relation to animal experimentation, the question about good news to the poor not only illuminates, but also complicates matters. If, as I suggested in framing the question, 'poor' is understood broadly, to mean those in any situation who are weak, vulnerable and marginalized, then patients and those whose lives are threatened by disease are clearly included. But to refer to another diagnostic

---

42 Barth, *Church Dogmatics*, vol. III.4, pp. 352–6.

43 Stephen R. L. Clark, *Biology and Christian Ethics*, Cambridge: Cambridge University Press, 2000, p. 286.

question, are non-human animals also our neighbours, and in view of the great imbalance of power between humans and non-human animals, should the circle of 'the poor' be extended to include them? Should a Christian imperative to give 'moral priority [to] the weak', as Linzey holds, lead humans to sacrifice their own interests and well-being rather than exploit animals?[44]

These questions seem to require us to balance the conflicting claims of two groups of 'the poor': vegetarianism might be bad news for some poor human populations, but good news for those creatures that they eat; medical research is often good news for patients with life-threatening diseases, but bad news for the non-human animals used. Attempts to resolve these competing claims with general, *a priori* answers risk doing so in one of two unsatisfactory ways. They might fall back on some kind of utilitarian calculus of the harms and benefits to both groups, which I suggested at the beginning of the chapter is a theologically unsatisfactory way to approach these questions. Or they might resort to circular arguments relying on stipulative definitions of the moral status of humans and animals, an ethical move which, I argued in Chapter 4, is subverted by the way in which the category of 'neighbour' is used in biblical texts such as the parable of the Good Samaritan (Luke 10.25–37).[45]

Rather than attempting to settle these questions in general and *a priori*, it might be theologically wiser to recognize that in each situation, it is a question of the command of God: is the taking of this animal life permitted or commanded? The fact that in the biblical texts cited by Barth, God *does* give humans permission to kill animals, suggests that the answer could sometimes be 'yes'.[46] To

---

44 Linzey, *Animal Theology*, pp. 28–44.

45 See above, pp. 114–18, and, further, Ian A. McFarland, 'Who is my Neighbor? The Good Samaritan as a Source for Theological Anthropology', *Modern Theology* 17.1 (2001), pp. 57–66.

46 This is not, of course, a matter of simply reading the command of God off particular texts. If it were, the argument might be vulnerable to the objection that it raises the alarming possibility of acts like child sacrifice conceivably being permitted or commanded

rule it out *a priori would* risk attempting a 'wanton anticipation' of God's promised good future. Barth might have been wrong about vegetarianism, at least as far as affluent modern Westerners are concerned, but his argumentation is sound. His point is much more convincing in relation to medical research, and in relation to those contexts in which lives depend on the nutrition to be had from meat or fish. But the *caveat* to God's permission – or to put it another way, the diagnostic question about sin and repentance – should prompt us to seek alternatives to the killing of animals whenever we can. And to the extent that we succeed, the boundary between faithful witness to God's good future and 'wanton anticipation' of it will shift. When aspects of biomedical research, for example, *can* be done without animals, then avoiding the killing of animals becomes a matter of simple faithfulness, not fanaticism.

A final *caveat*: self-interest easily clouds our judgement; it is always tempting to define 'faithfulness' as whatever we find easy, and 'fanaticism' as what we find too hard or uncomfortable. So a measure of suspicion and self-criticism in respect of these practical conclusions is in order. More generally, when one attempts to draw practical moral conclusions about issues such as these, there is inevitably a certain provisionality about them. But because we have to live and act in the world, we cannot endlessly defer decisions about the practical questions; we have to seek at least provisional answers. And even if the practical conclusions I have reached are wrong (which is quite possible), if answers are to be sought in the context of the theological tradition that I have been articulating, then it seems to me that the questions will have to be asked in something like the way that I have proposed.

(cf. Gen. 22.2). In fact, of course, Barth's hermeneutic is somewhat more sophisticated than that, and well able to resist such dangers. See Biggar, *Hastening*, pp. 97–122; cf. (on Gen. 22), Barth, *Church Dogmatics*, vol. III.3, p. 35.

7

Health Care Resource Allocation and the 'Recovery of Virtue'

Questions about the allocation of health care resources have been on the agenda of bioethics since its beginnings. One of the events said to have marked the 'birth of bioethics' was a report in 1962 in American news magazine *Life* about the Seattle Artificial Kidney Center's 'Admissions and Policy Committee', which advised who out of all the medically eligible candidates should be offered the new, life-saving but scarce treatment of kidney dialysis.[1] The *Life* article caused a national controversy in the USA, and the issues it raised were taken up in important early academic treatments of bioethics, such as Paul Ramsey's *The Patient as Person*.[2]

The *Life* article raised the issue of *micro-allocation* – how a scarce health care resource should be distributed between individual patients. Half a century later, the problem of micro-allocation has not disappeared from bioethics.[3] However, micro-allocation is only one level of the problem. There is also the

---

1 Shana Alexander, 'They Decide Who Lives, Who Dies', *Life* (9 November 1962), pp. 102–10, 115–28. For various perspectives on the 'birth of bioethics', see Albert R. Jonsen (ed.), 'The Birth of Bioethics', *Hastings Center Report Special Supplement* 23.6 (1993); see also Albert R. Jonsen, *The Birth of Bioethics*, Oxford: Oxford University Press, 2003.

2 Paul Ramsey, *The Patient as Person: Explorations in Medical Ethics*, 2nd edn, New Haven, CT: Yale University Press, 2002, pp. 242–52.

3 One particularly acute example, routinely rehearsed in the textbooks, is the shortage of donated organs for transplantation: when there are not enough suitable organs for all patients who need them, which patients should have priority, and how should that decision be made? See, for example, Tony Hope, K. W. M. Fulford and Anne Yates, *The Oxford Practice Skills Course: Ethics, Law, and Communication Skills in Health Care Education*, Oxford: Oxford University Press, 1996, p. 104; Tom L. Beauchamp and James F. Childress, *Principles of Biomedical Ethics*, 6th edn, New York: Oxford University Press, 2009, pp. 274–5.

complex and multi-layered business of *macro-allocation*, which raises such questions as how much of a nation's wealth should be spent on health care, and how that budget should be divided up between different sectors of the system, different specialties, different treatments and other activities. Different health care systems have different mechanisms for making these decisions. Since 1999 in the UK, for example, some aspects of macro-allocation have been in the hands of the National Institute for Health and Clinical Excellence (NICE).[4] Among other things, NICE assesses new treatments for clinical and cost-effectiveness, and issues guidance on whether those treatments should be publicly funded for patients in the National Health Service (NHS).[5] The difficulty and complexity of macro-allocation decisions are illustrated by the frequent controversy that NICE has attracted since its inception. Negative recommendations about new treatments are (not surprisingly) frequently criticized by manufacturers, clinicians and patient groups,[6] but more general criticisms have also been levelled at NICE since the outset. Argument has revolved around (*inter alia*) whether or not it is a device for rationing health care, whether rationing is necessary or desirable, and how transparent and rationally defensible NICE's methods of assessment are.[7]

---

4 For more information about NICE, see http://www.nice.org.uk/ (accessed 31 August 2010). Because the NHS in Wales, Scotland and Northern Ireland is under the control of the devolved governments in those nations, NICE advice is used in different ways in different parts of the UK.

5 See http://www.nice.org.uk/aboutnice/whatwedo/abouttechnologyappraisals/about_technology_appraisals.jsp (accessed 31 August 2010).

6 For two recent examples, see Anon., 'Asthma Drug Ruling "Nonsensical"' (12 August 2010), online at http://www.bbc.co.uk/news/uk-10948091, and Helen Briggs, 'Critics Condemn Bowel Cancer Drug Rejection' (24 August 2010), online at http://www.bbc.co.uk/news/health-11060968 (both accessed 31 August 2010).

7 See, for example, Richard Smith, 'The Failings of NICE' *British Medical Journal* 321 (2000), pp. 1363–4; various authors, 'The Failings of NICE', *British Medical Journal* 322 (2001), pp. 489–91; Richard Cookson, David Mcdaid and Alan Maynard, 'Wrong SIGN, NICE Mess: Is National Guidance Distorting Allocation of Resources?', *British Medical Journal* 323 (2001), pp. 743–5; Nigel Hawkes, 'Why Is the Press so Nasty to NICE?', *British Medical Journal* 337 (2008), p. 1906; Anon., 'NICE Ten Years On: Past, Present and Future', online at http://www.nice.org.uk/newsroom/features/NICETenYearsOn.jsp (accessed 31 August 2010).

As if that were not enough complexity to be going on with, there is a third level of the problem: however great the problems of providing equitable access to health care within any one Western country, they are massively overshadowed by the disparities in health care provision between rich and poor nations.[8] One aspect of this problem is the unavailability of essential medicines, vaccines and diagnostic tools in developing countries, both because of the high cost and patent protection of many existing drugs and because relatively little research and development activity is addressed to the diseases of poor countries. While some important steps have been taken to address these problems in recent years, major challenges persist.[9] Understandably enough, the international level of the problem is often simply omitted from discussions of health care resource allocation – an omission approved, for example, by Joseph Boyle, who argues that

> considerations about the relative lack of health care by many around the world do not provide much help for those thinking about how to allocate the resources of the system for which they are responsible. For these decisions are not likely to affect how much is available for those outside the system.[10]

However, this observation – true as it may be – can at most only be a relocation of the question: somewhere within the structure of our ethical analysis we shall have to find room to consider the just

---

8 See, for example, various authors, Theme Issue on Health Financing, *Bulletin of the World Health Organization* 86.11 (2008), pp. 817–908, online at http://www.who.int/bulletin/volumes/86/11/en/index.html (accessed 31 August 2010).

9 See, further, the website of the Médecins sans Frontières *Campaign for Access to Essential Medicines*, online at http://www.msfaccess.org/ (accessed 31 August 2010).

10 Joseph Boyle, 'Limiting Access to Health Care: A Traditional Roman Catholic Analysis', in H. Tristram Engelhardt, Jr. and Mark J. Cherry (eds), *Allocating Scarce Medical Resources: Roman Catholic Perspectives*, Washington, DC: Georgetown University Press, 2002, pp. 77–95, at p. 90.

distribution of health care goods between as well as within nations.[11]

These are, obviously enough, questions of distributive justice, but in what follows I suggest that standard accounts of distributive justice in health care are unsatisfactory in important respects, and sketch out some implications of an alternative approach based on a Christian understanding of justice as a virtue. While – for reasons that will become clear as the argument progresses – my account does not include detailed practical proposals, I comment briefly on its implications for all three levels of resource allocation identified above, including the international level. The chapter concludes with some remarks about the relationship between such a tradition-constituted account and the wider public forums in which resource allocation decisions are made in Western liberal democracies.

Justice and resource allocation: standard accounts

One of the more widely canvassed approaches to resource allocation makes use of a utilitarian calculus based on the quality-adjusted life year (QALY).[12] This is an attempt to measure the outcome of health care interventions in terms of both the length and the quality of the patient's life. To calculate the number of QALYs a patient enjoys, the number of years she lives is multiplied by a factor representing the health-related quality of her life, where 0 is equivalent to death and 1 to full health. The benefit of a health care intervention is expressed as the net gain of QALYs, and its

---

11 For a discussion roughly contemporary to Boyle's that does place it on the agenda, see Adam Wagstaff, 'Economics, Health and Development: Some Ethical Dilemmas Facing the World Bank and the International Community', *Journal of Medical Ethics* 27 (2001), pp. 262–7. There does appear to be a growing recognition that the international level of the problem cannot be omitted from discussion: for example, the latest edition of Beauchamp and Childress, *Principles of Biomedical Ethics*, contains a section on 'Global Health Policy and the Right to Health' not included in previous editions (pp. 264–7).

12 Alan Williams, 'Economics of Coronary Artery Bypass Grafting', *British Medical Journal* 291 (1985), pp. 326–9.

cost-effectiveness as the cost per QALY. This method could, at least in theory, be used in micro-allocation, by giving priority to those patients likely to gain the greatest number of QALYs,[13] and in macro-allocation, by prioritizing activities with low costs per QALY.[14]

As is well known, the QALY approach has been heavily criticized on a number of technical and moral grounds, and equally vigorously defended.[15] One particularly illuminating critique for our purposes is the claim that QALYs are 'ageist': that they unfairly discriminate against the old, because other things being equal, a younger person is likely to have more years of life left, and therefore stands to gain more QALYs than an older person receiving the same treatment.[16] Some therefore advocate giving a higher value to each QALY for older people so as to redress this alleged imbalance. Defenders of the QALY, however, argue that there is nothing wrong with the method, and that such weighting would itself be a form of discrimination, albeit one for which there might

---

13 Andrew Edgar et al. assert that 'QALYs are not designed to prioritize individual patients, but rather the funding of treatments': *The Ethical QALY: Ethical Issues in Healthcare Resource Allocations*, Haslemere: Euromed Communications, 1998, p. 67. But they do not give clear reasons for making this claim, which stands in tension with some of their own earlier discussion. For example, 'It is possible to argue that QALY gains from treating ill-health which is brought about as a result of individual's [sic] own behaviour ... should be of lower value than those from treating ill-health for whom [sic] the victim was blameless' (p. 56). But if such a weighting were to mean, for example, that heavy smokers as a group were given lower priority, other things being equal, than non-smokers for a particular treatment, this would obviously result in QALYs being used to prioritize individual patients.

14 Williams, 'Economics of Coronary Artery Bypass Grafting'. NICE guidelines state that QALYs should be used to assess the health benefits and cost-effectiveness of technologies such as new drugs: *Guide to the Methods of Technology Appraisal*, London: National Institute for Health and Clinical Excellence, 2008, pp. 38–9.

15 For a trenchant theological critique, see Michael Banner, 'Economic Devices and Ethical Pitfalls: Quality of Life, the Distribution of Resources and the Needs of the Elderly', in *Christian Ethics and Contemporary Moral Problems*, Cambridge: Cambridge University Press, 1999, pp. 136–62. A robust defence against some of the standard criticisms is given by Jack Dowie, 'Analysing Health Outcomes', *Journal of Medical Ethics* 27 (2001), pp. 245–50.

16 John Harris, 'QALYfying the Value of Life', *Journal of Medical Ethics* 13 (1987), pp. 117–23; Banner, 'Economic Devices', pp. 146–7.

be good arguments.[17] Others argue on a variety of grounds that it is perfectly legitimate to give the young priority for medical treatment, and it is even sometimes suggested that QALYs do not discriminate sufficiently against the old.[18] In other words, the critics of the QALY method from either side hold that it fails to measure up to some standard of justice, however conceived, while its defenders seem to think that what counts as just distribution in a particular situation must be learned at least in part from the QALY calculation itself.

An apparently very different approach is the attempt by Norman Daniels to give an account of just health care in terms of social contract theories such as that of John Rawls. Daniels argues that some kinds of illness prevent the fair equality of opportunity required by Rawls' and similar theories. A society ought to provide a system of health care which as far as possible prevents or cures those illnesses which obstruct fair equality of opportunity.[19] Arguments along these lines have been used to promote the notion that all citizens in a liberal society should have a right to a 'decent minimum' of publicly funded health care, and that all should have the right of equal access to health care.[20]

This theory, like the QALY approach, can be deployed in an attempt to settle questions about age-based rationing. According to Daniels, prudent deliberators, placed behind a 'veil of ignorance' which prevented their knowing how long or healthy a life they would enjoy, would choose a '*system that protected their normal opportunity range at each stage of their lives*'.[21] One implication is

---

17 Dowie, 'Analysing Health Outcomes', p. 249.

18 An argument summarized (though not endorsed) by Hope et al., *Oxford Practice Skills Course*, p. 102.

19 Norman Daniels, *Just Health Care*, Cambridge: Cambridge University Press, 1985, pp. 36–58. See also Norman Daniels, Donald W. Light and Ronald L. Caplan, *Benchmarks of Fairness for Health Care Reform*, New York: Oxford University Press, 1996, pp. 21–9.

20 Beauchamp and Childress, *Principles of Biomedical Ethics*, pp. 258–61.

21 Daniels, *Just Health Care*, pp. 86–113 (p. 103, emphasis in original). See also Norman Daniels, *Am I my Parents' Keeper: An Essay in Justice between the Young and the Old*, New York: Oxford University Press, 1988.

that resources should be put into home care and social support services for older people, and 'premature institutionalization' should be avoided. Daniels suggests, more tentatively, that another implication is to favour some kinds of rationing by age. It would be prudent to choose a system which maximized everybody's chances of living a normal span of life, rather than one which reduced the chances of reaching a normal lifespan but then prolonged, beyond normal, the lives of those who did make it to old age. The former kind of system might, conceivably, operate some forms of age-based rationing. It might, for example, restrict access to expensive life-saving interventions to those below a certain age. Daniels is, however, careful to distance himself from age-based rationing in general and to stress that his argument only applies 'under very special circumstances'.[22]

Social contract approaches, though, are as hotly contested as the QALY. As is well known, the Rawlsian theoretical base on which Daniels builds has been subjected to several different (and in some cases mutually incompatible) kinds of critique, for example from libertarians, communitarians and feminists.[23] Though Daniels' account does not depend exclusively on Rawls, some of these critiques are likely to apply, *mutatis mutandis*, to Daniels.

By now the suspicion may be developing that we are witnessing an example of what Alasdair MacIntyre memorably characterized as 'interminable' moral debate, symptomatic of the failure of the

---

22 Daniels, *Just Health Care*, p. 111. One important feature that distinguishes his account from more general proposals to ration by age is his proposal that we should think of ourselves as distributing resources not between different individuals of various ages, but between the different stages of the same individual's life. His proposal, therefore, would only apply in the context of a system 'that distributes resources over the lifetime of the individuals it affects', and would not justify 'piecemeal use of age criteria' by individual health professionals or institutions (p. 111).

23 For a libertarian critique, see Robert Nozick, *Anarchy, State and Utopia*, Oxford: Blackwell, 1974, pp. 183–231; for a communitarian critique, Michael J. Sandel, *Liberalism and the Limits of Justice*, Cambridge: Cambridge University Press, 1982; for a feminist critique, Seyla Benhabib, *Situating the Self: Gender, Community and Postmodernism in Contemporary Ethics*, Cambridge: Polity Press, 1992, pp. 148–77.

Enlightenment project.[24] This suspicion may be reinforced by the thought that both QALY and contractarian approaches to resource allocation are versions of the liberal attempt to devise a neutral, tradition-free framework within which individuals can pursue diverse and incompatible versions of the good life free from one another's interference. Both appear to rely on essentially procedural notions of justice and to prescind as far as possible from making substantive judgements about the human good. Yet this appearance may be illusory. MacIntyre has argued that liberal individualism, though it began as an attempt to devise a tradition-neutral framework for social negotiations of this sort, has itself become a tradition with 'its own broad conception of the good' and which in the public arena tends to exclude or marginalize other traditions.[25] If he is correct about this, then the standard approaches to health care resource allocation will themselves embody certain judgements about the human good which must at least be open to critique, extension or correction in the light of different accounts from different traditions.

The 'recovery of virtue'[26]

As is well known, MacIntyre's proposed solution to the failure of the Enlightenment project is to recover and reappropriate the tradition which it sought to displace: the tradition of virtue and the virtues articulated by Aristotle and his successors. In recent decades there has been no shortage of attempts to articulate an

---

24 Alasdair MacIntyre, *After Virtue: A Study in Moral Theory* 2nd edn, London: Duckworth, 1985, pp. 6–10. Daniels argues that his approach, while not utilitarian, should be attractive to utilitarians because it would tend to increase utility, even though it would not maximize it: *Am I my Parents' Keeper?*, pp. 94–5. However, utilitarians who were being true to their theory would presumably remain dissatisfied with Daniels' approach, even if they were prepared to settle for it as a political compromise.

25 MacIntyre, *Whose Justice? Which Rationality?* London: Duckworth, 1988, pp. 335–8.

26 The phrase is borrowed from Jean Porter, *The Recovery of Virtue: The Relevance of Aquinas for Christian Ethics*, London: SPCK, 1994.

ethic of health care using the language of virtue.[27] Some of these, it must be said, have operated with a fairly restricted understanding of what is meant by 'virtue': it has sometimes been treated, for example, as little more than a supererogatory excellence of conduct that goes beyond the minimum standards prescribed by rules and regulations.[28] But richer and more expansive accounts have been plentiful in the philosophical and theological literature. There have been virtue-based treatments of issues such as abortion and euthanasia.[29] There have been discussions of the virtues that should characterize physicians, nurses and patients.[30] There have been descriptions of medicine as what MacIntyre calls a 'practice', with its own internal goods, to sustain which the virtues are needed;[31] modern liberal societies, according to some authors, do not supply the necessary resources to cultivate those virtues and sustain the practice of medicine. Some such thought lies, for example, behind the claim of Hauerwas that to sustain its practice and render it intelligible, medicine needs a community very much like the Church.[32]

---

27 An early collection is Earl E. Shelp (ed.), *Virtue and Medicine*, Dordrecht: D. Reidel, 1985; for a more recent defence of the place of virtue theory in medical ethics, see Alastair V. Campbell, 'The Virtues (and Vices) of the Four Principles', *Journal of Medical Ethics* 29 (2003), pp. 292–6.

28 So, for example, Marc Lappé, 'Virtue and Public Health: Societal Obligation and Individual Need', in Shelp, *Virtue and Medicine*, pp. 289–303.

29 Rosalind Hursthouse, *Beginning Lives*, Oxford: Blackwell, 1987; Stanley Hauerwas and Richard Bondi, 'Memory, Community and the Reasons for Living: Reflections on Suicide and Euthanasia', in Stanley Hauerwas with Richard Bondi and David B. Burrell, *Truthfulness and Tragedy: Further Investigations into Christian Ethics*, Notre Dame, IN: University of Notre Dame Press, 1977, pp. 101–15.

30 Edmund D. Pellegrino, 'The Virtuous Physician, and the Ethics of Medicine', Martin Benjamin and Joy Curtis, 'Virtue and the Practice of Nursing', and Karen Lebacqz, 'The Virtuous Patient', in Shelp, *Virtue and Medicine*, pp. 237–55, 257–74 and 275–88 respectively; William F. May, 'The Medical Covenant: An Ethics of Obligation or Virtue?', in Gerald P. McKenny and Jonathan R. Sande (eds), *Theological Analysis of the Clinical Encounter*, Dordrecht: Kluwer Academic, 1994, pp. 29–44; Stanley Hauerwas and Charles Pinches, 'Practising Patience: How Christians Should be Sick,' in *Christians Among the Virtues: Theological Conversations with Ancient and Modern Ethics*, Notre Dame, IN: University of Notre Dame Press, 1997, pp. 166–78.

31 MacIntyre, *After Virtue*, p. 187.

32 Hauerwas, 'Salvation and Health: Why Medicine Needs the Church', in *Suffering Presence:*

Yet in all this discussion of virtue and medicine, the political and economic dimensions of the latter, those that are most relevant to arguments about resource allocation, seem curiously under-represented.[33] Much, though by no means all, literature on the virtues and medicine appears to reflect an assumption that virtue ethics is primarily relevant to the conduct and interactions of individuals, and that its relevance to the activities of public institutions is more doubtful. One effect of this is that the discussion of resource allocation is dominated by liberal conceptions of distributive justice, namely those of the marketplace.[34] But the tendency to restrict talk of the virtues to the realm of the individual is surely challenged by MacIntyre's analysis: a central feature of the story that he tells in *Whose Justice? Which Rationality?* is of the ways in which the virtues (specifically justice) have been instantiated by different political communities and their public institutions. If we are at all inclined to agree that liberal understandings of distributive justice have important shortcomings, it will be worth exploring what difference it might make to think of justice as a virtue in the context of a tradition other than the presently dominant one. Of course, if MacIntyre's diagnosis is correct, then any attempt to do so will meet the difficulty that modern Western political structures not only instantiate an impoverished understanding of justice, but allow relatively little space for the public practice of richer versions. This may partly explain the impression that the virtues have more to do with individual behaviour and relationships than with political structures

---

Theological Reflections on Medicine, the Mentally Handicapped, and the Church, Edinburgh: T & T Clark, 1988, pp. 63–83.

33 There are some counter-examples, for example Lappé, 'Virtue and Public Health', and Allen Verhey, 'Sanctity and Scarcity: The Makings of Tragedy', *Reformed Journal* 35 (1985), pp. 10–14 (reprinted in Stephen E. Lammers and Allen Verhey (eds), *On Moral Medicine: Theological Perspectives in Medical Ethics*, 2nd edn, Grand Rapids, MI: Eerdmans, 1998, pp. 974–9), but nothing like the same attention has been paid to these questions as to the other aspects of medical ethics alluded to earlier.

34 For example various authors, 'Economics and Ethics in Health Care', *Journal of Medical Ethics* 27.4 (2001).

and public institutions: that impression is a function of the political structures, not of the virtues themselves. One response to this situation would be to try and imagine a different set of political structures and institutions more hospitable to the articulation and practice of the virtues,[35] but to attempt such a project in a thoroughgoing way would take us far beyond the specific issue of health care resource allocation. What I shall attempt in the final section of this paper is the more modest task of thinking about ways in which a tradition-constituted understanding of the virtues might, so to say, infiltrate and enrich existing political structures, even when those structures are less than fully hospitable to it.

Justice as a virtue and resource allocation

There are some ways of exploring the relevance of the virtues to resource allocation which may initially seem attractive but which, I believe, will turn out to be false – or at any rate incomplete – trails. One is suggested by Tom Beauchamp and James Childress, for whom the content of moral obligation is largely dictated by the four principles of respect for autonomy, non-maleficence, beneficence and justice. The virtues are allowed to 'support and enrich' this framework, supplying dispositions to act according to the four principles and giving an account of motivation and character.[36] But they teach us little about the content of moral obligation; nor do they offer much by way of extension, challenge or correction of the substantive account derived from the four principles. Such a concept of virtue and character would, at best, allow us to add a portrait of the virtuous policy-maker or manager to those of the virtuous physician, nurse, patient and so on. It would tell us little or nothing, though, about the meaning and

---

35 This is, up to a point, what Ezekiel Emanuel attempts to do in the proposal discussed below.

36 Beauchamp and Childress, *Principles of Biomedical Ethics*, pp. 30–57 (p. 57).

content of distributive justice in health care, nor would it help us to resolve the presently interminable disagreements about resource allocation described earlier.[37]

Another route which we might find attractive, remembering MacIntyre's stress on communities in which the virtues can flourish, is Ezekiel Emanuel's 'liberal communitarian vision of health care'.[38] Emanuel, writing in a North American context, imagines a system in which the United States would be divided into thousands of 'Community Health Programs' (CHPs). Each CHP, by a process of deliberation among its members, would develop a 'shared conception of the good life' (p. 179), on the basis of which it would decide on its health care priorities and the allocation of resources. CHPs would have the power to determine their own membership and procedures for deliberation, though state and federal authorities would set limits to prevent unfair discrimination. Citizens would have a choice as to which CHP they joined, and would receive government vouchers for health care to be spent in their chosen CHPs. Some CHPs might be formed from religious communities with well-defined visions of the human good, while others would be more diverse and would have to clarify and articulate their conception of the good life by means of debate about celebrated cases in medical ethics (p. 180).

There is much that is appealing in this vision, particularly its promise that a variety of traditions would have space to instantiate their conceptions of the good and that citizens would be involved in serious deliberation about health care policy and practice. But it is unlikely to be free of the problems diagnosed by MacIntyre.

---

37 It is no accident that while there is some mention of the virtues in Beauchamp and Childress' chapter on 'Professional–Patient Relationships' (pp. 288–331), the chapter on 'Justice' (pp. 240–87), which contains their treatment of resource allocation, is framed entirely in terms of principles, rules and procedures. The understanding of virtue set out by Beauchamp and Childress may have some things to say about individual conduct and interpersonal relationships, but is silent on institutional and political questions.

38 Ezekiel J. Emanuel, *The Ends of Human Life: Medical Ethics in a Liberal Polity*, Cambridge, MA: Harvard University Press, 1995. Page numbers in brackets in this and the following paragraph refer to this work.

For one thing, it is far from clear that a CHP, unless formed by members of a highly homogeneous religious tradition, would find it possible to develop a shared conception of the good life. Emanuel's proposed method, to reach agreement by means of debate about medical cases and issues, could end up simply reproducing within the CHP MacIntyre's 'interminability' of moral debate. And on a larger scale, since the system is a device for enabling rival and incompatible conceptions of the good to coexist within the borders of one nation state, it faces some familiar tensions about the limits to the system's tolerance of rival conceptions of the good. These tensions are brought out by the question of whether it could allow a racist, sexist or ageist CHP to be set up. Emanuel makes it perfectly clear that he wishes to exclude this possibility, seeking to distinguish between positive conceptions of the good life that imply age, sex, race or religion-based selection for CHP membership and '[conceptions] of the good life based on the opposition to and denigration of others' (p. 240).[39] His proposal does not '[permit] all possible conceptions of the good life to be pursued ... [but] is compatible with many *worthy* conceptions of the good life' (pp. 240–1, emphasis added). But it remains somewhat unclear how we are to determine what counts as a 'worthy' conception of the good life, and what resources we have (beyond intuition and political fiat) for judging that some conceptions of the human good are so deeply flawed that they ought not to be put into practice, whether or not anyone is actually harmed by them.[40] Emanuel's proposal, then, remains prob-

---

39 The distinction between the two cases is illustrated by the following example: 'a Hispanic community might reject non-Hispanic applicants either because they want to perpetuate their particular traditions or for racist reasons. The first would be permitted and the second prohibited' (p. 239).

40 For example, suppose by way of a thought-experiment that a CHP based on an ideology of racial purity were set up in circumstances in which neither the citizens excluded from it, nor health professionals, nor any other member of the public, suffered any actual loss or harm as a result, and in which the wider liberal communitarian system was not thereby undermined. If we wish to say that nonetheless, the 'racial purity CHP' would embody such a distorted vision of the human good that it ought not to be permitted, my suspicion is that we will have to appeal to a 'thicker' account of human persons and their dignity

lematic, though there may be valuable things to be learned from it. But I now wish to sketch out a somewhat different way in which tradition-constituted conceptions of justice may be brought to bear on the resource allocation debate.

If we wish to learn what a Christian tradition might have to say about distributive justice in health care, in the nature of the case we will not simply be able to lift an influential account from the past and apply it to our present situation. Jean Porter makes this point in relation to Thomas Aquinas' discussion of distributive justice, which, as she observes, is too abstract and sketchy to offer much in the way of substantive practical guidance. We learn from Aquinas that the virtue of justice is directed to the common good, that distributive justice is concerned with the proper sharing of the community's goods among its members, that what counts as a just distribution will vary from one kind of political system to another, and that considerations of need, merit and desert all apply in determining what is a just distribution.[41] All of this hardly amounts to detailed guidance for policy-making, but as Porter argues, this reflects Aquinas' wisdom in recognizing that it would be impossible to deal in advance with the 'host of nice discriminations, delicate judgments, and gray areas' with which issues of distributive justice confront us: 'That is why a legislator, or indeed a private citizen, cannot be truly just unless he also possesses the virtue of prudence, which gives determinate content to the prin-

---

than is supplied by the liberal communitarian framework itself (cf. pp. 167–9). Emanuel believes that the rejection of racism is part of the 'overlapping consensus' to which both liberalism and liberal communitarianism, to differing extents, appeal (p. 39). But, as Duncan Forrester has argued about another aspect of the overlapping consensus (*Christian Justice and Public Policy*, Cambridge: Cambridge University Press, 1997, pp. 207–8), might our agreement about the unacceptability of racism not be rooted in the traditions, including Judaeo-Christian traditions, that still play a part in the formation of members of liberal societies? Perhaps – however egregiously Christians and churches have failed to live up to their traditions in this respect – the rejection of racism would be placed on a more secure footing if its roots in those traditions were more clearly recognized and explicated.

41 Thomas Aquinas, *Summa Theologiae*, ET ed. Thomas Gilby, 60 vols, London: Eyre and Spottiswoode, 1964–76, II-II.61.1-3, 63, 66.7; Porter, *The Recovery of Virtue*, pp. 124–54.

ciples of justice in the concrete circumstances of our lives.'[42]

Indeed, Porter goes so far as to say that for Aquinas, 'political prudence and distributive justice are in effect two components of one virtue by which rulers govern wisely and well', and that the more democratic a society, the closer the similarity between the kind of political prudence needed by rulers and that needed by every citizen.[43] If that is the case, it is worth asking what influences might help train members of a Christian 'community of character' in the political prudence that will enable them to judge soundly what ways of allocating health care goods will best serve the common good. Among these influences are themes from the Church's tradition, which are present either explicitly or implicitly in its Scriptures and which have been embodied in its practice with varying degrees of faithfulness and success, which could help shape its understanding and practice in relevant ways now. A few examples follow, though it will be obvious that this is far from a comprehensive list.

1. *A particular understanding of health and disease.* Norman Daniels builds his account of just health care on a 'biostatistical' model of health and disease, derived from Christopher Boorse, in which health is defined as the absence of disease, and diseases are understood in purely objective terms as deviations from species- typical functional norms.[44] This allows Daniels to argue that health care needs should be regarded as more important than many other kinds of need, since they must be met in order to

---

42 Porter, *The Recovery of Virtue*, p. 154. Note that here and in the following discussion, the word 'prudence' is used in its older sense, to denote the virtue called *phronesis* by Aristotle and *prudentia* by Aquinas, as distinct from the more commonplace modern sense, which is in play in the references to Norman Daniels' 'prudent deliberators' on p. 191 above.
43 Porter, *The Recovery of Virtue*, pp. 164–5.
44 Christopher Boorse, 'On the Distinction between Disease and Illness', *Philosophy and Public Affairs* 5.1 (1975), pp. 49–68, 'What a Theory of Mental Health Should Be', *Journal for the Theory of Social Behaviour* 6 (1976), pp. 61–84, 'Health as a Theoretical Concept', *Philosophy of Science* 44.4 (1977), pp. 542–73, and for a more recent defence, 'A Rebuttal on Health', in James M. Humber and Robert F. Almeder (eds), *What is Disease?*, Totowa, NJ: Humana Press, 1997, pp. 1–134.

protect the normal functioning that will give individuals access to a fair range of opportunities, and therefore that society has a greater obligation to meet health care needs than many other kinds of need.[45] But as I have argued elsewhere, Christians should not be satisfied with a biostatistical model of health. Instead, we are committed to a richer and more complex understanding, shaped on the one hand by the healing miracles of the Gospels and on the other by Paul's experience of the 'thorn in the flesh' (2 Cor. 12.7–10), which became an occasion by which he discovered more fully the strength of Christ. Taken together, these two influences suggest an understanding of health as a real and precious, but not the only nor the greatest, good. Disease and physical suffering are real and sometimes terrible evils, opposed to the loving purposes of God, yet can also be occasions for us to discover the goodness and love of God which reach beyond suffering and death. In our experience of disease and physical suffering, the two components of this dialectic of power and weakness are bound up together in ways too complex to be easily disentangled.[46] A community that embodied this understanding in its life together would see health care as a vitally important activity with a large and urgent claim on the community's resources. But it would also be wary of making an idol of health, or imagining that health was the only or the supreme good that it should pursue. It might, for example, discourage heavy investment in heroic life-prolonging measures at the margins of life, and devote more resources to '[caring] when it cannot cure'.[47] There are obvious links between

---

45 Daniels, *Just Health Care*, pp. 32–5.

46 Neil G. Messer, 'The Human Genome Project, Health and the "Tyranny of Normality"', in Celia Deane-Drummond (ed.), *Brave New World? Theology, Ethics and the Human Genome*, London: T & T Clark, 2003, pp. 91–115, and 'Towards a Theological Understanding of Health and Disease', forthcoming in *Journal of the Society of Christian Ethics* 31.1 (2011). My account draws extensively on Karl Barth, *Church Dogmatics*, ET ed. Geoffrey W. Bromiley and Thomas F. Torrance, 13 vols, Edinburgh: T & T Clark, 1956–75, vol. III.4, pp. 356–74.

47 Hauerwas, 'Medicine as a Tragic Profession', in *Truthfulness and Tragedy*, pp. 184–202 (p. 196).

this theme and another that I shall mention later, that of an appropriate response to tragedy.

2. *The sacrificial sharing of goods with those in need.* In Luke's portrait of the earliest community of believers (Acts 4.32–37), one sign that God's grace was upon them – perhaps the chief sign – was that 'there was not a needy person among them, for as many as owned lands or houses sold them and brought the proceeds of what was sold … and it was distributed to each as any had need' (vv. 34–35).[48] As Richard Hays points out, this vision of a new community characterized by the sharing of goods draws both on Aristotle's ideal of friendship, but extended to a larger scale, and on the Deuteronomic vision of God's covenant community.[49] Nor is this by any means an isolated text: Matthew's parable of the last judgement (25.31–46), Paul's collection for the church in Jerusalem (2 Cor. 8 and 9) and the Johannine insistence that love must be 'not in word or speech, but in truth and action' (1 John 3.17–18) are a few more examples of a ubiquitous theme in the New Testament. It is a theme that goes to the heart of New Testament ethics: Hays observes that this self-sacrificial sharing of goods 'is rooted in the paradigm of Jesus's death on the cross' (for example 2 Cor. 8.9, 1 John 3.16–18) and witnesses to the new creation inaugurated in his resurrection.[50] Furthermore, the call to sacrificial sharing does not appear to recognize territorial limits. Paul's advocacy of the collection for the Jerusalem church presupposes a solidarity that transcends geographical boundaries: my neighbour, it seems, is not only the person who lives nearby. This suggests that Christians should be dissatisfied with the tendency,

---

48 Richard B. Hays points out that the NRSV translation of this text somewhat obscures the connection between 'great grace was upon them all' (v. 33) and 'there was not a needy person among them' (v. 34) by leaving the word *gar* ('for') at the beginning of v. 34 untranslated: *The Moral Vision of the New Testament*, Edinburgh: T & T Clark, 1997, p. 123.

49 Hays, *Moral Vision*, pp. 122–5, citing Aristotle, *Nichomachean Ethics*, 1168b, and Deuteronomy 15.1–6.

50 Hays, *Moral Vision*, pp. 464–8.

observed earlier, to bracket the international level of the problem out of discussions of health care resource allocation.

Two questions, though, arise at this point. First, is this theme really concerned with justice and obligation, or with voluntary acts of generosity that might be encouraged but not commanded? In the language of the Thomist tradition, are we discussing the virtue of justice or of charity? The short answer is that the New Testament texts do not make a clear distinction between the two. While Hays holds that '[f]or the most part, the texts call the church to acts of sacrificial service far beyond what simple justice would require', he also acknowledges that Paul appeals to the notion of 'a fair balance' in trying to persuade the Corinthians to contribute to the collection (2 Cor. 8.13–15).[51] And questions about the *fair* distribution of goods among the needy arise quickly even in Luke's account of the early Church, in the argument between Hellenists and Hebrews (Acts 6.1–6). (It is worth noting in passing that the community's solution to this problem is to entrust the task of distribution to seven of its members chosen because they are 'full of the Spirit and of wisdom' [6.3]: prerequisites, perhaps, for the Christian 'political prudence' that will underpin sound judgement in matters of distributive justice.) In short, this New Testament theme suggests that the need of their neighbours places upon the members of the Christian community an obligation to share their goods so as to meet that need, even at considerable cost to themselves.

Yet this summary statement raises a second question. The theme of sacrificial sharing with those in need is presented in the New Testament as a matter for the community of Jesus' disciples, not (directly) as a proposal for how the state should order its economic life. So what relevance, if any, does it have for questions of health care distribution, which in contexts like ours are matters for secular political authorities? I leave this question aside for the time being, but shall return to it briefly in my final remarks about

---

51 Hays, *Moral Vision*, pp. 467, 465.

the relationship between Christian ethical claims and the wider arena of public policy and practice.

3. *The image of divine justice presented by Matthew in the Sermon on the Mount.* According to Duncan Forrester, a distinctively Judaeo-Christian contribution to public debates about justice is to be found in the structure of covenant relationships between God and his people, and among God's people. The covenant is unlike many modern notions of justice in that God's love is not conditional upon the people's faithfulness to the covenant, and that the justice of God cannot be separated from gratuitous generosity.[52] This is nowhere more clearly illustrated than in the thumbnail sketch of divine justice attributed to Jesus by Matthew in the Sermon on the Mount. Jesus here opposes the conventional wisdom that justice consists in doing good to one's friends and harm to one's enemies with the image of a God who is the maker and giver of all goods, and who gives them indiscriminately to all, regardless of merit or desert (Matt. 5.43–48). A generation ago, Paul Ramsey alluded to this image in the course of his argument for random selection in micro-allocation decisions when resources are too scarce for all to be treated:

> Men should ... 'play God' [not by using criteria of merit, desert etc. to decide who shall live, but] in the correct way: he makes his sun rise upon the good and the evil and sends rain upon the just and the unjust alike. This physicians do when in order to ensure equality of opportunity they devise a lottery scheme or adopt the practice of 'first-come, first-served' to determine who among medically equal patients shall be [offered treatment].[53]

---

52 Forrester, *Christian Justice*, pp. 208–10, 231–4.
53 Ramsey, *Patient as Person*, p. 256. It may seem strange to appeal to Ramsey in this connection, since he has been chided by Stanley Hauerwas for doing his medical ethics in an insufficiently theological way ('How Christian Ethics Became Medical Ethics: The Case of Paul Ramsey', in Allen Verhey (ed.), *Religion and Medical Ethics: Looking Back, Looking*

It has to be said, though, that while Ramsey discussed micro-allocation at length, he admitted defeat on questions of macro-allocation, saying, 'I do not know the answer to these questions, nor how to go about finding the answer.'[54] Explicating the relevance of this theme to macro-allocation and international allocation remains an unfinished task. However, it is possible to make a few suggestions. A policy of giving lower priority for certain treatments to some groups than to others on the grounds of merit or desert, rather than strictly clinical indications – for example, giving lower priority to smokers or heavy drinkers because they had brought their illness upon themselves, to the old because they had less to contribute to the economy than the young, or to non-citizens such as asylum-seekers because they had not helped to finance the system – would reflect a different understanding of justice than the one sketched here.[55] So does a state of affairs in which pharmaceutical research and development is directed largely to the diseases – and sometimes lifestyle issues – of wealthy nations, and neglects many of the major killer diseases of the developing world. Of course, such observations leave open the question whether, and how, Matthew's image of divine justice *should* influence public policy: they merely draw attention to the fact that some actual or conceivable policies and practices are expressive of very different notions of justice than the one to which this text points.

4. *An honest attitude to tragedy.* It seems clear that any imaginable community equipped with modern medicine will face the problem of scarcity, however generously its members share their

---

Forward, Grand Rapids, MI: Eerdmans, 1996, pp. 61–80) and by William F. May for offering an entirely deontological ethic with no account of virtue ('The Patient as Person: Beyond Ramsey's Beecher Lectures', in Ramsey, *Patient as Person*, pp. xxix–xliii, esp. pp. xxxiii–xxxvi). However, I think it could be argued that at this point (as, perhaps, at others), while many of his arguments are couched in terms of a rule-based deontological framework, his convictions are formed in important ways by his Christian tradition and its narrative.
54 Ramsey, *Patient as Person*, p. 272.
55 This is, of course, an over simplified way of stating the problem, since it can be a com-

goods with one another. There will always be more that could be done than the available resources allow. Choices will have to be made as to what is, and is not, done. It is often pointed out that these are *tragic* choices in the sense that the choice for one good is necessarily the choice against another. As Allen Verhey comments, tragedy in this sense is a consequence of our human finitude and cannot be eliminated by medical technology – nor, we might add, by any technique of public policy. However, while tragedy cannot be eliminated, it can be endured with the help of virtues such as '*cost-conscience*' which encourages the wise stewardship of medical resources and refrains from costly interventions of doubtful benefit, *truthfulness* which acknowledges the problem of scarcity and does not deny the necessity of tragic choices, *humility* which admits our limitations and saves us from placing unrealistic expectations on medicine (or indeed on public policy), *care* even when we cannot cure, and *piety* which sustains the other virtues and points to the Christian hope of a new age in which there will be no death, disease or pain.[56]

I have suggested that these four themes – a particular understanding of health and disease, the sacrificial sharing of goods, an image of divine justice that is indiscriminate in its favour and an honest attitude to the tragic choices that are a consequence of our

---

plex matter to disentangle judgements of the clinical appropriateness of certain treatments from discrimination according to merit or desert: see further Neil Messer (ed.), *Theological Issues in Bioethics: An Introduction with Readings,* London: Darton, Longman and Todd, 2002, pp. 191–4. It must also be acknowledged that some of the examples given here are at the boundaries of micro- and macro-allocation: the different levels of the problem are of course not sharply separable from one another, since what is done at any one level is likely to affect the others in complex ways.

56 Verhey, 'Sanctity and Scarcity'; see also Allen Verhey, *Reading the Bible in the Strange World of Medicine,* Grand Rapids, MI: Eerdmans, 2003, pp. 359–93. This theme, obviously enough, differs from the others I have identified in that it is less explicitly spelled out in biblical texts. However, as Verhey's treatments of it demonstrate, it is a theme that is thoroughly consonant with what Hays (*Moral Vision, passim*) calls the 'symbolic world' of the New Testament: there are obvious resonances, for example, with the eschatological tension between the 'already' and the 'not yet'.

finitude and mortality – emerge from the distinctive traditions of the Christian community and could help shape the 'political prudence' that would enable members of that community to form sound judgements about questions of distributive justice in health care. But this leaves unanswered the question of how that Christian 'political prudence' might engage with institutional and political decision-making processes that operate for the most part within a framework of liberal individualism.

Some Christians, of course, would be very wary of attempting such engagement. A theological case could be made that in a modern pluralist polity these distinctively Christian notions of justice cannot influence political decisions such as health care resource allocation in any direct or simple way. One version of this case might be the somewhat Niebuhrian thought that an attempt to introduce Christian notions of self-sacrificial sharing, indiscriminate generosity and so forth into the political debate would represent a confusion of love and justice that would, in the hard world of politics, be not only naïve but dangerous.[57] Such a thought would represent an important caution against overoptimistic attempts to practise Christian love in a secular public arena, but as critics have often pointed out, to maintain too sharp a distinction between love and justice can itself be problematic. While Niebuhr himself insisted that the 'impossible ideal' of love was needed to save justice from distortion and degeneration, Duncan Forrester observes that 'in the hands of theologically unsympathetic devotees ... [i]t proved easy for this understanding of justice to free itself from any kind of theological control, so that love as the impossible but relevant ideal disappeared over the horizon and justice became ... the interest of the stronger.'[58]

Forrester himself wishes to argue that without theologically informed notions, such as 'justice as generosity', society will not

---

57 For example Reinhold Niebuhr, *Moral Man and Immoral Society*, New York and London: Scribners, 1932, esp. pp. 257–77.
58 Forrester, *Christian Justice*, p. 219.

have a rich enough account of justice to support decent social relationships and public policies.[59] The critique of standard accounts of distributive justice in health care sketched out earlier would seem to bear this claim out, and would suggest that distinctively Christian concepts might challenge, extend and enrich the resource allocation debate. If that is so, then it is worth exploring possible modes of engagement of the theological account with public policy and practice. I close with three brief suggestions.

The first way is to *problematize* dominant approaches. For example, where technology assessments are made in part by means of QALY-based cost–benefit calculations, it behoves Christians as well as others to point out the deficiencies of such calculations. Again, Christians might well agree with Daniels and others that a 'decent minimum' of health care for all (at the very least) should be publicly funded, while holding that his argument for this rests on inadequate notions of health and of the human good. He may be right, or partly right, for the wrong reasons. While this is not a particularly constructive way to start, Christians have no reason to expect that their honest engagement in matters of public policy will always have the effect of helping the machine to run smoothly.

The second way is more constructive, though not necessarily more comfortable. It should be clear that the four themes I have identified are not in any straightforward sense contributions to a political theory, as that is commonly understood. Rather, they are directed to shaping the life of the Christian community as an alternative and counter-cultural politics, as Hauerwas and others have frequently pointed out.[60] One way – perhaps even the most

---

59 Forrester, *Christian Justice*, pp. 231–4.
60 For an instructive discussion, see Nigel Biggar, 'Is Stanley Hauerwas Sectarian?', in Mark Thiessen Nation and Samuel Wells (eds), *Faithfulness and Fortitude: In Conversation with the Theological Ethics of Stanley Hauerwas*, Edinburgh: T & T Clark, 2000, pp. 141–60. Hays stresses this point in his comments about Luke's vision of the early Church: *Moral Vision*, pp. 125–8.

powerful way – in which that community could influence political debate and practice would be by *embodying, and thereby witnessing to the possibility of, a different way of ordering our life together*. The hospice movement, at least to some extent and in some of its forms, demonstrates that Christian individuals, groups and communities can take actions that instantiate aspects of this Christian vision.[61] Local Christian communities could also act in various ways in line with the theological themes identified: they might share their own resources to support needed health care in their localities, or enter into partnerships with others to develop health care initiatives informed by these theological perspectives. Christian individuals who work in the health care system might also have their own vision and perspective shaped by these themes, and one would hope that this would be reflected in their own professional practice. This is where it could get uncomfortable, since they would then find themselves at the centre of any conflict between that vision and the practice of the system. The Church at all levels faces the challenge of supporting its members through such conflicts.

The Christian community should also be well placed to embody and witness to the concern for the international level of resource allocation which has been advocated in this paper. Churches, mission societies and church-sponsored non-governmental organizations already have considerable experience of international partnerships, which not infrequently include the sharing of health care personnel, expertise and other resources. Such partnerships can embody in practice the understanding that the neighbour who has a claim on my resources could be anywhere in the world.[62] There is almost certainly scope for strengthening,

---

61 See Shirley du Boulay, *Cicely Saunders: The Founder of the Modern Hospice Movement*, London: Hodder and Stoughton, 1984, for an account of the Christian motivation of one pioneer of that movement.

62 They should not, however, be understood merely as channels by which the 'Third World' can benefit from Western largesse, but rather as opportunities for Christian communities in all parts of the world to share their distinctive resources with one another

extending and developing these partnerships and increasing their visibility both within and beyond the confines of the Christian community.

The third form of Christian engagement is suggested by the thought that the National Health Service in the UK could be said to have a corporate ethos which includes discernible echoes of some of the theological themes I identified earlier. Those aspects of its ethos, though, are in tension with others less consonant with the Christian vision sketched here. For example, Geoffrey Rivett, in his history of the National Health Service of Great Britain, observes that the NHS was the creation of a particular time when "'we were all neighbours" ... [and the] underlying principle was that members of society were entitled to what they needed in health care and social support'. Yet this principle shows increasing signs of strain:

> Even within the limited confines of the health service there is conflict between, on the one hand, the older public service ethos and a belief in the need for solidarity in society, and, on the other, a belief in the primacy of the individual and an acceptance that not everyone will receive an excellent service.[63]

It may be that this 'older public service ethos' echoes, however inchoately, a Christian insight that my neighbour in need has a claim on whatever aid I can offer, even at the cost of some sacrifice on my part. If so, Christian individuals and communities may have a valuable role to play in articulating this insight, clarifying it, and encouraging and supporting its expression in the direction, organization and delivery of health care within the NHS. There

---

on an equal footing: see, for example, the statements of the Council for World Mission, online at http://www.cwmission.org/who-we-are (accessed 15 September 2010).

63 Geoffrey Rivett, *From Cradle to Grave: Fifty Years of the NHS*, London: King's Fund, 1997, pp. 470–84 (pp. 470, 484).

may be important 'theological fragments', as Forrester calls them,[64] to be contributed to debates about health care resource allocation.[65]

In this chapter I have alluded to some of the difficulties with standard approaches to health care resource allocation, and have made a few suggestions as to the shape of an adequate Christian response. These suggestions fall well short of a fully developed account, but that is at least in part because judgements about distributive justice in health care cannot fully be worked out in advance by means of armchair theorizing. Rather, they will be the fruit of a Christian 'political prudence' formed by the character of the Christian community. They must be developed and tested in the course of passionate and disciplined deliberation and practice within the Christian community, and equally passionate and disciplined engagement by that community with these questions as they arise in the public domain.

---

64 Forrester, *Christian Justice*, pp. 194–205.

65 See further Ruud H. J. ter Meulen, 'The Lost Voice: How Libertarianism and Consumerism Obliterate the Need for a Relational Ethics in the National Health Care Service', *Christian Bioethics*, 14.1 (2008), pp. 78–94, and above, p. 74.

8

Beyond Autonomy and Compassion: Reframing the Assisted Dying Debate

In many Western contexts, including the UK, assisted dying – physician-assisted suicide or euthanasia – never seems far from the public agenda. When legislation to permit it has been debated in the UK in recent years, two lines of moral argument have been particularly prominent. One is based on the principle of respect for autonomy, the other on an appeal to compassion. These lines of argument were much in evidence when Lord Joffe's unsuccessful Assisted Dying Bill was debated by the House of Lords a few years ago,[1] and it is safe to assume they will be equally prominent the next time assisted dying legislation is on the parliamentary agenda. Very often, autonomy and compassion are regarded by those on both sides of the argument as 'givens', in which case the debate turns on whether or not they require that the law should permit assisted dying. In this chapter, however, I shall argue that when Christians enter the debate, they should decline to accept appeals to autonomy and compassion as 'givens'. This is because both these arguments, in the forms in which they often appear in the assisted dying debate, turn out to assume views of human existence and the good which are – to say the least – highly problematic in theological perspective. Therefore, if legislation for assisted dying

---

1 Assisted Dying for the Terminally Ill HL Bill, 2005–06 (HL Bill 36), online at www. publications.parliament.uk/pa/ld200506/ldbills/036/2006036.pdf (accessed 16 September 2010).

is to be morally justified in a way that will be persuasive to the theological tradition that informs this book, it will have to be in very different terms from those used in the standard arguments. In fact, I very much doubt that this can be done; however, my purpose in this chapter is not to try and settle the argument about assisted dying, but more modestly to make a claim about the terms in which it should be conducted.

Respect for autonomy

The principle of respect for autonomy has become more or less axiomatic in Anglophone health care ethics, thanks in no small measure to Tom Beauchamp and James Childress' massively influential text *Principles of Biomedical Ethics*.[2] While respect for autonomy is only one of Beauchamp and Childress' four principles (the others being non-maleficence, beneficence and justice), at least some supporters of their approach argue that it should be 'first among equals'.[3] It certainly seems to have functioned in that way in some of the arguments in favour of the Joffe Bill that were submitted to the Parliamentary Select Committee set up to scrutinize that Bill. For example, the submission from the Voluntary Euthanasia Society (later rebranded as Dignity in Dying) began with a clear claim for patient autonomy: 'VES believes the patient should be the decision maker at the end of life irrespective of whether he wishes to prolong his life, or ask for medical help to die if terminally ill.'[4]

Many of the Bill's opponents also acknowledged the principle of

2 Tom L. Beauchamp and James F. Childress, *Principles of Biomedical Ethics*, 6th edn, Oxford: Oxford University Press, 2009, esp. ch. 4.

3 Raanan Gillon, 'Ethics needs Principles – Four Can Encompass the Rest – and Respect for Autonomy Should Be "First among Equals"', *Journal of Medical Ethics* 29 (2003), pp. 307–12.

4 Select Committee on the Assisted Dying for the Terminally Ill Bill, Report on the Assisted Dying for the Terminally Ill Bill, 2005–06, HL Paper 86-I–III, vol. II: Evidence, p. 1, online at www.publications.parliament.uk/pa/ld/ldasdy.htm (accessed 16 September 2010). Hereafter: Report on the Assisted Dying Bill.

respect for autonomy, but argued that in the case of assisted dying, it was outweighed by other factors like the risk of harm to vulnerable patients and to society. For example, the Association for Palliative Medicine argued that 'the appropriate scope of respect for individual autonomy requires further scrutiny and debate in the light of present-day circumstances of dying and in relation to the wider interests of vulnerable patients and society'.[5]

This dispute between VES and APM could be read as a disagreement, within Beauchamp and Childress' four-principles framework, about the appropriate balance between the different principles. The VES submission suggests that with regard to assisted dying, respect for autonomy is the over-riding principle, whereas the quotation from the APM implies that it is outweighed by other factors such as the risk of harm to vulnerable patients and to society: on this issue, non-maleficence trumps respect for autonomy. However, the disagreement might hang, not just on the relative weight given to respect for autonomy and other principles, but also on what is meant by autonomy, as we can see by dissecting the language of autonomy a little.

Like many others, Beauchamp and Childress trace the principle of respect for autonomy back to Immanuel Kant and John Stuart Mill. As Onora O'Neill has shown, this ancestry already signals some internal diversity and perhaps tension in their concept of autonomy. The Kantian idea that human action should be directed by self-governing reason rather than externally imposed authority is rather different from Mill's principle that 'the only purpose for which power can be rightfully exercised over a member of a civilized community, against his will, is to prevent harm to others'.[6] O'Neill believes that the conceptions of autonomy currently influential in bioethics owe more to Mill than Kant, and that a more Kantian understanding would be better for bioethics.

---

5 Report on the Assisted Dying Bill, vol. II, p. 141.

6 John Stuart Mill, *On Liberty* (1863), in *Utilitarianism, On Liberty, Considerations on Representative Government, Remarks on Bentham's Philosophy*, ed. Geraint Williams, 3rd edn, London: J. M. Dent, 1993, p. 78.

The picture could, however, be more complex and confused than this. In a highly illuminating analysis of autonomy language in bioethics and health care law, Mark Bratton has shown that many different conceptions of autonomy can be found in the literature – including, for example, self-ownership, self-legislation, self-control, freedom of choice, freedom from interference, and privacy.[7] We might suspect that these different meanings of 'autonomy' conceal a range of diverse and perhaps incompatible anthropological and ethical assumptions. Bratton suggests that these different conceptions of autonomy can be grouped into three 'readings' of autonomy, which he calls 'libertarian', 'empirical' and 'deontological'.[8] 'Libertarian' readings of autonomy are particularly concerned with *self-determination* and *freedom of choice*. They tend to emphasize the entitlement of patients to make decisions about their own treatment, and the obligation on health care professionals not to hinder those decisions even if they disagree with them. 'Empirical' readings are concerned with whether a patient's state of mind and circumstances make it possible for him or her to make autonomous choices. 'Deontological' readings are concerned with safeguarding patients against violations of their human dignity. They emphasize privacy and freedom from unwanted interference – as, for example, in the right to refuse unwanted medical treatment.

Bratton's analysis can shed light on disputes about whether respect for autonomy does, or does not, require provision for assisted dying. Some appeals to autonomy in the context of end-of-life care require only negative conceptions of the kind Bratton describes as 'deontological' readings, concerned with freedom from coercion and interference. The right to refuse life-prolonging treatment, for example, can be grounded on such a negative

---

7 Mark Bratton, 'The Many Faces of Autonomy', unpublished paper, Association of Teachers of Moral Theology, November 2007. I thank Mark Bratton for permission to cite this paper. See also Mark Bratton, 'Anorexia, Welfare, and the Varieties of Autonomy: Judicial Rhetoric and the Law in Practice', *Philosophy, Psychiatry and Psychology* 17.2 (2010), pp. 159–62.

8 Bratton, 'The Many Faces of Autonomy', pp. 14–16.

concept. This application of respect for autonomy commands very wide support in health care ethics. I certainly have no wish to argue that competent patients should be compelled to receive life-prolonging treatment against their will – though for reasons which will become clearer presently, I *am* inclined to ask whether 'autonomy' is the most helpful way of thinking about issues like treatment refusal.

Be that as it may, the VES submission quoted earlier makes a broader claim than this for patient autonomy: 'the patient should be the decision maker ... *irrespective of whether he wishes to prolong his life, or ask for medical help to die if terminally ill.*'[9] This appears implicitly to conflate different senses of 'autonomy'. A decision whether or not to have one's life prolonged medically could be supported, as I have said, by a negative 'deontological' conception of autonomy. The entitlement 'to ask for medical help to die', however, requires a more positive kind of 'libertarian' reading.[10]

What should a theologian working in a Reformed Christian tradition make of this debate? Implicit in a 'libertarian' reading of autonomy are notions of self-ownership, self-determination and self-realization. On this view, I am sovereign over my own, in-dividual, embodied human life, and should have the freedom to direct the project of my life as I choose. The limits of my freedom to choose the shape taken by my life-project are a matter of negotiation with my fellow members of society, about (among other things) whether the exercise of my self-determination harms others or limits their self-determination. It seems clear that this kind of conception of autonomy, at any rate, is problematic from a Reformed theological perspective. A well-known text from 1 Corinthians interrupts this discourse of self-determination: '[D]o you not know that your body is a temple of the Holy Spirit within you, which you have from God, and that you are not your own? For you were bought with a price; therefore glorify God in

---

9 Report on the Assisted Dying Bill, vol. II, p. 1 (emphasis added).
10 I thank Mark Bratton for drawing this point to my attention.

your body' (1 Cor. 6.19–20). This text originates, of course, in an argument about the kinds of sexual behaviour legitimate for Christians – but more broadly, it depicts a different kind of accountability for embodied human life and behaviour from that offered by 'libertarian' readings of autonomy. It suggests that the notion that I am free, within limits, to do what I will with my body is problematic in Christian perspective.

The text hints at the theological anthropology which grounds Paul's claim that 'we are not our own'. In so doing, it shows why the anthropology of self-determination implicit in 'libertarian' readings of autonomy is problematic for Christians. The phrases 'you were bought at a price' and 'your body is a temple of the Holy Spirit' signal an anthropology shaped by the creating, redeeming and sanctifying work of God. We are to understand ourselves as the beloved creatures of a good God, as sinners redeemed by God's saving work in Christ, and as recipients of the gift of the Holy Spirit, given us to transform us 'from one degree of glory to another' (2 Cor. 3.18) on the way to the ultimate fulfilment promised us in God's good future.

In a 'libertarian' conception of autonomy, the human good consists precisely in the freedom to choose and pursue one's own goods, goals and ends. By contrast, in the perspective of this theological anthropology, the true good of human beings consists in the fulfilment of God's good purposes in creating us, a fulfilment made possible by God's redeeming and sanctifying work. In this perspective, we might begin a discussion of ethics by asking how we are to *respond* to this work of God. So rather than framing the question of assisted dying in a discussion of autonomy, we might do better to attempt to map what Dietrich Bonhoeffer called 'the structure of responsible life'[11] as it should be lived in the difficult and painful situations that the Joffe Bill was intended to address. In short, what does it mean to respect and protect

---

11 Dietrich Bonhoeffer, *Ethics* (Dietrich Bonhoeffer, *Works*, vol. 6), ET. ed. Clifford J. Green, Minneapolis: Fortress Press, 2005, pp. 257–89.

God's gift of creaturely human life – or as Karl Barth formulated it, to obey the command 'Thou shalt not kill' (Exod. 20.13) – in these circumstances?[12]

Barth's divine command ethic offers an account in which ethics can and should be both 'systematic' and 'systematically open to correction', as Nigel Biggar puts it.[13] It is clear in Barth's writings that the command of God can be reasoned about, but at the same time we cannot pretend to complete certainty about what the sovereign God will command in any particular situation. In particular, Barth writes of 'boundary situations' (*Grenzfälle*), or exceptional cases in which the command of God can take unusual and unexpected forms. Thus, in relation to the protection of life, Barth holds that in the vast majority of situations, the command 'Thou shalt not kill' simply prohibits the taking of human life. However, he believes that there could be exceptional situations in which the taking of human life was permitted or commanded by God. Such cases of killing would not be suspensions of, or exceptions to, the command, but (to quote Biggar again) 'unusual [modes] of keeping it'.[14] In other words, they would be extreme situations in which the protection of human life required the taking of human life. Barth believes, for example, that there can be exceptional situations, of this 'life against life' kind, in which both abortion and killing in war might be permitted or commanded by God. However, he does not believe that there can ever be this kind of 'life against life' situation in which euthanasia could be permitted or commanded by God.[15]

It is quite possible, of course, that in terms of his own method and presuppositions, Barth is wrong to draw that conclusion. My

---

12 Karl Barth, *Church Dogmatics*, ET ed. Geoffrey W. Bromiley and Thomas F. Torrance, 13 vols, Edinburgh: T & T Clark, 1956–75, vol. III.4, pp. 423–7.

13 Nigel Biggar, *The Hastening that Waits: Karl Barth's Ethics*, Oxford: Clarendon Press, 1993, p. 35.

14 Biggar, *Hastening*, p. 34.

15 He does not discuss physician-assisted suicide, as distinct from euthanasia, but it is reasonable to assume that the same conclusion would apply.

purpose at present is not to try and settle that substantive question, but simply to argue that the issue should be framed in something like Barth's terms, rather than the standard category of autonomy. Christians ought not to be persuaded that assisted dying could ever be permissible unless they can be shown that it could in some cases be, as Biggar puts it, an 'unusual mode' of keeping the command 'Thou shalt not kill'.[16]

Suffering, compassion and love of neighbour

All this talk of responsibility and obedience to God's command, though, might seem harsh, inflexible and deficient in basic human sympathy in the face of the terrible pain, suffering and indignity experienced by some dying people. Stories of patients such as Diane Pretty, Debbie Purdy and Daniel James are frequently used to powerful effect in public campaigns in favour of assisted dying, as they were in support of the Joffe Bill.[17] Understandably enough, at least some opponents of that Bill seemed to accept the premise that compassion places us under an over-riding obligation to relieve suffering. Having done so, they had to argue that suffering can be relieved without resorting to assisted dying. The Association for Palliative Medicine's submission to the Select Committee on the Joffe Bill looks at first sight as though it should be read in this way:

---

16 This critique of autonomy-based arguments has been directed mostly at what Mark Bratton calls 'libertarian' readings of autonomy. Could 'deontological' readings of autonomy, more modest in scope and focused on the negative aspect of freedom from coercion or interference, still be serviceable in this theological perspective? Perhaps, in the sense that this theological ethic gives good reasons for requiring freedom from coercion or interference: obedience to God's command cannot be coerced, so those addressed by God must be given the freedom to respond. But my suspicion is that the language of 'autonomy' is so compromised by the associations and the kinds of confusion sketched earlier that it would be fraught with hazards for Christians to try and deploy it to give an account of freedom before God.

17 For a collection of such stories, carefully presented with an explicit campaigning aim, see http://www.dignityindying.org.uk/personal-stories.html (accessed 24 April 2009).

Relief of suffering is an important goal of medical care. However, palliative care cannot, and does not claim to be able to relieve all suffering. There is no sort of care that could ever alleviate all suffering (especially some expressions of social, psychological and spiritual distress), but the first step to addressing the majority of this suffering is to ensure effective support and skilled interventions are available to those who require them, rather than introduce a way to end these individuals' lives. The inability to relieve all suffering is inevitable and is part of the human condition. We believe that implementation of this Bill could increase suffering in vulnerable patients and their families by reducing trust, increasing fear and inhibiting patients from disclosing their concerns to doctors and other healthcare professionals.[18]

This paragraph acknowledges the importance of the relief of suffering, but argues that patients' suffering can be relieved *more* effectively by skilled palliative care than by assisted dying. There is more to it than this, though: as I shall observe later, it offers a more nuanced understanding of suffering and medical care than a hasty reading might suggest.

To return for the moment to the simple appeal to compassion often made in support of assisted dying: this appeal might seem to be reinforced by the biblical command, 'You shall love your neighbour as yourself' (Lev. 19.18), said by Jesus to be one of the two great commandments (Mark 12.28–31 par.). Paul Badham is one theologian well known for arguing that love of neighbour supports assisted dying, if that is what it takes to end a patient's pain and distress.[19] Now of course, it goes without saying that compassion *is* a major component of Christian love, and in a health care context, compassion *does* very often call for strenuous

---

18 Report on the Assisted Dying Bill, vol. II, p. 141.

19 For example Paul Badham, 'Euthanasia and the Christian Understanding of God', *Studies in Christian Ethics* 11.1 (1998), pp. 1–12; Paul Badham, *Is there a Christian Case for Assisted Dying? Voluntary Euthanasia Reassessed*, London: SPCK, 2009.

efforts to relieve suffering. But what seems to be implicit in many appeals to compassion is that our *over-riding* obligation, the one that trumps all others, is to relieve pain and suffering by any means at our disposal – including killing the sufferer, if that is what it takes. And I want to suggest that if we imagine this is what *Christian love* calls for, then we seriously over-simplify and distort the Christian understanding of love.

Some of the historical roots of this distortion have been traced by Gerald McKenny.[20] Part of the story he tells is that in the eighteenth century, the utilitarianism of Jeremy Bentham and others promoted a highly reductionist account of the human good. The human good was collapsed into happiness, understood as pleasure and the absence of pain.[21] While later utilitarians (including Mill) acknowledged that Bentham's account of happiness was over-simplified and attempted to enrich and nuance it,[22] at a more unreflective level his reductive assumptions have been influential on modern conceptions of the human good, and have from time to time found their way into Christian ethical argument – for example through the situationism of Joseph Fletcher and others in the 1960s.[23] If Christians understand the love of neighbour in terms of seeking one's neighbour's good, then it is easy to see how, under the influence of utilitarian thought, the command to love our neighbours can be collapsed into an over-riding obligation to relieve their pain.

Once again, though, if we go back to the sources of the Christian tradition, we shall discover how much of a distortion this is. As an example, let me take another text from Paul's Corinthian correspondence, part of his response to opposition from the rival

---

20 Gerald P. McKenny, *To Relieve the Human Condition: Bioethics, Technology and the Body*, Albany, NY: State University of New York Press, 1997, pp. 17–24.

21 Jeremy Bentham, *An Introduction to the Principles of Morals and Legislation*, ed. J. H. Burns and H. L. A. Hart, London: Athlone, 1970 (1789), p. 11.

22 Mill, *Utilitarianism* (1861) in *Utilitarianism, On Liberty, Considerations on Representative Government, Remarks on Bentham's Philosophy*, pp. 1–67.

23 Joseph Fletcher, *Situation Ethics*, London: SCM Press, 1966.

'super-apostles' who apparently boasted of 'visions and revelations', among other things, in an attempt to establish their superiority over Paul. The rhetorical strategy of Paul's response includes an attempt to subvert the simplistic notions of power, success and status that he finds in his rivals' boasts. So following his own vision experience, he tells how he has been given a 'thorn in the flesh' – maybe some physical illness, maybe some other kind of suffering and distress; in any event, something that caused him real and terrible suffering. Three times, he says, he pleaded with God to be relieved of this suffering; but he received the answer, 'My grace is sufficient for you, for power is made perfect in weakness.' 'Therefore,' he concludes, 'I am content with weaknesses, insults, hardships, persecutions, and calamities for the sake of Christ; for whenever I am weak, then I am strong' (2 Cor. 12.7–10).

The insights offered by this text are easily misunderstood in a modern culture whose basic assumptions about suffering and the good are so profoundly shaped by the kind of utilitarian view I sketched a moment ago. In such a context, it perhaps needs to be spelled out that this text is not in any simplistic way saying that suffering is good for the soul, or that God inflicts it upon us for our own good. Rather, Paul is saying some subtle and important things that unsettle some of our easy assumptions about the human good, suffering and love.[24] First, his experience of suffering is more complex and has more creative tension in it than the simple utilitarian picture can allow: his 'thorn in the flesh' was *both* a real and terrible evil *and* an occasion by which he has experienced God's love and empowerment more fully than before. Second, his story implies a richer and more complex account of *human goods*; in this account, the relief of suffering is of course a real and highly important good, but it is not the *only* good we should pursue. Nor is it in all circumstances the one that should

---

24 For what follows, cf. Barth, *Church Dogmatics*, vol. III/4, pp. 356–70, and Neil Messer, 'The Human Genome Project, Health and the "Tyranny of Normality"', in Celia Deane-Drummond (ed.), *Brave New World? Theology, Ethics and the Human Genome*, London: T & T Clark, 2003, pp. 91–115.

'trump' all others. Third, therefore, our understanding of what is meant by *the love of neighbour* also becomes richer and more complex. Of course, one crucial aspect *is* the relief of suffering; but it is not the only or, necessarily, the over-riding aspect. So at the very least, the vision of suffering, love and the good implied by this text suggests that those seeking to argue in Christian terms are *not* entitled to conclude that love of my suffering neighbour requires me to kill her if that is the only way her suffering can be stopped.

Such a Christian line of thought perhaps calls for a somewhat self-critical footnote. One implication of what I have said is that for some people in some situations, their good will be most fully realized not by total relief from suffering – which may not be possible – but by finding the resources to *endure* suffering and indignity. And this suggests the thought, made familiar by Stanley Hauerwas and others, that one of the most important contributions Christian churches can make to public debates about assisted dying is their practice.[25] Perhaps one of the most helpful and distinctive things that Christian communities can offer is simply to *be* the kind of communities that can give suffering human beings the resources to *endure* pain and indignity. Stories can be told of ways in which this has happened, to remarkable effect;[26] but it has to be said that Christian churches do not always live up to their calling in this regard. If their practice were better, their words might gain more credence.

---

25 See, for example, Stanley Hauerwas, 'Salvation and Health: Why Medicine Needs the Church', in *Suffering Presence: Theological Reflections on Medicine, the Mentally Handicapped, and the Church*, Edinburgh: T & T Clark, 1988, pp. 63–83.

26 The well-documented influence of Cicely Saunders' Christian faith on the practice of hospice care that she inaugurated is a case in point: see Shirley du Boulay, *Cicely Saunders: The Founder of the Modern Hospice Movement*, London: Hodder and Stoughton, 1984. As David Clark shows, however, there was a tension from the outset between Saunders' Christian vision and her aim to establish the practice of hospice care in the medical profession and health care system at large: David Clark, 'Originating a Movement: Cicely Saunders and the Development of St Christopher's Hospice, 1957–1967', *Mortality* 3.1 (1998), pp. 43–63.

Theology in public debates

It might be asked, though, whether this kind of theological and ethical objection to assisted dying ought to be translated into opposition to legislation that would permit it. In Chapter 2 I followed Barth and Bonhoeffer in arguing that one role of the state, understood in theological perspective, is to keep open a 'penultimate' space in which people can hear and respond to God's word. I emphasized that this claim should not be understood as a self-interested plea that the state should support the Church in the latter's pursuit of narrowly 'sectarian' goals. What is entailed by keeping open a space for response to the Word includes a range of concerns not dissimilar from those in view in the Catholic tradition's concept of the 'common good': Bonhoeffer's examples include feeding the hungry, housing the homeless and the establishment of a just political order.[27]

None of this suggests a simple correspondence between Christian ethical conclusions and legislation. If, as Barth puts it, the task of Christian ethics is 'to understand the Word of God as the command of God',[28] summoning human beings and setting them free to be all that they truly are in Christ, then no human agency can compel anyone's response to that liberating Word. Furthermore, since God is sovereign, the divine Word and command can never be fully contained within human systems or structures. As Barth remarks in the different context of abortion, legal rules are

> obviously useful, and even have an indirect ethical value as general directions to those involved ... [but] are not adapted to serve as ethical criteria, since obedience to the command

---

27 Karl Barth, *Church and State*, ET, London: SCM Press, 1939; Karl Barth, 'The Christian Community and the Civil Community', in *Against the Stream: Shorter Post-war Writings 1946–52*, ed. Ronald Gregor Smith, London: SCM Press, 1954, pp. 13–50; Dietrich Bonhoeffer, *Ethics*, pp. 163–70; see above, pp. 50–4.
28 Barth, *Church Dogmatics*, vol. III.4, p. 4.

of God must have the freedom to move within limits which may sometimes be narrower and sometimes broader than even the best civil law.[29]

However, this does not mean that there should be no connection between Christian ethical conclusions and the kind of legislation they should seek. If it is the law's business, theologically understood, to keep open a space in which citizens have the freedom to hear and respond to the command of God, this suggests that there must be limits to the law's interference in the decisions and actions of citizens. But it also means that the law must sometimes restrain citizens' decisions and actions, if they pose a threat to the very conditions that are needed for people to be *able* to hear and respond to God's word and command. In other words, the freedom of individuals to pursue their chosen aims and goals might have to be restrained by law if the pursuit of those aims and goals seriously threatens the social conditions in which all can flourish and move as far as possible towards their true fulfilment. In the debate over Lord Joffe's Assisted Dying Bill, advocates of assisted dying argued that individuals should be free to pursue the goal of a death that is as free as possible of pain and suffering. The Anglican and Catholic Bishops responded that if the law grants individuals this freedom, there is a serious danger that over time, society as a whole will come to respect human life – particularly the lives of the most vulnerable – less.[30] In other words, the effect of allowing this freedom could be that eventually all members of society will be *less* free to hear and respond to God's command to protect human life. If they were right, then Christians should oppose legislation in favour of assisted dying. Furthermore, this argument gives grounds for thinking that, as Nigel Biggar has argued, assisted dying *legislation* should be resisted even if Barth

---

29 Barth, *Church Dogmatics*, vol. III.4, p. 422.
30 Report on the Assisted Dying Bill, vol. II, pp. 488–91.

was wrong to conclude that *ethically* speaking, euthanasia could never be 'permitted or commanded' by God.[31]

The implication of all this is that Christians and churches do have a responsibility to engage, on the strength of their theological convictions, with debates about policy and legislation in this area. That being the case, how should they go about it: should they make explicit use of theological claims and perspectives, of the sort developed earlier in this chapter, or should they avoid using theological language and arguments for fear that their contribution will be written off as a sectarian view that ought not to influence public policy?

In Chapter 2 and elsewhere, I have claimed that there are good grounds to contest claims that public reason can or should be tradition-neutral, and that believers must leave tradition-based reasoning at the door when they enter the forum of public debate. Christians and churches should not be afraid to seek appropriate and tactically astute ways of talking about God in public.[32] If Christians do that in relation to debates like this one, they might find that some of what they want to say has got there before them – that for whatever reason, by whatever route, what Barth calls 'secular parables' of the kingdom of heaven are to be found in other contributions to the debate.[33] I close with one example: the paragraph about the relief of suffering quoted earlier from the Association of Palliative Medicine. I suggested earlier that the APM do not straightforwardly endorse the view of compassion of which I was also critical. In fact, they describe the relief of suffering as an 'important goal of medical care', but carefully avoid saying that it is the over-riding goal. They warn against the fantasy that

---

31 Nigel Biggar, *Aiming to Kill: The Ethics of Suicide and Euthanasia*, London: Darton, Longman and Todd, 2004, pp. 157–64.

32 See above, pp. 54–68, and, further: Nigel Biggar, 'Not Translation but Conversation: Theology in Public Debate about Euthanasia', in Nigel Biggar and Linda Hogan (eds), *Religious Voices in Public Places*, Oxford: Oxford University Press, 2009, pp. 151–93; Jonathan Chaplin, *Talking God: The Legitimacy of Religious Public Reasoning*, London: Theos, 2008.

33 Barth, *Church Dogmatics*, vol. IV/3.1, pp. 113–35.

all pain can be done away with: 'The inability to relieve all suffering is inevitable and is part of the human condition.' What this points to is a richer understanding of suffering and of care than is sometimes in play in these debates, an understanding in which the business of health care is sometimes to help patients endure their suffering, not to pretend that all suffering can be eliminated. There are obvious points of contact with the theological view that I have been advancing. It could be, therefore, that when Christians engage with these debates on the strength of their distinctive traditions, they will find more friends and allies than they sometimes fear.

Index